Disruptive Divas

MESSIAEN'S LANGUAGE OF MYSTICAL LOVE
edited by Siglind Bruhn

EXPRESSION IN POP-ROCK MUSIC
A Collection of Critical and Analytical Essays
edited by Walter Everett

JOHN CAGE
Music, Philosophy, and Intention, 1933–1950
edited by David W. Patterson

POSTMODERN MUSIC / POSTMODERN THOUGHT
edited by Judy Lochhead and Joseph Auner

New York Schools of Music and the Visual Arts
edited by David Patterson

Disruptive Divas: Feminism, Identity, and Popular Music
by Lori Burns and Mélisse Lafrance

Disruptive Divas

Feminism, Identity & Popular Music

Lori Burns
and Mélisse Lafrance

Routledge
New York and London

Studies in Contemporary Music and Culture
Joseph Auner, Series Editor

Published in 2002 by
Routledge
29 West 35th Street
New York, NY 10001

Published in Great Britian by
Routledge
11 New Fetter Lane
London EC4P 4EE

Copyright © 2002 by Routledge

Routledge is an imprint of the Taylor & Francis Group.

Printed in the United States of America on acid-free paper.

Library of Congress Cataloging-in-Publication Data

Burns, Lori
    Disruptive divas : feminism, identity, and popular music / Lori Burns and
    Mélisse Lafrance.
        p. cm.—(Studies in contemporary music and culture)
    Includes bibliographical references and index.
    ISBN 0-8153-3553-9—ISBN 0-8153-3554-7 (pbk.)
    1. Popular music—1991-2000—Analysis, appreciation. 2. Women in music.
3. Gender identity in music. 4. Feminism and music. I. Title: Feminism, identity,
and popular music. II. Lafrance, Mélisse. III. Title. IV. Series.

MT146 .B87 2001
782.42164'092'273—dc21   2001019249

Contents

General Introduction

As we enter a new century, many of the established historical narratives of twentieth-century music are being questioned or reconfigured. New approaches from cultural studies and feminist theory, methodologies adapted from such disciplines as literary theory, philosophy, and anthropology, and debates about the canon, postmodernism, globalization, and multiculturalism are profoundly transforming our sense of both what the repertoire of twentieth-century music is and how it should be understood. "Studies in Contemporary Music and Culture" provides a forum for research into topics that have been neglected by existing scholarship, as well as for new critical approaches to well-known composers, movements, and styles.

Volumes in the series will include studies of popular and rock music; gender and sexuality; institutions; the audience and reception; performance and the media; music and technology; and cross-cultural music and the whole range of the crossover phenomenon. By presenting innovative and provocative musical scholarship concerning all aspects of culture and society, it is our aim to stimulate new ways to listen to, study, teach, and perform the music of our time.

Joseph Auner

Acknowledgments

Lori Burns: I would like to thank the Social Sciences and Research Council of Canada, as well as the Faculty of Arts and Research Services of the University of Ottawa for grant support during the research of this project. A very special thank you is extended to Dr. Edison Amos, who generously granted copyright permission for Tori Amos's "Crucify." Sincere thanks also to the graduate students who worked with me over the past several years, especially Zacy Benner, Maya Chaly, Patrick Crosley, and Christina Linklater. My colleagues Murray Dineen and Paul Merkley, and our librarians Deborah Begg and Luc Bédard at the University of Ottawa, have all been and continue to be tremendously helpful and supportive. To my more distant colleagues who are always willing to discuss tricky matters, I offer my gratitude: John Covach, Walter Everett, Ellie Hisama. It is also a pleasure to express my appreciation to my coauthor in this endeavor, Mélisse Lafrance, for her brilliant thoughts and her fierce commitment to her work. Finally, I humbly offer my deep gratitude to my family (my parents and siblings, and my own children and husband), for all of their patience and love.

Mélisse Lafrance: I am deeply grateful to my family, immediate and extended, for their love and support throughout the drafting of this manuscript. I am equally indebted to the Oxford group: Tamar Blickstein, Dominic Brookshaw, Oliver Davis, Stephen Forcer, Amelia Glaser, Christina Howells, and Robert McGill for their unwavering intellectual stimulation and invaluable friendship. Heartfelt thanks also go to Charlotte Ross, for her patient readings, her insightful suggestions, and her precious companionship. Finally, I would like to extend my sincere appreciation to David Carlson, Sonia Sikka, and Geneviève Rail, who remain my best friends and my most cherished mentors; and to Lori Burns, for believing in my strength of mind and spirit and for being an invaluable coauthor.

Preface

Disruptive Divas: Feminism, Identity, and Popular Music concentrates on four female musicians who have influenced contemporary popular culture in courageous and, at times, unexpected ways. Tori Amos, Courtney Love, Me'Shell Ndegéocello, and P.J. Harvey have impelled and disturbed the boundaries of "acceptable" female musicianship in ways both sociocultural and musical, and are thus important objects of inquiry for cultural as well as music theorists. In order to understand the expressive potential of their music, we have combined these disciplinary perspectives to analyze selected popular songs. Before launching into a discussion of the book's critical and analytical approaches, however, we thought it would be useful to address our primary objectives and to describe the conceptual tensions that arose as we sought to realize these objectives.

Primary Objectives and Critical Stance

In this book, we investigate how these four female musicians negotiate their manifold axes of identity through popular musical expression. We have selected a group of artists who, by means of their creative work, ultimately disrupt dominant discourses of sex, gender, race, and creed. Hence, *Disruptive Divas* undertakes, first and foremost, to interpret the chosen popular songs for their disruptive meaning and potential.

This primary undertaking, however, provokes our first theoretical dilemma. That is, reading these mass-produced cultural forms for their subversive potential inevitably implies that such mass-produced forms on some level can articulate resistance politics. This formulation is, of course, not unproblematic. In fact, it constitutes one of the most significant points of polemical tension in *Disruptive Divas*. We could not have written this book without believing that the articulation of resistance politics is possible through forms mediated by late capitalist patterns of consumption, even if that articulation invariably involves the employment of contaminated resources and the creation of effects both oppositional and hegemonic. Consequently, we attempt to account for the subversive potential of certain popular songs without celebrating the economic processes through which they were generated. Applauding the countercultural possibility of a cultural form without applauding the means through which it was produced and made accessible is, of course, something of an argumentative balancing act, but in our view one worth pursuing. To completely refuse to address this music simply because of its ties to capital is to dismiss the media through which most people gain most of their cultural literacy.

The second point of tension is created by our selection and utilization of diverse and at times seemingly disparate theoretical frameworks to analyze the songs in question. This has, once again, involved utilizing argumentative balancing acts. These balancing acts have consisted of, for instance, positing the plurality of interpretations while privileging a particular form of interpretation, applying a conventional method of systematic analysis while asserting unconventional analytic results, or asserting the indeterminacy of sociocultural processes while recognizing their relatively stable patterns. *Disruptive Divas* is characterized by many such conceptual tensions and epistemological negotiations, though they are in no way accidental. These tensions have been evoked in an effort to yield the most inclusive and productive analyses possible and to avoid the almost irresistible tendency toward "grand" and/or universal modes of theorizing.

In a sense, then, the present volume might be read as a disruptive project in terms of both its objects and modes of inquiry. While the musicians disturb and destabilize dominant discourses, norms, and values, we also disrupt disciplinary mores and blur conjectural boundaries through our transdisciplinary approach and our unconventional theoretical appropriations. These disciplinary disruptions, though, do not come without some practical complications. The combination of sociocultural and musicological perspectives, two vastly different approaches to the analysis of popular music, begs the question of expositional strategy. How do two scholars exploiting immensely disparate theories and concepts go about assembling their analyses in coherent argumentative form?

We have tentatively resolved this dilemma through the use of two methodological tactics. First, we have ensured the coherence of our analyses by working almost simultaneously throughout the process of analytical development. In other words, each author uses the other's engagement with the text as a yardstick for the salience and legitimacy of her own discussion. For example, Mélisse was ready to disregard the bridge of the song "Crucify", because it appeared, at first glance, textually uninteresting. However, Lori believed that the bridge was one of the most important musical moments of the piece. After considering its musical value, Mélisse was persuaded to revisit her interpretation and discovered that the bridge did indeed comprise an essential moment of narration. This is simply one example of how we have endeavored to render our analyses more inclusive and complete through transdisciplinary cooperation and collaboration.

The second tactic relates to the actual writing process. Although we work together to select the most important narrative structures and themes, we are nevertheless examining considerably different phenomena. Consequently, our analyses are kept relatively discrete. The running heads at the top of each page will be constant reminders to the reader of who is "speaking" at any given point.

We begin in chapters 1 and 2 with individual expositions of our theoretical positions and interpretive methodologies. This section of the book is vitally important, as it clarifies our own disciplinary orientation and responds to the existing literature in our fields. In these chapters the reader will find detailed explanations of the theoretical frameworks used to interpret the music and the issues (both cultural and musical) that are evoked by that music. The remaining chapters offer in-depth criticism and analysis of the selected artists and their music, from both the sociocultural and music-theoretical perspectives. This book is not intended as a survey of women in popular music. Rather, *Disruptive Divas* is theoretically, methodologically, and analytically grounded, in an attempt to produce "close readings" of the chosen songs. The music will be discussed in the context of the artist's contributions to her chosen musical style and genre, but we will not discuss related artists or musical trends to any significant extent. The artists and songs we have selected explore a range of textual themes and musical styles, and our critical/analytical chapters, while anchored and embedded in culturalist perspectives, are dedicated primarily to the illumination of each artist's social message and individual musical offering.

The artists we have selected represent a variety of musical styles and genres, but all of the music is from the 1990s. The themes that run through this repertoire include gender consciousness, sex/gender performance and performativity, agency and resistance, social relations of domination and subordination, representations of the "female" body, religion, sexuality, desire, race (especially "whiteness" and "blackness"), as well as how each of these phenomenal articulations are produced, sustained, and understood within a contemporary Western popular cultural imaginary. We begin our reflection with a discussion of Tori Amos. In her song "Crucify," Amos negotiates the leitmotifs of gender consciousness, gender performance and performativity, self-surveillance, and agency and resistance, while simultaneously interrogating dominant discourses of femininity and Christianity. In her songs "Violet," "Asking for It," and "Jennifer's Body," Courtney Love (the lead singer and songwriter of the group Hole) also takes on the politics of sexual violence, while in other songs ("Doll Parts," "Miss World," and "Plump") she attacks male supremacist beauty standards by depicting the "female" body as a fragmented postmodern commodity, consistently reterritorialized and reinvested with oppressive norms and desires. Me'Shell Ndegéocello, in "Mary Magdalene," navigates questions of textuality, meaning, and power, while interrogating discursive regimes of race, gender, sexuality, and desire in Christian doctrine. Like Amos and Ndegéocello, P.J. Harvey, on her album *Is This Desire?*, also approaches the situation of women in Christian societies by satirizing key components of Christian symbolism and exposing their relationship to patriarchal gender binaries and resultant cultural matrices of desire.

In sum, this book endeavors to read these musical works for their disruptive, subversive, and countercultural potential. It also attempts to disrupt the conventional mores of academic disciplinarity by combining cultural and musicological perspectives. And, finally, *Disruptive Divas* seeks to evoke actively the tensions and negotiations involved in the production of our analyses in order to produce the most transparent and circumspect arguments of which we are capable.

Terminology and Music Resources

At the very inception of this project, we recognized that very few readers would be able to comprehend *equally* the cultural-critical and music-theoretical analyses. It is our hope that the reader, despite individual training, will be able to find value in both the sociocultural critiques and the musical analyses. We have not sacrificed disciplinary integrity for the sake of complete comprehension by all readers. Rather, we would like the reader to have patience through the passages that require an expertise not yet (or perhaps never to be) acquired, with the ultimate reading goals of gleaning the general nature of the theoretical argument and discovering the intersections between the two primary disciplines.

The terminology employed in the cultural-critical sections of the book is either as straightforward as it can be, or will be explained throughout the book. However, it is worth making a few remarks about the terminology employed in the musical-analytical sections. In these passages, chords (harmonies) are identified either by means of root and chord-quality labels using uppercase letters and arabic numbers (for instance A^9 as a ninth chord on A), or by means of roman numeral function labels (upper- and lowercase) and arabic inversion symbols (for instance, I–ii_6–V). Harmony will always be discussed in the context of a mode or key (for instance, Dorian, Aeolian, Mixolydian, Ionian), as popular music operates within a modal/tonal harmonic framework. Specific pitches in register will be designated with the following system: for example, middle C on the keyboard is C^4, the octave below is C^3, and the octave above is C^5.

All of the songs we analyze are based on the verse-chorus formal organization that is common to popular music.[1] The division of a song into discrete sections is a very important aspect of our analysis, and our interpretations will emphasize the specific placement of a lyrical theme or a musical strategy in one of these sections. In the lyrics, the *verse* is the section that, through its changing content (there might be several statements of the verse with different lyrics), usually advances a specific and sometimes personal narrative, while the *chorus* (heard several times in identical form) offers a more global social statement and often encapsulates that statement with a concise poetic line that will be the title line of the song. Some songs include a *pre-chorus*, also a section of fixed content (rarely altered and with minor textual changes), which sets the stage for the chorus. A *link* is a short instrumental passage that connects two sections. A *bridge* is a contrasting section to the verse, sometimes entirely instrumental, sometimes with a brief lyrical reflection. It is usually the last set of new ideas to be heard, as the material following the bridge is based on the chorus and possibly pre-chorus. A *coda* is a concluding section, most often repeating the chorus material and fading out. In the music, many possibilities exist for style of expression, but we can generalize that the verse and chorus will be contrasted by means of the modal or tonal centers, melodic and harmonic strategies, rhythmic emphasis, and instrumental effects.

Some of the musical examples are transcriptions of particular passages, and some are reductive graphs, "summaries" if you will, of the contrapuntal and harmonic content of a given song's musical sections. (Appendix 2 explains the notational style of the reductive graphs.) Although these reductions will be used for illustrative purposes, they do not show the totality of the musical content. The analytical discussions will refer to instrumental and vocal effects that cannot be charted. The graphic analyses are based on transcriptions from the particular source CD. Transcription is a controversial issue for popular music analysis, as many recorded versions of a given song might exist, and performance versions might be significantly different from the recorded versions. Certain songs are available in song-sheet publication (the music of Tori Amos and Hole); the reader is encouraged to use those scores as a partial guide to the music, with the caveat that these song sheets do not transcribe all variants or all subtleties of rhythmic and harmonic presentation.

One of the issues that arises in the transcription of popular music is the choice of meter and the ascription of measure numbers. Because the formal musical analysis is conducted within a methodological framework that relies on concepts such as phrase length and phrase expansion, the reader will find references to measure numbers.

Song Lyrics

It would be too cumbersome to present the lyrics for an entire song in the body of an analytic chapter; thus, appendix 1 reproduces the full lyrics to the songs that are analyzed in detail in this study. In this format, it is also possible to add CD reference cues and formal labels (verse, chorus, and so on). The reader is encouraged to refer to appendix 1 during the analytical discussions.

What's Love Got to Do with It? Affective Engagements and Objects of
Inquiry

At the outset of this investigation, we established a set of criteria for
selecting the female musicians to be studied. Having devised the criteria,
however, we nevertheless found ourselves in a difficult situation: we still
had to choose from a relatively large pool of "disruptive" female musicians. To resolve this dilemma, we decided to take a few more factors into
consideration when selecting our objects of inquiry.

First, we decided that we wanted this cultural and musical commentary to capture the spirit of the 1990s. In that we wanted our volume to
function as somewhat of a snapshot of this epoch, the pool of musicians
from which we would choose our objects of inquiry narrowed considerably. Thus, even tremendously interesting musicians such as Annie
Lennox and Tracy Chapman became less pertinent to our project, as
their most important moments of subversion transpired in the 1980s.[2]

Second, to present the veritable range of poetic and aesthetic sensibilities organizing women's popular musical forms in the 1990s, we felt
compelled to select musicians whose works would allow us to explore
multitudinous themes and concepts. To do so, we were obliged to select
musicians who were distinct from one another in terms of the questions
and problematics they explored. For this reason, there are many female
musicians whose work we consider courageous and groundbreaking that
is, however, not discussed in the present volume (for example, k.d. lang,
Ani Difranco).

Third, we selected musicians whose work profoundly engaged us.
We chose, for the most part, works we loved. Some may scoff at our decision to study those whose music we love rather than to conduct "unbi-
ased," "value-neutral" investigations of music and musicians. Regardless
of what conventional positivists may maintain, however, we argue that
when one is studying music—an object of inquiry that communicates in
intensely personal and often unconscious, unknowable ways—one must
not be indifferent to it.[3] In fact, to truly discern the operations and
effects of music, the critic requires an epistemological standpoint highly
attuned to music's affective circuits rather than a standpoint that is
allegedly "detached" and "objective." In contrast to mainstream scientific
mores, then, cultural and musicological analyses uninformed by the
affect that inhabits music and one's affective engagement with music
lack both rigor and responsibility. Indeed, these purportedly objective
approaches fail precisely because in attempting to "bracket" affective

engagement with music, the theorist becomes unable to feel, hear, and discern exactly that which makes music "a distinctive signifying practice" (Shepherd and Wicke 1997, 5) and an "irreducible form of human expression" (2). The theorist becomes, in essence, unable to recognize how music is made to mean. On this topic, neo-Marxist Antonio Gramsci declares:

> The intellectual's error consists in believing that it is possible to know with-out understanding and especially without feeling and passion... that the intellectual can be an intellectual... if he is distinct and detached from the people nation without feeling the elemental passions of the people, under-standing them and thus explaining and justifying them in a particular histor-ical situation, connecting them dialectically to the laws of history, to a superior conception of the world... [feelings] and passion become under-standing and thence knowledge. (quoted in Simon 1991, 98–99)

The deeply engaged spirit of our analytical strategies does not, in our view, preclude them from being rigorous and thoughtful. If anything, the intimacy we share with these musical works allows us to perform closer and more critical readings of them, as it provides us with a sophis-ticated conduit through which to understand some of the more subtle and involved musical-textual moments. It is worth noting, however, that we are not the first to admit to selecting music that we love for analysis. In fact, John Shepherd illuminates this penchant, among others, in his book *Music as Social Text*:

> At one level, the book could be read as the attempt of a [white middle-class] male to uncover the conditions of his own musical pleasures. That level is undoubtedly there. However, I make no apology for it. On the one hand, it seems to do no harm to analyze the conditions of one's own existence. On the other, I would not wish to claim any privileged position for the nature of this analysis. While the analysis may well be privileged in terms of my own posi-tion in the academic world and of the dominance of male discourses within that world, I am not convinced that the analysis as such precludes different arguments originating from other social locations. (1991, 3)

While neither one of us would embrace the same form of interpreta-tive pluralism advanced by Shepherd—and Lori will elaborate on this point in her exposition—we do agree that despite the meticulous nature of our analyses, what you will find in the following pages is but one pos-sible interpretation of the works in question. In this sense, you will no doubt discover a good deal about the authors, as well as the musicians, as any act of interpretation invariably engages and discloses psychic elements of both parties.

LB and ML
Ottawa, December 2000

1

A Cultural Studies Approach to Women and Popular Music

Mélisse Lafrance

This book represents an effort to make sense of the multitudinous mechanisms through which four women have contested the discursive regimes of sex, gender, and race organizing late-twentieth-century mass culture. The at once profoundly compelling and fiercely insurgent narratives of artists Tori Amos, Me'Shell Ndegéocello, Courtney Love, and P.J. Harvey appear to dispute the claim made by some critical and postmodern theorists "that all expression, even the most rebellious forms, is tamed and made completely inauthentic by its 'incorporation'... into multinational corporate capitalism" (Nehring 1997, xi).[1] In fact, these musicians agitate, destabilize, and, at times, appall prevailing cultural politics in incisive and powerful ways.

This first chapter endeavors to communicate the spirit in and through which this book was actualized. To do so, I will explicitly introduce a number of the theoretical concepts and epistemological positions organizing my critical approach. This introduction will thus be broken down into four parts. First, I will address the title of the book itself and the conceptual sensibilities structuring it. More specifically, I will discuss what I understand by the phrase *disruptive divas*, and how such an understanding logically invites the employment of feminist frameworks informed by contemporary theories of identity. Second, I will describe the methodological approach employed in this book. I will strive to outline the fundamental tenets of a cultural studies approach to the popular, as well as to illustrate how I have drawn and borrowed from these approaches to apply them to the study of women and popular music. Third, I will elaborate the processes through which I have made sense of the creative works in question through a critical discussion of the problematics of interpretation. That is, I will bring into relief the theoretical strategies that have allowed me to analyze these works, and to figure them in the oppositional politics of signification and representation. And fourth, I will close this chapter with some remarks on the links that can be forged between cultural studies and musicology.

DISRUPTIVE DIVAS, FEMINISM, AND IDENTITY: PRIMARY TERMS AND CONCEPTS

Disruption

The musicians included in this book were selected according to the extent to which they disrupted mass musical culture. The extent of their disruption has been gauged by several practical and theoretical criteria. Though arbitrary in nature, these criteria have served to delimit what, for Lori and myself, "counts" as disruption in popular culture and who enacts and personifies it in engaging ways. All of the disruptive divas included in our analysis have, at some point during the 1990s, disrupted the musical expectations placed upon them by the mainstream media and the conventional listener. We chose to structure the book as a "snapshot" of the 1990s not only for methodological efficacy, but also because we hope to show that social relations are not fixed relations between statuses but, as Dorothy Smith writes, "an organization of actual sequences of action *in time*" (1990, 160).

The first and foremost constituent of disruptive musical expression present in all of the works included in this volume involves the creative interrogation of dominant normative systems on the part of the artist through a range of musical techniques (that is, lyrical and sonic). All of the artists were selected because, in our view, they adopt marginal, countercultural positions in and through their creative work. The second requisite to be considered a disruptive musical presence is that the artist's music disquiet and unsettle the listener. For instance, Tori Amos's complicated and often obscure symbolic incursions into the regulatory technologies of Christianity and male supremacy tend to make her music disconcerting. We argue that the troubled quality of an engaged listener's response to Amos's work (and indeed all the work of those profiled herein) is produced by the artist's articulation of allegedly private and largely silent (and indeed *silenced*) gynocentered traumas. The widespread discomfort produced by Amos's articulation of such traumas indicates that they assume a meaningful systemic and "public" quality, rather than merely an individualistic and "private" one. In brief, then, the female musicians selected for this volume were chosen because they tend to make their audiences uncomfortable.[2] This book represents an attempt to understand the significance of such discomfort from sociocultural and musicological perspectives.

The third constituent of disruptive musical expression pertains to the artist's manipulations of conventions and styles, which play on the listener's expecations and understanding of established codes. For instance, unexpected instrumental and/or vocal strategies, or a failure to resolve tensions or expectations in the musical or narrative structure, can function to disrupt musical and narrative norms, ultimately destabilizing the conventional listening experience. Lori will discuss such potential musical disruption at length in chapter 2.

The fourth constituent of disruptive musical expression relates to the technical and creative operations of music making. All of these female musicians were (and in some cases still are) among the most important creative actors in their experiences of musical production. While many female musicians remain excluded from the myriad production processes that culminate in an album, the music produced by our selection of artists is, I believe, a closer expression and reflection of their own concern, frustration, and rage, as they were actively involved in the music's realization. These musicians' seizure of both the creative and productive reins, as it were, constitutes a formidable and formerly inaccessible vehicle of gynocentered self-expression and is thus an important consideration in any reflection on the autobiographical "female voice" as it is disseminated in popular culture.

As regards the female voice in popular culture, I concur with Elspeth Probyn when she writes that "the use of the autobiographical can be made to question implicitly the relation of self to experience, researcher to researched, and the production of knowledge itself" (1993, 105). Moreover, I agree with her when she posits, "a feminist cultural studies approach to the autobiographical reveals the voice as strategy" (120). It is precisely the diverse dimensions of such vocal (that is, narrative, discursive) strategies that are explored in the present volume. Nonetheless, in the following chapters, the notion of the female voice is explicitly and implicitly challenged through many different argumentative mechanisms. These mechanisms include, for instance, reflections on the mediated nature of the subject and the text, ruminations on the conceptions of subjectivity inscribed through autobiographical texts, and complications of the "truths" produced through autobiographical narrative. In my view, such explorations and problematizations of the female voice in popular music will show that "if worked upon and worked over, these personal voices can be articulated as strategies, as ways of going on theorizing" (120).

Finally, all of these female musicians were selected because they have assumed, and in many cases continue to assume, an important presence in *popular* music. Although there are many feminist and lesbian rock and punk groups that are arguably more subversive than the artists we selected (for example, the Riot Grrrls, Babes in Toyland, and others), we remain most interested in how mass culture either wittingly or unwittingly produces, negotiates, and mystifies popular artists who seemingly undermine it. An analysis of the more culturally marginal feminist and lesbian music scenes is an essential academic task,[3] but it is not included here due to our interest in the musical destabilization and disruption of dominant popular culture.

Feminism

To assess the disruptive value of admittedly exceptional female musicians requires a theoretical framework attuned to the manifold sociocultural relations of domination and subordination, marginalization, and social differentiation currently organizing contemporary popular culture. In addition, this theoretical framework must be sensitive to the complex machinations of power in and along all axes of individual and collective difference, such as sex, gender, race, ethnicity, and creed. Finally, it must offer interpretative strategies that posit neither unrestricted agential voluntarism nor complete subjective determinism on the part of the female musicians in question—a framework that enables and restores a fundamental belief in human agency while remaining alive to the fissures and contradictions of such agency.[4]

I have found in a particular configuration of feminist cultural studies a methodological approach that appears to satisfy all of these prerequisites. While I may exploit multiple feminist theories in each chapter, the discussion in its entirety is characterized by certain positional continuities. First, I do not confine my investigative schematic to only one epistemological formation, nor do I feel that it should be neatly subsumed by only one notional category (for instance, postmodern feminism or socialist feminism). I have therefore gone to great pains to extract the richest and most pertinent insights from a range of feminist theories and approaches. To do so, I have applied some of the more contemporary postmodernist, poststructuralist, and psychoanalytic feminist theories to my interrogations of these musicians. I have also sought to integrate the recent indispensable insights of queer, black, and postcolonial feminisms into my analyses. Finally, I have revisited a good deal of movement (or second-wave) feminist scholarship on questions related to women and their situation in popular culture. This last body of work has gone out of "scholarly style" for many perfectly legitimate reasons: it tended to essentialize sex/gender categories, it sometimes left the question of subjective agency unproblematized, it often presumed a universal (and universalizing) conception of the female subject, it frequently neglected axes of difference other than those of sex/gender, and it occasionally positioned women as incurable victims of patriarchal conditions (see Brooks 1997, Butler 1990, de Lauretis 1988). Doubtless, these problems represented significant theoretical shortcomings that quite reasonably limited the application of movement scholarship. I want to argue, however, that in either wholly abandoning or effacing many of the cogent and well-founded insights produced within the time and space of second-wave feminism—as a good deal of contemporary feminist theorizing has—certain feminist theorists may have done themselves and the late-twentieth-century feminist movement a disservice. I in no way mean to suggest that all feminist theorizing should have direct, accessible, and/or practical applications to the feminist movement. Nor do I intend to posit that all feminist theorizing should either exploit or celebrate the insights of movement scholarship. I do feel, however, that fewer and fewer feminist treatises speak to the radical potential of feminist consciousness channeled through popular aesthetic forms. It is this fiery radicalism that I hope to communicate through the use of certain movement feminist texts.

Recalling the incisive radicalism of movement feminism in our investigative enterprises is important if only to gauge the highly problematic prevailing representations of sex, gender, and feminism currently haunting the popular landscape. As some feminist scholars have already noted (Cole and Hribar 1995, Lafrance 1998), the popular imaginary is increasingly characterized by "postfeminist" positions, articulations, and representations. As Cole and Hribar posit,

> While movement feminism generated spaces and identities that interrogated distributional and relational inequalities, meanings, differences, and identities, the post feminist moment includes spaces that work to homogenize, generate conformity, and mark Others, while discouraging questioning. . . . Those spaces are established in the realm of the popular and include, for example, the news, films (from *Fatal Attraction* to *Thelma and Louise* to *Disclosure*), television programs . . . advertisements . . . and celebrities such as Madonna, Jane Fonda, and Camille Paglia. . . . Regardless of the limitations of the political spaces available in the post feminist imaginary, in the post feminist moment, the politics associated with movement feminism seem troubled, less compelling and outdated. (356)

The postfeminist moment, then, appears to be characterized by a shift away from movement feminism's anger at social relations and formations of inequality. Consequently, the postfeminist moment is characterized by an embrace, on the part of both women and men, of an allegedly new egalitarian order (Cole and Hribar 1995, Lafrance 1998). And, it is worth noting, feminist scholarship is not immune from like-natured postfeminist impulses. Indeed, much of the scholarly criticism leveled at postfeminist academe appears to be related to specific yet highly influential forms of postmodern theorizing and their effect on academic formulations of oppositional struggle. Here I will take a moment to delineate those elements of postmodern theorizing that have been perceived by some as particularly problematic for the elaboration of feminist strategies.

Drawing on Geraldine Finn's *Why Are There No Great Women Postmodernists?* I argue that one's engagement with the so-called crisis of modern Western epistemological authority depends a great deal upon one's position within the time and space over which it has ruled. Those heavily invested in and rewarded by its authority, such as the "great" postmodernists (most of whom are moneyed, white males), may well be profoundly disturbed by the collapse of modern Western grand narratives. Modernist myths of Reality, History, Freedom, Reason, and Man, however problematic, not only benefited moneyed, white male scholars, but also attributed preeminence and value to their experiences. Of course, in so doing, these myths also "disappeared" marginalized and disenfranchised members of alleged "minority" groups. It is small wonder, then, that the great postmodernists have framed the disintegration of such myths in apocalyptic terms. The apocalyptic terms in which these theorists have formulated contemporary moments are made manifest through the many conceptual casualties storied by "official" postmodernism, such as "the end of the known and signifying universe . . . the end of History as such . . . the death of *the* Subject (as if there were only ever One), the loss of *the* Social, the disappearance of *the* Real, the absence of *the* Signified, the end of *all* Politics" (Finn 1993, 127). Within the confines of postmodernism, the disintegration of modernist certainties is translated into, as Finn puts it, the disintegration of "*all* certainties and *all* possibilities of certainty and thence of *all* judgment . . . into a position . . . which (I want to argue) abdicates ethics and politics and intellectual responsibility in the name of their contemporary impossibility" (127). Cultural studies scholar Dick Hebdige has also criticized the postmodernist "line that we are at the end of everything" (cited in Nehring 1997, 11). Indeed, he asserts that white male postmodernists have responded to the increasing presence of disenfranchised groups in academia by resolving to "take it all—judgment, history, politics, aesthetics, value—out the window with them" (11).

Wendy Brown (1987), Jane Flax (1987), Nancy Harstock (1987 and 1990), and Neil Nehring (1997) concur with Finn (1993) and Hebdige (1987) in positing that certain influential strands of white male postmodernism (for instance, those of Jacques Derrida, Roland Barthes, Jean-François Lyotard, and Jean Baudrillard) tend to both paralyze oppositional politics and reverse much of the recognition hard won by women, queers, and racial and ethnic minorities. In a now well-quoted assertion, Harstock demands, "Why is it that just at the moment when so many of us who have been silenced begin to demand the right to name ourselves, to act as subjects rather than objects of history, that just then the concept of subjecthood becomes problematic?" (1990, 163). More specifically, Nehring has indicted postmodernist and poststructuralist theorizing related to the study of women and popular music, asserting that "[under] the rule of postmodern theory, even feminist literary scholars who deign to examine mass and popular culture typically turn to Madonna—not out-and-out angry but ambiguous (supposedly) and thus a more suitable subject than [angry feminist musicians such as] the Riot Grrrls for postmodern treatises on the instability and fragmentation of all communication" (1997, 120).[5]

Though I am not necessarily in agreement with all of the views expressed in the previous paragraph, there can be no doubt that these theorists challenge some of the assumptions of postmodernist scholarship in meaningful ways. Yet, I am not convinced that these challenges truly enable the feminist scholar to improve and/or refine her conceptual tools. In my view, they tend to leave the theorist with two choices, neither of which is particularly desirable: on the one hand, the feminist scholar can refuse postmodernism's sensibilities and return to a past/passed analytic style; on the other hand, she can exploit the resources of postmodernism, but only at the expense of resistance struggle. In this book, I attempt to avoid this impasse as I endeavor to engage a constellation of approaches, productively examining what can be worked with and worked over, and discarding that which might be seen as deleterious to a progressive and inclusive feminist theoretical strategy.

My transdisciplinary approach to feminist theorizing is evidenced throughout the book. For instance, to make sense of Tori Amos's song "Crucify"—a work pertaining to the concrete and metaphorical crucifixion of women in Western Judeo-Christian culture—I discuss its internal structure of meaning and trace its representations of gendered agency, resistance, rage, and violence. To do so, I draw upon theoretical trajectories as diverse as Foucauldian feminist theory (for instance, Balsamo 1996, Bartky 1993, Bordo 1993 and 1995, Cole and Hribar 1995, Fisher and Davis 1993), radical feminist theory (for instance, Daly 1968, 1973, and 1978, Reuther 1974), sexual difference feminist theory (for instance, Butler 1989, 1990, 1993a, and 1993b), and postmodernist feminist theory (for instance, Flax 1990, Fraser and Nicholson 1990). Again, while these theories may at first glance appear somewhat irreconcilable, when taken together they produce a rich and involved interpretive schematic.

Courtney Love is the angriest disruptive diva profiled, and I consider my analysis of her work to be very important precisely because both her musical approach and her political purpose have been unforgivably perverted by the mainstream press. Love's album *Live through This* is a formidable feminist manifesto shamelessly admonishing male supremacist acts of violence against women and the patriarchal body tyranny to which women are routinely subjected. In this chapter, I draw primarily on movement feminist theories of masculinist violence and domination (for instance, Edwards 1987, Kelly 1987, MacKinnon 1989), as well as on feminist postmodernist theories of the fragmentation and commodification of the female body in late capitalism (for instance, Bordo 1993 and 1995).

In my analysis of Me'Shell Ndegéocello's piece "Mary Magdalene," I see Ndegéocello rereading and rewriting the biblical "story" of Jesus and Mary Magdalene by writing herself—a black and openly bisexual woman—into a cultural text whose interpretations are frequently mobilized to legitimate sexism, misogyny, racism, homophobia, heterosexism, and the derision of bodies materialized and conditioned by norms of femininity. Because the chapter focuses so intimately on acts of rereading and rewriting, I use feminist literary and poststructural theories to underscore the resistant possibilities introduced by the reappropriation of dominant cultural texts (for instance, Althusser 1969, Derrida 1976, Johnson 1997, Moi 1985, Saussure 1974, Weedon 1997). However, because this piece also overtly implies questions of race and desire, I apply critical analytical strategies forged by black feminist criticism and critical race theory (for instance, Frankenberg 1993, hooks 1992a and 1994, Morrison 1992, Snead 1994) and queer studies (for instance, Goldman 1996).

For the P.J. Harvey chapter, the approach taken is somewhat different. In general, I see the Harvey album *Is This Desire?* as an exposition of the complicated nature of human desire. The album is also, however, a fairly synchronous reflection on how desire has been regulated by dominant discursive regimes of sex/gender. In my exegesis, I combine poststructural and psychoanalytic approaches (for instance, Derrida 1976, Lacan 1977, Moi 1985) in order to understand the impossible circuitry of desire disclosed in Harvey's songwriting. I complement this analysis with lesbian, feminist, and queer theories on sexuality and desire (for instance, Butler 1990 and 1993, Weeks 1996).

The works examined in this volume are at times quite abstract, and at times viscerally angry. Insofar as it is possible, then, I intend to focus on both their abstract and angry qualities in equal measure. Their abstract qualities must be discussed at length, as they reveal the extent to which popular female musicians are producing sophisticated critiques of contemporary culture within the confines of mass cultural media. And, in view of the massive social disapproval of gynocentered anger, this music's angry quality must also be highlighted. As Nehring posits, anger is "already a significant cognitive discovery—even just the possibility of being angry, [is] a critical matter particularly for young women" (1997, 108). Carol Tavris also asserts that anger "is essential to the first phase of a social movement. It unifies disparate members of a group against a common enemy; the group becomes defined by its anger" (1989, 264). She goes on to explain that "[out of] private, unarticulated experience [arises] a feeling of power. [Anger] creates the hope of change" (271–72).

To do justice to both the rage and the intensity of this music, the theoretical framework seeks to marry the more abstract nature of some contemporary academic feminism with a number of the still valuable contributions of insurgent second-wave feminist literature. Ultimately, the present approach is—at the risk of sounding cliché—a tapestry of many different modes of feminist analysis and critique attuned to the potential of feminist subversion through popular music yet mindful of its constraints and potential perverse structural and discursive effects. My approach draws out the pertinent elements of diverse feminist theories without necessarily embracing them in their epistemological totality.

Identity

Before closing this section of the chapter, I would like to address explicitly the question of identity as it relates to popular music made by women. In this volume, I conceptualize identity as inextricably linked to the sociocultural processes of its construction and, subsequently, the agential possibilities and constraints introduced through that construction. I will digress momentarily here to repeat a number of ideas systematized by Judith Butler, as they have influenced my position on the tensions embedded in a feminist conception of gendered identity.

In "Gendering the Body: Beauvoir's Philosophical Contribution" Butler reads Simone de Beauvoir's "explicitly feminist account of bodily experience" (1989, 253) to understand the processes of gender acquisition and performance, as well as the relationship between sex, gender, and desire. Butler problematizes the Beauvoirian concept that "one is not born, but becomes a woman" (254) by investigating its existential and ontological bases. First, Butler asks who is the "I" who "becomes" and who is (she) before she begins becoming? Of what is her identity constituted if not of a socially predetermined gender? Butler writes, "If it is the case that the body is always already gendered, if personhood is coextensive with gender itself, then what sense does it make to appeal to a subject who maintains an ontological status prior to gender itself?" (255). For Butler, Beauvoir's notion of becoming a woman is problematic because it presupposes the existence (and indeed the possibility) of a pregendered state in which an individual resides until she makes the leap from natural facticity to historicity. Second, Butler problematizes the issue of "becoming" and its intimation of agency and choice. Butler questions the possibility of "choosing" to perform femininity when gender relations seem inescapable and deeply entrenched.

Butler resolves the first problem (the trajectory of becoming) by explaining that "for Beauvoir, acculturation is not a fact or even a precondition, but a peculiar kind of achievement" (255). This suggests that the process of gender acquisition is an active one. The second problem is resolved when one understands that the process of becoming cannot have teleological closure, and thus it must be constantly renewed. The constant and active effort required to sustain and reify our own gender attests not only to the historical contingency of gendered modalities of being-in-the-world but also to the possibility of resisting and subverting such modalities. Hence, Butler is careful to underscore Beauvoir's distinction between inevitable and/or coercive complacency and forced but nonetheless chosen complacency (that is, Otherness). Rather than stating that women are essentially destined to be oppressed, Beauvoir posits that women are forced to choose to be the Other—forced, in essence, to choose against themselves—because of the social discipline they would face if they chose any other course of action. In this sense, women are active producers of their gendered identities, albeit not free producers.

Smith elaborates a similar conception of women as active yet unfree subjects. Smith's contribution, however, remains particularly pertinent, as it also provides a way of understanding how cultural texts *actually* intervene in everyday productions of self. In *Texts, Facts, and Femininity* (1990), Smith posits that femininity is constituted by the social relations and effects of discursive mechanisms that are already mediated by texts. In and through these social relations and effects, contends Smith, women participate actively in their constructions of identity but do not necessarily evade broader matrices of cultural and economic power. Smith explains,

> Women are not just the passive producers of socialization; they are active; they create themselves. At the same time, their self-creation, their work, the uses of their skills, are coordinated with the market for clothes, makeup, shoes, accessories, etc., through print, film, [music], etc. The relations organizing this dialectic between the active and creative subject and the market and productive organization of capital are those of a textually mediated discourse. (161)

Smith's conception of the inextricable relationship between identity and (inter)textuality and Butler's account of gender and subjectivity might be seen as two of this volume's keystone concepts. Indeed it will become clear that the overall orientation of the Butler/Smith schematics buttress the presentations, productions, and negotiations of the female artists discussed here. The value of Butler's and Smith's work for this book lies, I believe, in the fact that both of their accounts allow for an agential gendered subject without effacing the ever-present regulatory technologies of sex/gender regimes.

To negotiate the tensions embedded in modalities of gender experience and to discern how such modalities operate on a broader scale, one requires analytical tools designed to illuminate the functions (and the dysfunctions) of popular cultural processes. I believe that these analytic tools are found within the disciplinary framework of feminist cultural studies.

ON "DOING" CULTURAL STUDIES

> Partly cultural studies matters because it is about how to keep political work alive in an age of shrinking possibilities. [It also] matters that the field of cultural studies is open and unstable and contested. For cultural studies assumes that history—its shape, its seams, its outcomes—is never guaranteed. As a result, doing cultural studies takes work, including the work of deciding what cultural studies is, of making cultural studies over again and again. Cultural studies constructs itself as it faces new questions and takes up new positions. (Grossberg 1992, 18)

As Lawrence Grossberg reveals, cultural studies is a diverse ensemble of investigative enterprises (Blundell, Shepherd, and Taylor 1993, Dines and Humez 1995, During 1992, Grossberg 1992, Grossberg, Nelson, and Treichler 1992, Hall 1992, Kellner 1995). The mutable nature of the theoretical, methodological, and epistemological formations that characterize this particular approach are, however, undergirded by certain relatively stable objectives. In an attempt to resume the more stable objectives of cultural studies, Grossberg has elaborated a list of problematics that, in his estimation, appear to typify most cultural studies projects. For Grossberg, cultural studies seems to be buttressed by eight central problematics. Of these eight problematics, at least five reside at the heart of *Disruptive Divas*. These five problematics, namely "epistemology and interpretation, agency, the structure of cultural formation, power, and the specificity of cultural struggle" (Grossberg 1993, 32), are explored, nuanced, and complicated in *Disruptive Divas* through a reflection on how each intersects with popular music made by women.

Douglas Kellner also endeavors to summarize the fundamental elements of a cultural studies approach. He proclaims, "At its strongest, cultural studies contains a threefold project of analyzing the production and political economy of culture, cultural texts and the audience reception of those texts and their effects" (1995, 8). Although our volume does not devote a proportional analysis to the first objective—that is, the political economy of popular music—our analysis does focus on the examination of cultural texts and the multitudinous modes of their reception. (I will return later to a discussion of why our volume has not opted to profile a proportional analysis of the political economy of popular music.)

Foremost on our cultural studies agenda, then, is indeed the "analysis, interpretation and criticism of cultural artifacts" (Kellner 1995, 6). Popular cultural artifacts, such as television shows, films, and music, constantly surround the individual in her everyday life. Given the omnipresence of popular cultural artifacts, we tend to be instructed by them in many complex ways. They inform our production of thought, behavior, and affect while simultaneously establishing the parameters of acceptable and unacceptable ways of being. In this sense, popular cultural artifacts are profoundly pedagogical. But as in any pedagogical dynamic, the conditions of reception are never guaranteed. That is, the recipient does not always decode the meanings encoded in the cultural artifact—its preferred meanings—in preferred and dominant ways. As Gail Dines and Jean Humez conclude, "specific audiences can either accept those meanings that are preferred by the text or produce negotiated or even oppositional readings of their own" (1995, 3). Yet despite the potential for negotiated or even oppositional readings, it seems fairly clear that many individuals—compelled in large part by the pedagogies of sexist, racist, and homophobic mainstream media—do not produce subversive readings of musical forms.

Mass media regimes continue to read even the most disruptive musical works in ways that marginalize, disarm, and/or efface their subversive potential. These dominant readings underlie the urgency of our project and essentially underwrite its primary objective: to employ a combination of feminist and cultural theory in order to produce a diverse yet coherent collection of *oppositional* readings of the works in question. That is, in reading the present collection of cultural artifacts for their feminist, antiracist, and queer resistance narratives—both lyrical and musical—I also am attempting to disrupt dominant discursive regimes of meaning in popular music. Of course, the present treatise will have neither the distribution nor the impact of highly marketed mass cultural images and commodities. My disruptive analyses and critiques will, however, align this volume with the "intrinsically critical and political dimension to the project of cultural studies that distinguishes it from empirical and apolitical academic approaches to the study of culture and society" (Kellner 1995, 7).

Let us return now to a discussion of the political economy of popular music and its place in this volume. We have not conducted a proportional analysis of the political economy of popular music. This methodological choice in no way indicates that we deem the political economy of cultural texts less important than either their interpretation or their reception. But we chose to focus on questions of textual interpretation and reception, rather than textual production, for two reasons. First, neither Lori nor I could have undertaken to perform all three of the analytical tasks delineated by Kellner within the purview of a single book. Second, the political economy of mass-produced aesthetic forms has been belabored at length by a considerable number of scholars: from the critical theorists (for instance, Adorno and Horkheimer [1969] 1993) to the feminists (for instance, Bordo 1995, Kaplan 1983, 1987, and 1988) to the modernists (for instance, Kant [1790] 1951) and the postmodernists (for instance, Grossberg 1992, Jameson 1983 and 1991).

Economic analyses are, of course, essential to our discernment of mass culture's processes and effects. According to Nehring, however, some of these influential economic theories tend to view even the most rebellious popular cultural forms as almost entirely colonized through the logic of consumer capitalism or determined by flows of trans- and multinational capital. Nehring has thus quite rightly underscored the numerous difficulties with modernist *and* postmodernist theories of aesthetics that deride cultural forms produced within the commercial sphere. Drawing on Andrew Goodwin (1992), Nehring posits,

> The whole problem with mass-culture critics, for two centuries now, is their impossible desire that art be "authentic" or exist outside commerce, which turns into *despair* when that impossibility becomes apparent. The romantic agenda simply no longer makes sense, as the "supposed contradiction between art and commerce" has become "increasingly artificial." (1997, 30; emphasis added)

The despair of which Nehring writes is made manifest in works such as *We Gotta Get out of This Place: Popular Conservatism and Postmodern Culture*, by Lawrence Grossberg. In this treatise, the author posits the near impossibility of subversion through popular music. Because we take an antithetical position—that is, we assert the viability of a marriage between insurgent politics and popular musical forms—I thought it might be appropriate to comment briefly on Grossberg's work. After all, Grossberg himself points out that "any position is always engaged in and constituted by responses to debates with other positions" (1993, 22).

Grossberg opens *We Gotta Get out of This Place* with an emphatic introduction to the questions organizing his deliberation. He writes,

> [This book] is not an optimistic look at the possibilities of popular culture but a pessimistic speculation about the role that popular culture is playing in the contemporary reorganization of power in the United States. This book questions the role of passion and its absence in contemporary political struggles and cultural studies. It is about the relations of theory, politics and passion: How is culture, as both an object and source of passion, implicated in power and how can we understand that relation? (3)

Grossberg goes on to propose that the subversive potential of popular musical forms is increasingly disconnected from political realization, and that in fact "rock is losing its power to encapsulate and articulate resistance and opposition" (9). For Grossberg, "rock" is losing its ability to articulate resistance politics because of its ties to multinational capital—through which the production of "authentic" musical subjectivities is allegedly impossible. Grossberg explains, "In the end, rock, like everything else in the 1990s, is a business. The result is that style is celebrated over authenticity, or rather, that authenticity is seen as just another style. . . . Within the emerging languages of these formations, authenticity is no better than and no worse than the most ironically constructed images of inauthenticity" (234). For Grossberg, then, the machinations of power in the popular sphere operate as a closed circuit, wherein the artist—in view of her ties to consumer capitalism—is guilty of inauthenticity regardless of her musical intentions and/or message.

Nowhere is Grossberg's arguably defeatist thesis more evident than in his cursory discussion of Tracy Chapman, an African-American popular musician who has released many albums rife with fierce and penetrating critiques of white supremacy and patriarchal gender relations. Grossberg characterizes Chapman's success as an ostensibly "authentic rocker" as indicative of the postmodern "proliferation of authenticities" (235), which are, according to him, little more than an assemblage of consumer-driven fads. By way of example, Grossberg writes:

> Tracy Chapman's "authenticity" would seem to be of the *rockist-folk kind*, but the form of her success, and the fact that *she has obviously been produced* and marketed by and for commercial interests (which are not necessarily the same as her own intentions) seems to locate her authenticity elsewhere. (235; emphasis added)

Grossberg's analysis of Chapman's work seems flawed to me for several reasons. First, what exactly does Grossberg mean when he says that Chapman's authenticity is of the "rockist-folk kind"? In my view, such a vague and unqualified statement not only says nothing of Chapman's exceptional artistic trajectory but it also effectively obliterates her vital and sustained black feminist musicianship. In addition, his statement "she has obviously been produced" is both presumptuous and factually incorrect (if one interprets the word *produced* as pertaining to the actual processes of sonic production). With the exception of her very first album, Chapman has not been "produced" at all. Even a casual glance at the back cover of any of her albums reveals that *she* has either produced or coproduced each one of her musical works. Finally, as regards the last component of Grossberg's assertion, I find it difficult to dismiss Chapman's subversive potential or "locate her authenticity elsewhere" simply because she has been "marketed by and for commercial interests." Certainly her record company attempts to sell as many of her albums as possible for purely financial reasons, but this does not, I would argue, preclude her albums from producing countercultural effects.

To be sure, the mass production and sale of any commodity consolidates late capitalist formations that both directly and indirectly perpetuate classist, racist, sexist, and homophobic discursive and structural regimes. Yet "[while capital] has been increasingly successful in co-opting, recycling and remarketing previous forms of oppositional expression, it has nonetheless afforded more space at the national and local levels within which individuals are frequently able to maintain a degree of autonomy in relation to the transnational" (Blundell, Shepherd, and Taylor 1993, 8). It is precisely this "degree of autonomy" on the part of subjects purchasing Chapman's work that gets lost in Grossberg's discussion. There appears to be very little room in his analysis for how the consumer actually engages with and/or responds to the musical product. Can anyone really listen to Tracy Chapman's work—work chronicling the physical and sexual abuse of women, racist police brutality, and corporate greed and exploitation—with passing indifference? If, according to Grossberg, even Chapman's work is merely representative of a postmodern constellation of consumer-driven "authenticity gimmicks," then I cannot think of a single popular cultural form that, within the confines of Grossberg's analytical logic, could possibly articulate political resistance. In his productivist theses of popular aesthetics, then, Grossberg effectively forecloses any possibility of resistance through mass cultural forms. On this subject, Nehring draws on Linda Hutcheon's (1989) discussion of postmodernism, and posits,

> In its pessimism about the power of multinational corporations to absorb or co-opt any expression of dissent, much of postmodern theory only reinforces

a sense of hopelessness, a conviction of the inevitability of the status quo. Thus "postmodernism ultimately manages to install and reinforce as much as subvert the conventions it appears to challenge,"... and its apparent criticism belies "its own complicity with power and domination." (1997, 22)

In a different article, Grossberg himself admits that in popular culture's complex vectors of power, consumption, and meaning, oftentimes one both "wins" and "loses" simultaneously. He writes, "A practice not only may have multiple and even contradictory effects within a single (for instance, ideological) register but across a range of different registers as well. Thus a particular articulation can be both empowering and disempowering; people can win something and lose something" (1993, 62). When it comes to Tracy Chapman, and all of the female musicians examined in the present volume, feminist, queer, antiracist, and/or left-leaning consumers both win and lose when we purchase countercultural musical products. We win because these musicians ignite us, educate us, and infuse us with a sense of oppositional solidarity. But we also lose, because in purchasing these musical products we invariably reproduce exploitative capitalist relations of consumption. Certainly, within the context of the present chapter, I am neither willing nor able to discuss the relative merits of either "winning" or "losing" in such a complex landscape of consumer capitalism. I am here, however, to attest to the fact that I have been qualitatively moved—from a very young age—by artists such as Tracy Chapman and those discussed in *Disruptive Divas*. I have been emotionally and politically challenged, pained, motivated, and, as Nehring puts it, "steered into fully conscious radicalization" (1997, xxiii) due, in large measure, to their musical contributions. Surely the obvious transformative potential of popular music must be valuable in and of itself to the study and understanding of cultural formation and struggle.

Hence my analysis does not explicitly address the political economy of the cultural artifacts being studied. And although I do believe that popular cultural forms can produce transformative effects, I am deeply mindful of the dangers associated with overestimating the political potential of subversion-through-consumption. I therefore concur with Dines and Humez when they state,

> We would agree that audience resistance alone cannot serve as a counterbalance or substitute for political efforts, either to get mainstream producers to change imagery or, ultimately, to achieve a more democratic system of media

ownership and access. But as long-term battles are being waged on the political fronts, we would also advocate taking a view of ourselves as media audiences that is grounded in respect for our own agency, values and intelligence.
(1995, 4)

To summarize briefly, my component of this project attempts to (a)
read disruption, subversion, and opposition in selected musical works;
(b) approach these musical works as complex, contestable, and polyse-
mous cultural artifacts to be analyzed, interpreted, and criticized; and (c)
focus on how a given cultural artifact, such as popular music, can be
decoded and understood through a reader- or listener-centered
hermeneutics in order to elucidate the multifarious and at times contradictory narratives that organize it. While this may sound relatively
straightforward, it will become important at this point to delineate the
assumptions from which I am working and, equally, those against which
I am working as I interpret the texts in question.

THE PROBLEMATICS OF INTERPRETATION:
READING POPULAR MUSIC

Reading resistance in cultural texts and indeed reading cultural texts
from the reader's perspective rather than from the author's perspective
requires some discussion primarily because reader-oriented criticism
remains marginalized as a hermeneutic strategy in popular media
accounts of musical works. That is, the mainstream press often tries to
understand the works of popular musicians primarily through an
author-centered approach—an endeavor that is undergirded by the
assumption that authorial intention is the key to discerning the meaning
of a work. In this section I will argue against a strictly author-centered
approach to understanding a textual work. To do so, I will highlight a
number of the debates pertaining to textual interpretation that have
transpired in literary and cultural studies.

Smith (1990) begins her chapter "Femininity as Discourse" by setting
forth her view of the ways in which text and discourse are made to mean
within a social context. She writes,

We are part of a world a major segment of which is mediated by texts; forms
of discourse have emerged that are vested in social relations and organization; reason, knowledge, concepts are more than merely attributes of individ-

ual consciousness, they are embedded in, organize, and are integral to social relations in which subjects act but which are not reducible to the acts of subjects....Discourse and ideology can be investigated as actual social relations ongoingly organized in and by the activities of actual people. (160)

Smith's argument constitutes a succinct articulation of why—given the inherently cultural character of text and discourse—creative works cannot be interpreted in sole relation to their "authorial origins." Even if one agrees that diverse forms of textuality inform the ways in which creative works are made to mean, however, one may still be left with a number of thorny questions. For instance, if one does not use the author's intention as the yardstick by which to appraise creative works, then what standard of evaluation should be used? How can one interpretation be seen as any better than another? What does a reader-oriented hermeneutic imply for broader conceptions of language and meaning? These are some of the questions upon which I shall reflect in this section. It is worth noting, however, that I will be using a good deal of literary critical terms, as the authors upon whom I draw in this section are primarily students of literature. Yet, in that I am performing "readings" of the works in question, I believe that the following remarks—born as they were in a tradition of literary study—are nevertheless highly pertinent to the enterprise of understanding popular lyrics.[6]

Author-Centered Reading versus Reader-Centered Reading

Many critics have remarked that the modern discussion of authorial intention as it relates to acts and/or methods of interpretation was inaugurated by Wimsatt and Beardsley's landmark article "The Intentional Fallacy." In this article, Wimsatt and Beardsley posit that a critic's overall approach to and view of literature (or texts in general) is always mediated by his or her conception of authorial intention. With respect to their own conception of authorial intention, Monroe Beardsley and William Wimsatt propose that "the design or intention of the author is neither available nor desirable as a standard for judging the success of a literary work" (1954, 3). The intention of the author is undesirable as a standard of interpretative judgment because, according to these authors, "the poem [or work] belongs to the public. It is embodied in language, the peculiar possession of the public, and it is about the human being, an object of public knowledge" (5). These polemical utterances collide quite significantly with E. D. Hirsch's vehement treatises (1969 and 1976) on

the problematics of authorship. Through a critical analysis of these treatises, I will show that for Hirsch—an important figure in the interpretation debate—texts are not figured as essentially "public" in any way.

In *Validity in Interpretation* and *The Aims of Interpretation*, Hirsch
attempts to rescue the preeminence of authorial intention in literary
criticism. In ardent opposition to the early proponents of more reader-
oriented schools of thought (that is, New Criticism), Hirsch posits that
the banishment of the author has "frequently encouraged willful arbi-
trariness and extravagance in academic criticism and has been one very
important cause of the prevailing skepticism which calls into doubt the
possibility of objectively valid interpretation" (1969, 2). In a slightly tau-
tological afterthought, Hirsch adds: "These disadvantages would be tol-
erable, of course, if they were true" (2–3).

By exploiting theoretical and methodological schematics akin to and
inspired by Husserlian phenomenology, Hirsch posits that the meaning
of a literary work is fixed and stable and indeed that it is identical to
whatever mental object the author intended at the moment of composition. While Hirsch avows that there may be a plurality of valid interpretations, such valid interpretations must move within "the system of
typical expectations and probabilities" permitted by the author's meaning. Moreover, Hirsch concedes that a work of literature can be made to
mean in different ways, depending on the reader and his or her temporal
and discursive location. But these different, non-author-centered meanings are not, in fact, meanings—they are "significances." Thus, for Hirsch,
where meanings are immutable and for all intents and purposes determined by the author, significances are changeable and open to historical
variation.

Interestingly—in what appears to contradict the unyielding posi-
tivism of his earlier assertion regarding objectively valid and true interpretations—Hirsch confesses that one can never know with absolute
certainty that he or she has fully ascertained the author's meaning. It is
thus entirely possible, according to Hirsch, that a critic may one day
apprehend, in all its fullness and complexity, the true meaning of what
an author intended at the moment of composition but never be in a position to know with absolute certainty that he or she has accomplished
such an impressive feat of interpretation. For Hirsch, then, knowing anything of value about the meaning of a literary work necessarily involves
a simultaneous not-knowing. This epistemological aporia strikes me as

particularly problematic, even if it appears to be smoothed over by Hirsch's proposition that meaning is not an affair of words, but one of consciousness. This contention implies that meaning is, like Husserl's, prelinguistic, willed by the author through a "ghostly, wordless mental act which is then fixed for all time in a particular set of material signs" (Eagleton [1983] 1996, 58).

Yet subsuming meaning under a rubric of the prelinguistic does not resolve the manifold difficulties that continue to haunt Hirsch's position. For instance, the constitution of the authorial "wordless consciousness" is not at all elucidated by Hirsch and therefore continues to pose problems for his attempts to salvage the legitimacy of critical appeals to authorial intention. While Hirsch acknowledges that because consciousness is by nature elusive, it is untenable to suggest that the critic should endeavor to somehow access the consciousness of the author and reconstruct the thoughts and sensibilities that characterized the moment of redaction. Despite this acknowledgment, however, Hirsch asserts that one can come relatively close to discerning the author's compositional intentions by restricting himself to the analysis of the "intrinsic genre" of the text, which basically refers to the general literary norms, codes, and conventions that could be said to "have governed the author's meanings at the time of writing" (Eagleton [1983] 1996, 59). Hirsch also suggests that the ideal critic can to a fair extent reconstruct the author's meaning of a work by confining him or herself to the appraisal of what he calls "verbal meaning." However, in defining verbal meaning, Hirsch excludes so many other dimensions of meaning—such as psychologistic meaning, meaning experience, extratextual meaning, and subject matter meaning—that the Hirschian critic is left only a tremendously narrow definition of meaning with which to work.

The implications of Hirsch's distinction between meaning and significance could also be construed as dogmatic when considered in sociocultural terms. Because for Hirsch all meanings exacted from a text that do not conform with the author's own are expelled from the supreme rubric of meaning and indeed relegated to the inferior and less pertinent realm of significance, Hirsch could be branded with the charge of elitism on a number of counts. In a quintessentially Marxist critique, literary and cultural theorist Terry Eagleton maintains that Hirsch's conceptualization of meaning and textuality is authoritarian and juridical, and that by conferring upon the author the ultimate truth-function, Hirsch is effectively policing the dissemination, transformation, and multiplication of the signified. Eagleton writes,

> The aim of all this policing is the protection of private property. For Hirsch an author's meaning is his own, and should not be stolen or trespassed upon by the reader. The meaning of the text is not to be socialized, made the public property of its various readers; it belongs solely to the author, who should have the exclusive rights over its disposal long after he or she is dead. ([1983] 1996, 59–60)

While Hirsch does not concede that his author-centered approach is elitist, authoritarian, and/or juridical, he does admit that it is arbitrary. For him, using the author's meaning as the standard by which we interpret a text is not the only possible hermeneutic course of action; it is, however, the most desirable for both scientific and ethical reasons. Scientifically, discerning the author's intention is the best critical strategy, as it constitutes the only stable and universal textual norm and is therefore the only reliable means by which one can reasonably interpret a given work. This method is obviously rife with problems, especially in view of the multitudinous difficulties associated with isolating authorial intention through phenomenological methods. Hirsch's rationale for appealing to authorial intention on ethical grounds, however, is equally problematic. According to Hirsch, remaining loyal to the author's meaning is morally right if only because, in his words,

> When we simply use an author's words for our own purposes without respecting his intention, we transgress..."the ethics of language," just as we transgress ethical norms when we use another person merely for our own ends. Kant held it to be a foundation of moral action that men should be conceived as ends in themselves, and not as instruments of other men. This imperative is transferable to the words of men because speech is an extension and expression of men in the social domain, and also because when we fail to conjoin a man's intentions to his words we lose the soul of speech, which is to convey meaning and to understand what is intended to be conveyed....An interpreter, like any other person, falls under the basic moral imperative of speech, which is to respect an author's intention. That is why, in ethical terms, the original meaning is the "best meaning." (1976, 90–2)

It is at this point that I would like to extend Eagleton's ([1983] 1996) cogent critique of Hirsch's elitism to encompass other considerations. Construing the encouragement and valorization of alternative and/or marginal textual interpretations as forms of unethical literary conduct, as Hirsch does, presupposes that the maintenance of "original" meanings is not only an ethical good in and of itself, but that it is in the best interests of both the literary/cultural community and society at large. In response to this assumption, I posit that any form of blind submission to the original meanings of texts, canonical texts in particular, can be and often is deleterious to both scholarship and culture on at least three counts. First, if Foucault is right when he posits that modes of dominant discursivity both produce and reinforce unequal relations of power—and if conventional interpretations of canonical literature constitute a particular form of dominant discursivity—then it seems irresponsible to uncritically privilege "original" or "preferred" interpretations of canonical literature. To do so is, in my view, conceptually analogous to continuing the saturation of the literary and cultural imaginations with the prejudices, concerns, and sensibilities of what, in the final analysis, is a minute, unrepresentative, and highly homogeneous group of usually white, heterosexual, moneyed male writers.

Second, Hirsch's justification for privileging authorial meanings rather than alternative meanings rests on the postulation that "men" should be conceived as ends in themselves, and not as instruments of other "men"; or, put differently, that readers should respect the integrity of the writer's original idea rather than selfishly appropriate it for their own ends. Once again, Hirsch's assertion is undergirded by the presupposition that the authors in question have conducted themselves in an ethical fashion throughout the writing process and that, by extension, they have not used others to meet their own creative needs. Although I am quite sure that many authors have written and do write ethically, the fact remains that a good many of the modern West's allegedly great writers deal frequently in sexist, racist, and homophobic thematics, and in doing so, undoubtedly use Others for their own creative advancement and affirmation. It is precisely for this reason that feminist, queer, black, and postcolonial cultural and literary critics have begun, over the course of the last few decades, to thoroughly reread the canon. Such processes of resignification have been necessary to disentangle the multifarious ways in which canonical writers have at times mythologized culturally marginalized groups.

Finally, because writing is so often a vocation for society's most privileged, the need to, in Eagleton's language, deprivatize its meanings seems all the more urgent. Very often the only creative avenue for meaning-making open to disenfranchised groups, or groups frequently omitted by forms of literary culture, consists in subversive or alternative readings of dominant works. These reading practices must, in my view, be construed as legitimate forms of discerning meaning. To reduce them, as Hirsch would, to the inferior realm of significance would merely perpetuate the West's long legacy of privileging the "truths" of the ruling classes.

My views on the importance of a reader-centered approach have been generally conditioned by poststructuralist conceptions of language and signification. These conceptions are systematized and applied by theorists of the reader-response school and will be underscored below.

Reader-Response Criticism

Disgruntled with modernist forms of literary criticim that attributed absolute primacy to authorial intention, French theorists such as Barthes and Foucault began to question not only the legitamacy of an author-oriented hermeneutics, but the entire etiology of "the author." According to these two theorists, viewing the master key of textual meaning as somehow housed by the author's intention is both elitist (because it perpetuates the view that meaning-making is the preserve of those privileged few who write) and linguistically and semiotically impossible (in that language is always already indeterminate). Barthes's interrogation of the author is perhaps the most radical; he writes,

> [A] text is made of multiple writings, drawn from many cultures and entering into mutual relations of dialogue, parody, contestation, but there is one place where this multiplicity is focused and that place is the reader, not, as was hitherto said, the author. The reader is the space on which all the quotations that make up a writing are inscribed without any of them being lost; a text's unity lies not in its origin but in its destination . . . the birth of the reader must be at the cost of the death of the Author. ([1970] 1974, [1970] 1974, 150)

While Foucault's examination of the author is more cautious than Barthes's, he nevertheless brings into relief the historical nature of attributing the source of textual meanings to a single author. Having exposed the radically constructed nature of the figure of the author, Foucault extols a vision of society wherein literature would circulate anonymously—free from interpretative constraints related to the author-function. These two views are, quite obviously, a sharp departure from the author-centered hermeneutics of theorists such as Hirsch.

Shortly after the works of Barthes and Foucault, German and particularly Anglo-American critical theorists also began demanding the enfranchisement of the reader's perspective.[7] This collective demand, albeit diverse and at times contradictory, can be broadly described as the "reader-response" school; it encompassed the works of theorists such as Wolfgang Iser, Stanley Fish, Hans Robert Jauss, Jonathan Culler, Jane Tompkins, Frank Kermode, and many others. Essentially, the theoretical move to "read the reader back in" to exercises in interpretation is buttressed by two central clusters of epistemological premises, which can be seen as fundamentally skeptical of a modernist and/or formalist hermeneutics. First, reader-response criticism challenges the privileged position of the work of art and seeks to undermine its priority and authority not only by displacing the work from the center and substituting the reader in its place, but by putting in doubt the autonomy of the work from linguistic, cultural, and economic processes. Second, this form of criticism endeavors to bring into relief the impossibility of objectively true interpretation by showing that one's relationship to reality is not a natural or immanent knowledge but a hermeneutic construct, that all perception is already an act of interpretation, that the notion of a text-in-itself is empty, that a work cannot be understood in isolation from its results, and that the subject and object are invisibly bound. Thus, broadly conceived, reader-response criticism can be seen not only as an attempt to understand the reading experience and its conditions, but also to collapse the modernist divide between reading and writing, leading ultimately to a view of *reading as writing,* as textuality (Freund 1987).

Reader-Oriented Criticism and Popular Cultural Texts

Although this discussion may appear most pertinent to those interested in strictly literary questions, its basic premises can be applied to the reading of popular music. However, while it is true that literary works have traditionally been the preserve of white, moneyed men, the same cannot necessarily be said of popular musical works. Indeed, the production of popular musical forms has, since its inception, encompassed and even relied on the contributions of those who inhabit the marginalia of dominant culture (for instance, women and people of color). This fact, however, does not occlude the relevance of a reader-oriented criticism. If anything, the fact that women and people of color have been tolerated, and even celebrated, in popular culture (as opposed to being pathologized, as they are in most other spheres of public life, such as those of education, religion, and the family) renders a reader-oriented approach all the more vital.

I am arguing that the success of culturally marginalized groups in popular music necessarily begs the following questions: What does the marked presence of such groups in the popular musical sphere accomplish, articulate, and/or imply for prevailing discursive and economic processes? How has a sexist and racist dominant culture produced such a vast audience willing to engage with the narratives of those oppressed by its own machinations? How have the transnational corporate technologies of popular media—from *Rolling Stone* and *Billboard* to MTV— attempted to contain, reformulate, and benefit from the contributions of nonwhite and female musicians by influencing the way the listener engages with their works? How do culturally marginalized groups of readers make a cultural text mean in ways that trouble and/or contradict dominant or "preferred" textual meanings? A reader-oriented approach to understanding popular music enables the scholar to tackle these kinds of questions—questions that would be neither plausible nor thinkable within a hermeneutics of authorial intention.[8]

A reader-oriented approach allows us to see how the meaning of any one cultural text is unstable, indeterminate, and multifaceted. Once one has established the tenuous nature of textual meaning, one can expose the subversive potential of individual acts of interpretation by understanding musical texts in ways antagonistic to dominant readings. So while we dispense with the dream of "objectively valid interpretations" when we embrace and valorize the reader's manifold textual engagements, we gain the ability to read insurgence in works that have been hitherto domesticated by the tactics of a sexist, racist, and homophobic media culture.

MAKING SENSE OF POPULAR MUSIC: CULTURAL STUDIES MEETS MUSICOLOGY

As someone whose intellectual formation has been structured primarily by the theoretical sensibilities of cultural studies, I have at times been alarmed by conventional musicological analyses of popular music. As several contemporary musicologists have recently avowed (McClary 1991, Shepherd 1991, Shepherd and Wicke 1997, Solie 1993, Walser 1992 and 1993b), traditional musicological accounts of popular musical forms tend to ignore "the most basic questions about what pieces of music can express or reflect of the people who make and use them, and thus the differences between and among those people" (Solie 1993, 3). Because much musicological theory does not endeavor to address such fundamental questions, its analyses tend to essentialize and/or idealize the works of music under scrutiny (Shepherd and Wicke 1997, Solie 1993). Consequently, theorists schooled in the humanities and the social sciences have taken up the analysis of popular music in order to explore its implications as a signifying practice (Grossberg 1992, Nehring 1997).

Yet embedded within these analyses of popular music are a number of important problems and limitations. Although these analyses focus on textual, systemic, and semiotic problematics neglected by conventional musicologists, cultural analyses neglect the unique mechanisms through which music is *made to mean*. That is, they treat popular music—and the study of it—as though it signifies in ways akin to any other popular cultural artifact (Shepherd 1991, Shepherd and Wicke 1997). This tendency is evidenced by the "content-analysis" approach of most nonmusicological studies of popular music. This particular methodological approach—borrowed from disciplines like sociology and psychology—focuses primarily on the lyrical components of a popular musical work. When applied to music of any kind, this approach has two noteworthy implications: On the one hand, the disproportionate amount of attention paid to the work's lyrical aspects tends to result in a dismissal of the work's musical (that is, sonic and tonal) elements and the role they play in processes of signification. On the other hand, the content-analysis approach to song lyrics tends to treat the narrative elements of popular music as though they operate and signify in the same way as language. Thus, when cultural theorists employ a content-analysis approach to the examination of affect and meaning in music, they invariably sever the text under scrutiny from its intrinsically musical environment. Indeed, according to Shepherd and Wicke, many nonmusicological scholars of popular music treat the lyrical content of a musical work "as if there were no alternative but to assume that it signifies in the circumstances of its historical contingencies, as if it were language (which it clearly is not)" (1997, 3).

If musicology has tended to privilege the study of music while ignoring the meaning of such music within specific sociocultural contexts, then cultural studies has privileged the study of music's meaning within specific sociocultural contexts while ignoring the ways in which music actually contributes to the generation of meaning. In their dismissal of either the text or the music, neither approach seems entirely appropriate to the study of popular musical forms. Indeed, to produce a truly comprehensive account of popular musical artifacts, the theorist must be sensitive to both the textual and musical constituents of a musical work.

The present volume strives to overcome the disciplinary limitations of both musicology and cultural studies by engaging both methodological trajectories simultaneously. In essence, our goal in *Disruptive Divas* is to forge and apply an approach that conceptualizes music as a distinctive signifying practice that is nonetheless constituted socially and culturally (Shepherd and Wicke 1997). Rarely have two scholars, one trained in cultural studies and the other in music theory, worked together to produce such integrated close readings of popular songs.

2

"Close Readings" of Popular Song: Intersections among Sociocultural, Musical, and Lyrical Meanings

Lori Burns

My interpretive work explores how a cultural-critical study can be merged with a music-theoretical analysis. I have developed an analytic method that allows me to explore music and text relations in popular songs, but that is also internally coherent and systematic within the discipline of music theory and analysis. This work responds to and engages a wide range of literature in the disciplines of music theory and musicology, including studies of text/music relations, popular music analysis, and feminist musicology. In addition to that musicological orientation, I am informed by the cultural-critical approach taken by my coauthor in this project. This requires a balancing act, and I often have the sense that I am walking a tightrope between the two disciplines of music and cultural studies, or between formalism and poststructuralism. In the following pages, however, I shall explore some of the questions and problems that I encounter in this exercise, as well as offer my solutions in the form of a well-defined analytic method.

My approach to the analysis of the music itself is formalist in the sense that I discuss the musical relations of pitch and rhythmic structure, with a special focus on the formal organization of the song and its harmonic and voice-leading progressions, as if these were fixed and internal to the work of music. However, I believe that I can claim a "post-structuralist" orientation, as I do not assert absolute or fixed meanings, and I am sensitive to the context of specific musical events within a structure. As I shall discuss below, the study of formal details in the analysis of popular music is often criticized by scholars who advocate an exclusively sociocultural approach. However, music theorists are beginning to look carefully at this repertoire, believing that they have something valuable to offer to the investigation of what constitutes meaning in popular music, and wishing to make that contribution not only to the discipline of music theory, but also to the general field of popular music studies.

Alongside my formalist music-analytical focus stands my lyrical-interpretive focus; that is, my interest in the extramusical meaning of a popular song, and, in particular, the ways in which issues of gender are negotiated. Thus my analysis is not merely an effort to understand the musical form as structure, but rather to determine the ways in which that structure "enacts" or animates the lyrics and their social message.[1] It is thus the intersection of musical meaning and lyrical meaning that is the focus of my analytic exercise.

Music theory and its practitioners are not always welcome visitors to the field of popular music studies. The theories are accused of being too rigid to do justice to individual pieces of music, and the music theorists are accused of forcing the music to fit the paradigms defined by the theories.[2] The criticisms come from cultural studies experts as well as musicologists. In the following pages, I will discuss the issues that arise in this debate, and position myself more clearly on the issues in order to set the stage for my analytic methodology.

MUSICAL ENGAGEMENT AND DISCIPLINARITY

Within the larger fields of musicology and music theory, the study of popular music is in a burgeoning state of development. With the work of Richard Middleton, Allan Moore, and Stan Hawkins in the United Kingdom and Robert Walser, Susan McClary, John Covach, David Brackett, Walter Everett, and John Shepherd in North America, popular music has been established as a repertoire to be respected and studied within the academy. Although there seems to be general agreement that we have much to gain by studying popular music, scholars have engaged strenuously in the debate over *how* we should study this music.

The first issue that a music scholar faces upon encountering the literature of popular music studies is that another academic discipline is heavily invested in the study of this repertoire. Cultural theorists have been writing about the social significance of popular music for many years (for instance, Frith 1981, Grossberg 1992, Kaplan 1983 and 1987, Lewis 1990), and we in the field of music can learn a great deal from this literature. However, it is not within a cultural theorist's particular expertise to discuss the musical content—an understandable *lacuna*, yet a frustrating one when the author not only avoids objectified discussion of the music but goes so far as to negate the value of the music in the communication of meaning. I will quote a fairly lengthy passage from Neil Nehring in order to illustrate an extreme example of discipline negation:

> Given my interest in encouraging a better appreciation of the interplay between emotion and reason in the reception of popular music, I do not intend to do musicology in the next chapter. I don't find technical description of music all that revelatory anyway; I only feel a compelling need to know the chords when I want to play along on my guitar, and they're usually easy enough to discover—rock and roll, after all, continues to be the same three chords over and over, or it wouldn't be rock and roll. . . . The rather dramatic claims that even the best musicologists make for the effect of chord progressions and musical modes, moreover, invariably seem inflated and unconvincing. Robert Walser does anticipate all these objections: "To argue that critical scrutiny of the details of rock music is inappropriate because people don't hear that way is like arguing that we can't analyze the syntax of language because people don't know that they're using gerunds and participles." But gerunds and participles have never gotten anyone particularly excited, of course. (1997, 149)

Nehring dismisses the potential for music to bear meaning in this repertoire. We witness here the difficulties of crossdisciplinary work. Nehring's lack of interest in reading technical music analysis is understandable, given his disciplinary orientation (he is an English professor in the United States); however, his evaluation of rock harmony would surely irritate most music theorists. I am personally disappointed by the fact that, while I am open to the benefits of his sociocultural investigation, he is clearly not open to the benefits of a musical one. As a colleague of mine once put it, this is not a question of border crossings, but rather of border patrol.[3]

To be fair, Nehring's deprecation of musicology is not representative of the entire cultural studies community. In fact, a good number of cultural theorists acknowledge the importance of music-technical analysis even if they do not or are unable to integrate such analysis into their own investigations of popular music (for example, Frith in Shepherd 1991). Some cultural theorists have even included musicological contributions in their collections on popular culture (for example, Frith, Goodwin, and Grossberg 1993).

Although the musicologists and music theorists who study popular music generally agree that the "music itself" should be discussed, the arguments continue over how this should be done. The criticisms generally come from within the discipline of musicology and focus on the discourse of music theory. Such debates engage the definition, identification, representation, and interpretation of musical structure and impinge on the very content of music-theoretical discourse.

Philip V. Bohlman, for instance, criticizes the music theorist's interest in analysis and in notation, both of which are negatively cast as methods of essentializing music. Using rap music as an example of music that resists analysis, he questions the role of music theory in popular music interpretation: "What would we study as rap's music? What would we learn by transcribing rap performances, putting its notes on the page? . . . Rap music resists essentializing as 'music.' Its symbols are literary, ideological, and political, not the depoliticized symbols of a repertory or musical system" (1993, 430). Because he is frustrated with the limits of traditional theoretical methods, Bohlman tosses out both the theory and the music that the theory is attempting to explain. He says in so many words that rap music is *not* music. A further point to make about Bohlman's remarks is that the symbols of a musical system—and presumably by this he means notation and terminology, which are written representations of our theoretical understanding of the music—are by no means "depoliticized." Indeed the theoretical language that has developed over the centuries to account for Western music is itself an important and influential part of musical culture.

John Shepherd and Peter Wicke call for a consideration of affect and meaning in popular music, yet they are extremely critical of music-theoretical approaches to the analysis of the music. They believe that musicologists and music theorists

> have been able to contribute little... to the question of how music signifies, and how, exactly, musical experience is constituted. This is because music theory and music analysis have taken as their starting point not musical experience, but the production of music. They have in other words been more concerned with how the notes are "placed" than with their effect once placed. (1997, 139)

This statement is typical of the criticisms of music theory that occur in the field of popular music studies. It suggests that a theoretical stance will necessarily preclude a creative listening/interpretive experience, that theorists are more concerned with theories than with music. Shepherd and Wicke go on to criticize the discourse of music theory more specifically when they identify their complaint with theoretical parameters such as mode, harmony, and rhythm:

> [T]hese concepts and their accompanying categories and terminologies are constructs: linguistic constructs which constitute discourses essentially extrinsic to the sonic events of the music they describe. Since the categories are *not* intrinsic to the sounds of music, they can *of themselves* be of little assistance in specifying the cultural character of those sounds in music. (1997, 147)

Arguably, music theory has been constructed as an external means of examining internal music relations. However, the conceit and an essential tenet of the discipline of music theory is that the work we do to construct our theoretical discourse has its basis in empirical observation. As David Lewin wrote in 1968 and then reiterated in 1991, music theory "attempts to describe the ways in which, given a certain body of literature, composers and listeners appear to have accepted sound as conceptually structured, categorically prior to any one specific piece" (1991, 112). Here, Lewin risks being criticized as a "formalist" for admitting to such a standard of objectivity or musical autonomy. A musicologist of postmodern sensibilities might also point out that a formalist approach does not take into account the larger social context of a given work. Because of these criticisms, formalist analysis has been dismissed for its potential to contribute to the understanding of affect and meaning in music.

With my analytic method, I propose that there is a value to working within the traditional discourse of music theory, as long as one holds the concomitant agenda of examining and possibly reshaping and remodeling that discourse. Matthew Brown has offered a brilliant working metaphor for this intellectual activity:

> [E]mpiricists resemble sailors at sea on a leaking boat. Instead of rebuilding their boat from the keel up in a dry dock, they fix the leaks while adrift on the open water. As each plank is replaced, the remaining timbers keep the craft afloat. But once each leak is patched another appears; bit by bit the boat becomes transformed, being carried along by nothing but the evolving conceptual scheme itself. (1997a, 336)

Brown's parable suggests the importance of the practical as well as imaginative responses to solving theoretical problems. It also affirms the evolutionary process of methodology, and the value of the empirical process itself.

A theoretical system—a constructed discourse—can be formally limiting, if one applies the system too rigidly. But surely the solution to this problem does not exist in the total dismissal of the formalist approach to music and its language. Feminist theorists have debated the use of existing theoretical discourses at length, taking on the texts of, for instance, Sigmund Freud and Michel Foucault; indeed this research lies at the very heart of the feminist critical enterprise. Hazel Rowley and Elizabeth Grosz examine the role of Freudian theory within the feminist literature, and make the following claims:

> Freud's work tended, between the 1930s and 1970s, to be regarded as misogynist, ahistorical, and acultural. Many feminists saw it as a rationalization and justification of relations of domination and subordination between the sexes, for they claimed that Freud explains men's and women's relative social and psychical positions in terms of their anatomy. Nevertheless, instead of simply abandoning psychoanalytic theory and seeking alternative models of psychical development and functioning, feminists have remained commited to the reform, rereading, or reinterpretation of psychoanalytic doctrine in an attempt to use it to describe and explain the ways in which males and females acquire their socially ordained sexual roles and their correlative psychical attitudes and structures. (1990, 175)

Rowley and Grosz emphasize reform, rereading, and reinterpretation as important critical activities for a theorist who wishes to develop a new understanding out of an existing discourse. These activities require the kind of creativity and experimentation that Matthew Brown invokes with his boat story. Nadine Hubbs also emphasizes "imagination" as the intellectual tool that will help us "bridge the gap between musical discourse and musical experience" (2000, 8).

Not that music theorists have been lacking in imagination. Despite the negative stereotype of music theorists as cold, scientific formalists, "musical experience" is of great import for anyone working within the discipline of music theory. In defense of my discipline, I would contend that, for the music theorist who is working toward a systematic explanation of a composition or group of compositions, the music itself (and thus the musical experience) *is* the focus of the enterprise.

One of the threads common to recent "defenses" of music theory (for instance, Agawu 1997, Matthew Brown 1997a, Burnham 1997, Everett 2000, Guck 1997a, Hubbs 2000, McCreless 1997) is the proclamation of an engagement with the music. Scott Burnham speaks of "handling the goods" (1997, 325), stressing the importance of a tactile knowledge of music and comparing the music theorist's relationship with music to the English literary critic's relationship with words:

> But in the end, like anything else truly worth cultivating, knowing music takes time, and your average theorist is someone who has taken the time to learn music as a functional language. Imagine practicing the criticism of English poetry if you yourself could not automatically form meaningful utterances in the English language. (1997, 327)

Marion Guck's honest account of her analytic experience is anything but cold and formalist. Since I first heard her say these words they have had a lasting effect on my own analytic response:

> And doing this work gives me great pleasure: I make myself all ears, give myself up to the piece, let it carry me away. When the sounds of the piece end, I carry myself back by asking "just what was that like? What could I tell someone else so that they too could hear that effect?" I play it at the piano, I make up momentary dances—I give myself up to it now as it has become part of me. (1994, 38)

As Guck implies when she wonders how she will verbalize her experience, the particular aural engagement of a professionally trained music theorist will necessarily be different from that of other listeners—

including other music theorists as well as listeners with less theoretical expertise.

Theoretical expertise is a distinct challenge in the analysis and discussion of popular music, because not all listeners are informed to the same extent by the academic discipline of music theory. But Walter Everett asserts the value of his music analyses despite an inequality on the theoretical playing field:

> My aim is to illustrate that because rock musicans express their originality according to all significant musical parameters, a working understanding of all of these basic elements (whether nurtured by an expensive tuition through peer-reviewed programs in theory, analysis, and musicology, or developed by a bright independent performer with good ears) can be both appropriate and useful for a full appreciation of the literature's expressive import. I'll demonstrate expressive manipulations of formal construction, vocal and instrumental colorings, rhythmic relationships, melodic devices, and tonal systems, without once ever considering whether the composers, arrangers, artists, or engineers might have been fully conscious of how I might hear what they were doing. The only question of value to me is what might profit the imaginative *listener's* consciousness. (2000, 271)

Everett defends his choice to study particular musical elements when he says, "my pure and simple interest has been, and continues to be, talking about the expressive musical effects that gratify me, and learning from others who do the same in their own ways" (2000, 270). Some of the parameters that he mentions (formal construction, rhythmic relationships, tonal systems) require a strong theoretical foundation and, indeed, Everett has himself received such an education and has chosen to work as a professional music theorist.

It is difficult to write music-theoretical analysis in such a way that a general reader can follow the argument. The analytic methods, terminology, and notation are complex and require familiarity. Hubbs says that she strives for "accessibility" when she creates her musical examples, but maintains that "we will need to cultivate some form of musical notation in our pop-rock discourse, if it is to pursue meaningful illumination of musical issues; the challenge lies in rethinking, adapting, perhaps reinventing conventional notation and modes of graphic representation, for optimal transparency and illustrative effect" (2000, 12). I applaud the innovative spirit of this stance, and I agree that we as music theorists ought to strive for clarity, but there is a limit to such generosity. (I also ask, rhetorically, if all disciplines are so generous as to simplify in layperson's terms what they have been trained to perceive as a substantive element of their discipline, be it a Foucauldian concept of power relations or a Marxist analysis of socioeconomic organization.) As Hubbs proceeds to discuss an example of music, she uses graphic notation that incorporates pop chord labels, and there is certainly no guarantee that all readers will understand these symbols. She also writes descriptive passages such as the following: "It presents a B-minor ground bass proceeding by measured but inevitable chromatic descent to V, and then moving toward drawn-out resolution—on a tonic chord clouded for two beats by the voice's suspended ninth "(2000, 16–17). The reader trained in music theory can appreciate every detail in this technical description. Indeed it is a very clearly written analytic passage, which allows me as a reader to "hear" what she is hearing; that is, I can follow with my inner ear the very harmonic progression and contrapuntal gesture that she describes. Thus, her analysis has meaning for me and reaches me, even though it may not reach all readers in the same way. Hubbs communicates something of value with her analysis, and there is an audience for her ideas. I would not like to see her or any other music analyst eliminate such content from their work, but would rather see a more generous spirit on the part of the reader who is trained in another discipline. Just as I may have to struggle and ultimately accept defeat as I read certain passages in the scholarship of another academic discipline, I believe that a reader who wishes to have access to the larger conceptual framework of an interpretation could learn to have patience for the technical passages. Crossdisciplinary or interdisciplinary work is ill conceived when the individual disciplines have to eliminate substantive content in order to achieve total accessibility for all readers. Mélisse and I prefer to think of our efforts as a collaboration that allows us to work together as well as to work apart. This is one of the many reasons why we have chosen to write as individuals rather than to merge our commentary into a seamless whole.

MUSICAL CONTENT AND "TRADITIONAL" MUSIC THEORY

Rather than reader competence and accessibility, the more serious problem with the use of music-theoretical terminology has to do with the care and consistency with which we use labels and symbols within a theoretical system, and with the very question of the degree to which a traditional system can be applied to popular music. The terms and analytic values that we apply to tonal music were developed to account for European art music and need to be carefully adjusted and refined. Yet many musical principles carry over from one harmonically conceived repertoire to another, and there are many theoretical tools that can be put to good use.[4] After all, the same call for theoretical refinement could be made as an analyst moves from studying baroque to classical music (different styles), or even from studying Robert Schumann to Clara Schumann (similar styles but different particulars). John Covach supports the use of traditional methods for popular music with the caution that wholesale application could produce distortions:

> It seems clear that attempting to force popular music into models created for the analysis of Western European art music is bound to produce distortions. At the same time, however, asserting that an entirely new approach to musical analysis needs to be devised especially for popular music seems extreme. One problem with developing entirely new modes of analysis specifically for popular music is that it presumes that popular and art music are entirely different from one another, but this certainly need not be the case. (1997b, 85)

As Covach suggests, it would be excessive to discard traditional analytic methods entirely in favor of an original method. I have to wonder what that method would comprise and how long it would take for the rest of the scholarly community to learn how to communicate effectively with it. We have enough to debate as it is; using traditional methods at least we know what we're speaking of and can attain a sophisticated level of critique within a familiar discourse. We do, however, need to be cautious about wholesale application; as I have suggested throughout this chapter, traditional methods need to be interrogated and modified in order to accomplish repertoire-sensitive analysis.

In addition to working with and adapting existing methods, we also need to devise new analytic parameters in order to account for the stylistic and expressive content of popular music. In this regard, several authors have begun to identify the musical elements or parameters that ought to be discussed in popular music analysis (for example, Middleton 1990 and 1993, Allan Moore 1993, Walser 1993b). In the interest of distinguishing styles or song-types, Richard Middleton discusses the "gestural layers" of popular music, which for him comprise the "groove," the

vocal phraseology and melodic intonation, the "micro-gestures associated with many individual sounds," the chord sequences, and the texture,
which would include a consideration of the technical sound "mix" of the
recording (1993, 180–81). The discussion of these individual features
requires some usage of traditional terminology and methods of evaluation, especially for the phrase analysis and harmonic interpretation,
which are the main elements of any traditional music-theoretical analysis. (I will return to Middleton's usage of traditional harmonic analysis
presently.) By considering the "groove," and the special timbral effects
(instrumental and vocal) as well as the textural organization, Middleton
opens up some important analytic avenues for the study of popular
music. Here, one might say that he goes beyond traditional methods and
reveals a sensitivity to the popular style.

Similarly, in his study of heavy metal music, Robert Walser borrows
certain analytic tools from conventional theory, but also devises new
parameters for this particular style. He identifies his analytic framework
to include (in this order of discussion) timbre and guitar distortion, volume, vocal timbre, mode and harmony, rhythm, melody, and guitar solos
(1993b, 41–51). In the areas of mode and harmonic analysis, as well as
that of melody, Walser borrows many traditional concepts, but his analytic emphasis on timbre, volume, and guitar techniques allows him to
explore many important aspects of heavy metal style.

Allan Moore devises a more abstract model for the reduction of a
musical texture into individual elements or layers:

> The model stratifies sound-sources into four layers. The first is an explicit
> rhythmic layer, where precise pitch is irrelevant. This layer is the preserve of
> the drum kit and other percussion. The second layer is formed by the music's
> deepest notes (those with lowest frequency), and which can be thought of as
> a low register melody. This layer is normally restricted to the bass guitar. A
> third layer is formed from higher frequency melodies, whether sung or
> played by a variety of instruments. This layer corresponds to the common-
> sense understanding of "tune." The fourth layer fills the registral gap between
> the second and third by supplying harmonies congruent to each of these (I
> shall tend to refer to the function of this layer as that of "harmonic filler").
> (1993, 31–32)

Apart from the rhythmic layer, this four-layer structure privileges the
role of harmony and counterpoint in the creation of a musical texture. In

essence, the music is reduced to a soprano and bass counterpoint with its harmonization, an abstraction of musical structure that derives from historical contrapuntal and harmonic theory and that might suggest a kind of Schenkerian orientation.[5] Moore makes it quite clear that an analyst can privilege such a structure yet maintain a sensitivity to other features of the music. Once he has described the four-layer structure, he discusses the musical elements that would be active within this texture. His subheadings for his lengthy theoretical discussion are as follows: notation, instrumental roles, rhythmic organization, the voice, harmonic patterns and formal structures, open-ended repetitive patterns, the open-closed principle, and composing at the instrument (1993, 33–55). As with the Middleton and Walser definitions of musical content and structure, Moore combines traditional emphasis on harmony and form with an analytic sensitivity to elements that allow the popular music style to be discerned.

Implicit in all of these authors' analytic methods is the notion that while an individual parameter may be isolated for theoretical discussion, its function and meaning are dependent on its context within the remaining musical texture; that is, all of these elements interact, and although an analyst may illuminate a particular feature, it is with an understanding that meaning is affected by all parameters simultaneously. As Moore says, "the process of analytical reduction is only valid if it is completed by putting the elements together again" (1993, 31). The *degree* to which an analyst explicitly combines all of the elements is subject to individual interest and analytic goals, but all of these authors certainly aim to keep the whole picture together, as is evident from their analytic commentary. I place emphasis on the word *degree* here because the question of analytic weight or privilege is important, and therein exists the potential for the analyst to be criticized: as music scholars we do not all agree on the issue of analytic weight, as is evidenced by the negative criticisms (discussed earlier) launched at music theorists for worrying too much about pitch structure.

Concern for pitch structure is most evident in the analysis of harmony and voice-leading, and this is where the debate often heats up. For popular music analysis, the traditional theoretical system that is criticized the most is Schenkerian voice-leading analysis. Some theorists have applied this technique to popular music (Mathew Brown, Lori

Burns, Everett, Kaminsky, Koozin), but there has been a great deal of criticism of this approach.[6] Middleton (1990, 192–97) and Allan Moore (1993 and 1995) carefully outline their concerns with the limitations of Schenkerian analysis for charting modal harmonic relations, different melodic/contrapuntal strategies, and the sectional formal organization of popular song. Middleton and Moore are critical of the method, but they leave open the possibility that, *in modified form*, voice-leading reduction could be applied to popular songs.[7] They imply that any practitioner of Schenkerian theory would force the music to fit the system without any regard for the individual identity of the chosen music. In order to correct this misunderstanding, Covach points out that authors who have tackled the problems of reductive voice-leading analysis for popular music have not simply forced the music into strict paradigms, but rather have attempted to show that popular music "also has musical characteristics that are all its own" (1997b, 83). In other words, reductive analysis can be modified to accommodate the distinctive features of popular music harmony, melodic design, and form.[8]

Schenkerian analysis is not the only "traditional" method that assumes tonality to be based upon certain paradigmatic progressions. Functional harmonic analysis, represented by Roman numerals within a key, is also an interpretive and hierarchical system. For instance, the functions "tonic," "subdominant," and "dominant" carry with them their own set of expectations for how the harmony will function and relate to the surrounding harmony. In popular music, those expectations may or may not be fulfilled. Another analytic limitation of the functional harmonic system is the tonal bias toward major and minor keys, insufficient for popular music, which frequently uses modal scales and harmonies. Thus the analyst who chooses to work with harmonic labels does not achieve a position of analytic neutrality any greater than the voice-leading analyst.

And in any case, analytic "neutrality" does not seem to be the desired stance. Most popular music analysts are more interested in the interpretation of meaning in a given song than in any abstract harmonic or structural relationships. However, they do rely on traditional labels to make their interpretive assertions. As an example, here is a lengthy passage from Middleton's analysis of a Bryan Adams song, "Everything I Do (I Do It for You)":

> The subdominant chord and the IV–I progression play a big part in this song. . . . The gestural equivalent of the plagal progression seems to me to be something like a "benediction," the arms opening and descending to reassure, absolve, bless. . . . Over the whole song, the role of the plagal effect is to modify the otherwise strong I–V–I tendency which Schenkerians could easily find in the *Ursatz* (. . . Schenkerians could easily locate a 3–2–1 *Urlinie* as well—but this is not surprising in a genre with deep roots in European bourgeois tradition). A hint of Gospel ecstasy tempers ballad desire and aspiration. The most explicit focus for this desire is Bryan Adams' voice. Husky, limited in high frequencies . . . rich in dissonant "noise," this places us in the (imagined world) of concrete reality. (1993, 185–86)

This is a very interesting example of analysis, because in one short passage Middleton engages many different analytic concepts: he describes harmonic events using traditional labels and interprets the social meaning of the harmony; he suggests yet dismisses a possible Schenkerian interpretation (dismisses it too easily, I might add, as he does not pursue it in detail); he comments on and interprets genre and stylistic content; and he identifies specific vocal strategies, also interpreting them for their communication of meaning in the song. Middleton's response to the "music itself" is very passionately described, and thus might distract the reader from the traditional content that lies at the heart of his analysis. Yet that foundation exists nonetheless.

Similarly, in Walser's description of the events in Van Halen's "Runnin' with the Devil," he responds to harmony, mode, and counterpoint as significant bearers of meaning when he writes,

> In particular, the chords move from a typically metallic Aeolian bVI–bVII motion through a surprise transformation to the tonic major. The main gesture is a syncopated suspension of a power chord on bVII (D) over the pulsing bass tonic (E); the E serves as a pedal point that clashes with the D, creating desire for resolution while guaranteeing it. But the resolution is simultaneous with a modal shift that occurs every two measures and constructs an affective transcendence. Every two bars we are lifted out of the familiar negative Aeolian terrain into the perfect resolution of the major mode's tonic. Immediately thereafter, we are plunged again into Aeolian gloom and then carried up out of it once more. (1993b, 52)

As in the Middleton analysis, we find in Walser's words some engaging ideas about how harmony and counterpoint contribute to the meaning of the song. However (and this is where my disciplinary orientation shows), the traditional tools that are invoked are not subjected to systematic investigation. Middleton and Walser privilege "meaning" in their discussions, and thus attempt to deemphasize the structural content by not interrogating it to any extent. Thus, the theoretical tools are used rather vaguely or indirectly. They lend authority to the discussion, but because they are meant to be downplayed, they are not questioned from a theoretical standpoint. The technical descriptions in such analyses are also cursory, in the sense that the musical events are not described in adequate detail to communicate to me, the reader, precisely what is happening in a musical passage. As a reader of such analyses, I would look for a more systematic discussion of the elements so that I could hear what the author was hearing and so that I could then make the desired connection between musical expression and lyrical content. A further criticism is that the musical elements are handled individually; to describe harmony in one passage and melody or contrapuntal techniques in another is to separate two parameters that are, for me, intricately dependent on one another. Here once more is the question of putting the elements back together again. For instance, in Middleton's analysis of the Bryan Adams song, he distinguishes the individual musical parameters (rhythm, harmony, and so on), representing each as a "gestural" layer in a graph. There is a theoretical and analytical value to stratifying the layers of structural content. But here the individual layers are not subsequently reintegrated into a coherent and systematic analysis. I am not entirely sure from the graph or the description how all of the individual gestures interact and thus how they convey the text.

What Do Music Theorists Want?

As a music theorist reading an analysis of a popular song, I would like to see the detailed analytic ideas more deliberately and systematically interpreted. When I read an interpretive claim about a particular harmony, I would like to study the contextual functions of that harmony throughout the entire song, which would include not only the vertical but also the linear domain. In particular, I would like to consider how the vocal melody interacts with the harmony to create a contrapuntal structure. Ultimately, I would like to be able to understand in what sense that contrapuntal structure *animates* the lyrical meaning of the song, by examining in detail the association of a harmonic or contrapuntal event with a specific textual idea. A voice-leading analysis can put into play the contrapuntal manipulations of a harmonic progression such that it is possible to identify which musical "voice" in the instrumental and vocal texture is doing what work, a concept that will emerge as essential to my analytic approach. Thus my own analytic approach puts fair emphasis on structural voice-leading analysis, and my reductive technique owes a considerable debt to traditional Schenkerian structures. As I have stated, I do see the value of considering the music of popular music through the lens of existing theoretical systems. My analytic method also responds, however, to the criticisms of strict formalism and demonstrates particular ways in which music theory can provide a vehicle for the careful and sensitive interpretation of musical meaning.

Beyond harmonic and voice-leading analysis, I am also interested in the rhythmic/metric, timbral, and textural layers of musical expression, and especially in how they interact with the contrapuntal structure. These factors contribute a great deal to the meaning conveyed by the song. Like Middleton, Walser, and Moore, I am very sensitive to the signifying power of musical effects. Where my work differs from theirs is in the analytic weight that I ascribe to harmony and counterpoint—that is, in the degree to which I investigate those parameters and privilege them in my analytic assertions.

"MEANING" IN MUSIC: TOWARD A CULTURALLY INFORMED ANALYSIS

What permits an analyst to make the claim that a particular musical event has social significance? In the preceding discussion, I emphasized traditional techniques because they play such an important role in our theoretical discourse and thus in our interpretive process. Musicologists and music theorists are equipped with a large tool kit of analytical techniques, and an equally large set of assumptions about musical meaning. This was evident in the passages I cited from Middleton and Walser: Middleton invoked the religious significance ("benediction") of the plagal, or subdominant-tonic progression; Walser asserted the aggressive character of an Aeolian progression. What is at work here is the reliance upon shared musical experience and understanding: the concept of *musical codes and conventions*. For my analytic method, codes and conventions are of enormous import. Middleton (1990) offers a very careful discussion of musical codes in the popular style.[9] I think it is worth the effort to outline his theoretical discussion, and to bring out those points that will be important springboards for my own analytic method.

Codes and Competences. In his general definition of *code*, Middleton identifies three important concepts. First, in the process of musical communication, the participants' (sender's, receiver's) level of *competence* is a crucial consideration (1990, 173).[10] As I discussed earlier when I explored the notion of musical engagement from the point of view of discipline orientation, this competence level will depend on the participants' training, interests, and motivations. In the field of music analysis, different elements (codes) can be emphasized to varying degrees of technical explanation. Second, Middleton suggests that, in any given musical moment, there is an entire *range* of codes in operation (involving pitch, rhythm, and so on), giving rise to what he calls a "multi-parameter system." He goes on to say that these simultaneously enacted musical codes "may not always reinforce each other but may be out of phase or contradictory" (173). This is an invaluable perspective for me, as it suggests the potential for fluidity of meaning, for the juxtaposition of different ideas in order to create irony, or for a disruption of meaning (more on this presently). Third, Middleton proposes that codes vary in *strength*: "That is, the patterns they organize may be familiar and predictable—heavily coded—or they may be rather ambiguous and unpredictable—subject to weak or newly invented codes" (173). This distinction offers a rubric for considering the degree to which an artist works with a set of stylistic norms or conventions (heavily coded) or develops original musical ideas (newly invented codes). The potential to offer social commentary exists within both compositional options. Musical conventionality would not necessarily be aligned with societal conformity—after all, working with a set of conventions does not necessarily mean that all the "rules" will be followed.

Middleton identifies two levels of code interpretation: primary and secondary signification. Primary signification comprises a fundamental conception of "content [as] defined through its structure" (1990, 222). At this level, meaning is created by a number of factors, including (a) the very words we use to describe the music, or the discourse of music commentary, (b) the internal references to music that occur within the music itself (borrowing, quotation, parody), and (c) the grammatical significance of individual events, taking into account positional values, or context. Secondary signification operates at the level of *connotations*: the meaning of specific effects, structures, gestures, styles, and genres (232).[11] Here Middleton invokes the commonly received meanings attached to specific musical elements, such as "a cadence equals repose," "an AABA form generates the constructs of equivalence and contrast," and "punk is associated with aggression" (232).

Code Manipulation. Any conception of musical codes and conventions implicitly relies upon the paradigmatic definition (*codification*) of musical constructs. For example, the langue of Western tonality has been codified by theorists into "rules" or "norms," including the musical features of the "reposeful cadence" mentioned by Middleton. It is never assumed that all compositions will express the paradigms in a typical formation, but theorists can identify variants and "normalize" such variants as being derived from the paradigm. "Normalization" can be a contentious issue if the theoretical paradigm is applied so strictly as to override the distinctive features of the musical event. I would argue, however, that one can evaluate and mobilize formalist analysis more positively. If the music is analyzed according to strict paradigms and is found to conform, then that is worth noting and possibly even interrogating. If the music distorts conventions and codes, that is especially worth consideration: What part of the structure has been manipulated? Where does the music rupture, resist, break away, defy convention? The concept of code or convention *manipulation* is thus integral to my investigation.[12] The choices made by a composer can be clues to the meaning of a song, and the way in which the actual music negotiates its way through the system of conventions gives it the power to enact the text.

Contradictory Meanings and Oppositional Readings. Another problem with the interpretive reception of musical conventions is that, although the conventional meanings *do* exist, they may not be intended to bear that conventional meaning in a given musical composition. A conventional structure might be presented in typical paradigmatic formation, but the context (of surrounding music, text, or style of presentation) might work against the expected meaning in order to create an *oppositional reading.* The source of this potential site for contradiction exists in the certainty that an abstract musical construct cannot have an absolute, fixed meaning. As Walser claims,

> There is never any essential correspondence between particular musical signs or processes and specific social meanings, yet such signs and processes would never circulate if they did not produce such meanings.... This is a poststructural view of music in that it sees all signification as provisional, and it seeks for no essential truths inherent in structures, regarding all meanings as produced through the interaction of texts and readers. (1993b, 29)

"Ideological" Readings. One of the categories of secondary signification listed by Middleton, *ideological choices*, is defined as "particular, preferred meanings, selected from a range of possible interpretations: drug readings of psychedelic songs like 'Lucy in the Sky with Diamonds'; attributions of conservative political meanings to the styles of Country music songs" (1990, 232). To a certain extent, I connect with this category because of how it invokes the analyst. My interpretations are indeed developed out of a particular stance and inclination; this study had its origins in my wish to investigate the feminist thematic content in popular music by women. However, the terms *ideological choices* and *preferred readings* strike warning bells for me, as they suggest that an analytic stance could be chosen or dismissed depending on the perspective of the analyst. I agree that different analysts might discuss different aspects of the same song, and thus might read that song in distinct ways. But different interpretive perspectives do not necessarily result in diametrically opposed analyses. As Walser says, "the range of possible interpretations may be theoretically infinite, but in fact certain preferred variant readings are commonly negotiated.... So while meanings are negotiated, discourse constructs the terms of the negotiation" (1993b, 33). In other words, music can "mean" different things to different listeners, but given the particulars of a texted song, it cannot mean just anything. My analyses will be offered from my particular scholarly and social perspectives, but they are not flights of fancy, subjective stories invented to suit my own ideological agenda. Rather, the musical content of my analyses is systematically consistent within the discipline of music theory, just as the textual content of Mélisse's analyses is systematically consistent within the fields of literary, cultural, and feminist theory. Our personal positions do influence us tremendously, but we must emphasize our scholarly and discipline-based positions as well.

I must also stress that a feminist orientation is not something that can be dismissed as nothing but a personal or ideological agenda. The songs that we have chosen for study could not possibly be analyzed without adopting a feminist stance: as Mélisse has suggested, the feminist content of these songs is readily apparent and cannot be responsibly bracketed. It is intriguing to reflect on the question of listener responsibility or *obligation*. In his recent exploration of social meaning in popular music, Eric Clarke (1999) suggests that the perception of music can be compared to the concept of the "subject-position" in film criticism, in which "a perceiver is encouraged, or obliged, by the film to adopt a particular attitude to what he or she is witnessing" (352; emphasis mine). He does admit the influence of a spectator's unique personal stance, yet asserts that "there is a limit on this potentially infinite plurality which can be attributed to properties of the film itself-understood within a shared cultural context" (352).

Feminist Interpretations of Codes. Susan McClary (1991 and 1992) offers a feminist critique of certain music-theoretical codes and conventions. She illustrates the ways in which theoretical constructs have described and prescribed musical meaning and she uses that understanding of the relation between theory and practice to illuminate the individual characteristics and feminist strategies of selected compositions. McClary's solution to the problem of finding a culturally informed method of analysis has been to develop and critique what already exists as a common compositional and theoretical language. Invoking the role of the composer, she says: "Beginning with the rise of opera in the seventeenth century, composers worked painstakingly to develop a musical semiotics of gender: a set of conventions for constructing 'masculinity' and 'femininity'" (1991, 7). She also emphasizes historical theorists' role in the construction of a gendered musical discourse, citing examples of theoretical formulations that define musical constructs in terms of a binary opposition (such as a strong or weak cadence, a major or minor mode) that explicitly includes gendered qualities (strong as masculine, weak as feminine) (10–12). In addition, McClary investigates gendered and sexualized accounts of narrative processes in music, including models of tension and release, the designation of musical thematic content as masculine and feminine, and the exploration of those roles through a narrative process of opposition and conquest (12–15). By working with the very tools of dominant discourse, she sheds new light on traditional musical language and exposes its sociopolitical potential. My analytic approach owes a great debt to the pioneering work of McClary as well as to other feminist music scholars who have used traditional music-theoretical techniques to illustrate themes of gender and sexuality in given works.

In addition to that of McClary, the writings of Suzanne Cusick (1993, 1994a, and 1994b), Ellie Hisama (1995 and 2000), and Ruth A. Solie (1992) all reveal a commitment to music analysis as primary in the investigation of textual meaning. The degrees to which these authors espouse a formal technique vary, in part because of the training of each (of these selected four, three are professional musicologists and one is as a music theorist), but also because of the different goals of each investigation. When we write about music, we can and do focus on many different aspects of the work. However, regardless of the extent to which a system is explicitly applied, the mere implication of the analytic system is sufficient to demonstrate the importance of music analysis to the professionally trained writer about music: Cusick (1994a) uses Schenkerian reductive techniques to explore the narrative of Claudio Monteverdi's *Arianna's Lament* from a feminist point of view; Hisama uses a highly formalist theory of contour relations to investigate the politics of race in Ruth Crawford's "Chinaman, Laundryman"; McClary investigates the feminist narrative potential of the large-scale tonal design in Madonna's "Live to Tell"; and Solie discusses harmonic and key strategies in Robert Schumann's *Frauenliebe und Leben* to illuminate the female subject's voice within a patriarchal narrative. These and other authors have begun to demonstrate the great potential of music analysis to buttress a textual or cultural interpretation.

ANALYTIC METHOD

Analysis and interpretation of popular song require the careful study of the individual lyrical and musical content, followed by an integrated reading of these two domains. During the first stage of individual lyric and music analysis, I attempt to remain neutral in the evaluation of content. I attend to each parameter on its own and save the discovery of connections or contradictions until the interpretive stage of my work. In the following pages, I will outline first the individual lyrical and musical parameters that I consider, and second the theoretical categories that I find pertinent to the interpretation of meaning in these feminist popular songs.

During the musical analysis, I am sensitive to the unique features of the given artist's style. Indeed, the songs that I analyze derive from different styles and genres, so one might suggest that I would need a different analytic method for each piece. However, I would argue that the musical parameters that I consider are sufficiently general and flexible to accommodate the different genres, styles, and idioms. The particular ways in which a musical composition engages these parameters—form, harmony, melody, counterpoint, texture, and rhythm and meter—constitute the distinguishing features of a musical style.

My lyric analysis is a combination of my own efforts to examine the elements of a song's lyrics and my coauthor's critical examination of the text. When Mélisse offers a reading of the text from an interdisciplinary perspective (literary, feminist, and cultural theory), one might ask why I also conduct a lyric analysis and how our readings interact. Mélisse explores the theoretical implications of the text and its engagement with cultural and feminist themes. One might say that her criticism operates at the level of textual content and signification, while my analysis operates at the level of language, grammar, and structure. With Mélisse's exploration of the theoretical, political, and cultural implications of the song lyrics in mind, I study how these messages are conveyed through the formal, narrative, and grammatical organization of the lyrics. Equipped with both a critical-thematic reading and an analytical-structural reading, I have a thorough text analysis on which to base my close reading.

Content Analysis: Lyrical and Musical Elements

Form in Lyrics and Music. Despite the different styles and genres explored in this study, all of the music I discuss is based on the verse/chorus popular song formal model.[13] When analyzing the form of a song, one must consider the text and music simultaneously (despite my earlier claim that I distinguish the parameters). The subdivision of the song into different sections (verse, pre-chorus, chorus, bridge) is clearly articulated by both lyrics (for instance, through a change of perspective or subject) and music (for instance, through a shift in texture or mode). I am particularly attentive to the sectional divisions of the song, and to the precise location in which particular musical or lyrical strategies occur. For formal analysis, it is also important to consider the use of text repetition and contrast, expansion and contraction, as well as the musical treatment of these lyrical features: one can consider where lyrics are repeated with musical repetition or with musical contrast.

Story. My first path through the lyrics is to consider the overall story that is told, or information that is provided. I look for the identification of the characters involved and the description of the location, as well as the actions or situations.

Narrative Voice and Perspective. Equally important to the story itself is the question of how the story is told, by whom, and from what perspective. The narrative voice will be established through the use of grammatical devices such as verb tense (past, present, future) and conjugation (first person, third person), as well as noun and pronoun choice (he/she, I/you). These and other devices help to position the subject and to clarify his or her motivations, desires, or conflicts. In addition, these grammatical devices can help to distinguish the different characters or roles that emerge in the narrative.

Vocabulary and Thematic Content. In any poetic analysis, a close attention to vocabulary is essential, as it is an important element in the determination of meaning. To investigate thematic content, one can consider the symbols, images, discursive formations, and sociocultural institutions invoked through the choice of particular nouns, but one can also be sensitive to the choice of verbs as a means of engaging those themes.

Figures of Speech. Literary devices such as metaphor, hyperbole, sarcasm, irony, and rhetorical devices can contribute in large part to the poetic meaning of a text. These can be used to create humor or irony, which are direct means of inciting the audience's emotional or critical response. In the lyrics we have chosen for study, these devices can be especially important as methods for conveying disruption or resistance.

Harmonic Content. The theoretical literature on rock/pop harmony has developed significantly in the past several years. Although it is a diverse harmonic language, theorists have come to identify and, to a certain extent, codify harmonic patterns in rock and popular music. There has been a great deal of interest in the connections and distinctions between classical and popular music harmony, and contentious debates continue over the applicability of analytic systems to the latter, when originally conceived for the former. It is not my intention here to review these debates, nor shall I define the elements of rock/pop harmony.[14] Suffice it to say here that the language incorporates both tonal and modal harmonic procedures, which means that the analyst must take care when discussing issues of harmonic directionality and stasis, dissonance and consonance, or harmonic closure.[15] My analyses will be sensitive to these issues and will draw attention to interesting patterns of harmony in their musical contexts.

Vocal Melody and Phrase Design. The vocal melody is a prominent part of the texture in a popular song, as the musical "voice" that carries the song's lyrics. Many different melodic styles are possible in popular music, from the goal-directed tunes derived from the Tin Pan Alley style to the more fragmented and partially spoken lines of hip-hop. Again, it is not my goal here to define popular music melodic conventions; rather, I will address the particular strategies manifest in the individual songs chosen for analysis.[16] My analytic method places great emphasis on the voice and its relation to the remaining musical texture.

Harmonic and Voice-Leading Structure. One of the most useful methods for the study of counterpoint and voice-leading is reductive analysis, yet its application to popular music is often criticized severely, as I have already discussed. My own reductive method is derived from Schenkerian theory, but it has been developed especially for popular music in order to accommodate the unique harmonic, melodic, and formal features of that repertoire (Burns 2000). It is a valuable tool not only for revealing that unique content, but also as a notational representation of the song, to provide a visual aid to accompany my prose descriptions of the musical events. For the interested reader, appendix 2 reviews my reductive method and defines my notational symbols.

Texture and Instrumental/Vocal Strategies. The songs chosen for this study feature many different instrumental and vocal strategies, that have great affective power in the communication of musical meaning. In this first stage of musical analysis, I attempt not to interpret these strategies but simply to identify them in each section of the song; for instance, to remark that the voice is hushed with an acoustic guitar accompaniment in the verse, whereas the voice is loud and harsh against a highly distorted electric guitar in the chorus.

Rhythmic, Metric, and Hypermetric Organization. Rhythmic emphasis and metric design are integral components of popular song composition and performance. It is important in this regard to emphasize that the rhythmic presentation is not confined to the drum kit; rather, the vocal melody and harmonic articulation contribute in large part to the rhythmic design. In my analysis, I am interested in the kind of emphasis that derives from rhythmic and metric regularity, as well as from irregularity. For instance, the voice typically moves in and out of sync with its accompaniment, sometimes anticipating harmonic change and sometimes delaying the arrival of a melodic pitch in relation to the supporting harmony. Another common strategy is a metric expansion immediately before a section change. These and other devices are important components of musical expression.

Interpretive Analysis: Conceptual Framework and Theoretical Categories

During the interpretive stage, the analyst juggles the relative prominence of lyrics and music. To what extent, if any, does one domain supersede the other? Do the words control how we perceive the music, or does the music control how we perceive the words? I find it useful to consider the words and music as mutually dependent for their ultimate meaning. Individually, a musical code or lyrical symbol might be loaded with the potential to "mean," but if its meaning is to be interpreted, it cannot be separated from its song context. That is not to say, however, that I would always argue for a conception of unity between words and music. An exclusive conception of musical-lyrical unity would suggest that the role of the music is to depict precisely what is being uttered in the lyrics. Although instances of such close agreement can be found, I am also interested in instances of musical or textual irony, contradiction, or moments of discursive fracture that might contribute to an *oppositional reading*.

The following interpretive categories provide a theoretical framework for such *intersections* between words and music. These categories are conceptual tools for mobilizing a traditional analysis of musical and lyrical elements, and for the reinterpretation and modification of traditional theoretical discourse. These categories are my response to the call for imagination as a bridge between discourse and music. The first group of categories stems from a musical perspective and attempts to address the ways in which the music might signify the lyrics; the second group derives from a lyrical or social perspective and attempts to address the ways in which a lyrical theme might be represented by the music. Two sides of the same coin, these two groups are distinguished in order to clarify the perspectives from which one can consider the complex relationship between words and music. The musical categories are defined very broadly so as to be applicable to a wide range of popular songs; however, the textual thematic categories are more specific to songs that explore issues of society, gender, sexuality, and identity.

Musical Meaning (in Relation to Lyrics)

Codes, Conventions, Styles. I have already discussed extensively the importance of musical codes, conventions, and styles to the discourse of music theory. My particular approach to the interpretation of musical idioms is to eschew the assumption of fixed meanings and instead consider a specific musical strategy in the context of the lyrics. In this regard, my understanding of *code manipulation* is very important. At times, a musical construct will be used in its *conventional meaning*; for instance, when a slow, minor-mode march is meant to connote "funeral." At other times, however, a particular musical construct might be associated with a textual theme that sets up a contradiction; that is, the *associative meaning* might not be consistent with conventional meaning—as when a funereal, minor-mode passage is used to set a passage affirming life. By creating such an association, the composer would be working against conventional meaning, but would nevertheless be relying on that conventional meaning in order to create ironic expression. I consider carefully the *context* of these associative meanings; that is, how they are carried through the composition, and with what consistency they are handled. The interpretive process is complicated by the problem that a poetic idea might not be treated consistently within the text, nor a musical construct within the music. This becomes further complicated if one is attempting to attach interpretive significance to the close connection of a poetic idea with a musical motive. If the constructs are not given a fixed meaning within their own individual domain (lyrics or music), then how is one to attach fixed meaning to the word-music relation? Such complexity, however, opens up the possibility for ambiguity and fluidity. It also makes possible different forms of musical commentary on a text (literal versus ironic, for example).

Contrasting Values. Analysts often describe strategies of musical contrast using a term that invokes a binary opposition. For instance, a cadence is strong (or weak); a harmonic progression is directional (or static).[17] These contrasting values are inherent in most music-theoretical systems and are so ingrained that the music analyst would usually take them for granted. The musical processes that these interpretive values address are significant in their power to express, and thus I do not eschew these values. However, I do attempt to be sensitive to these assumptions and to question the oppositional terms. I will list here a few of these values, although the list could be extended:

Strength/weakness
Tension/resolution
Consonance/dissonance
Stability/instability
Stasis/directionality
Fulfillment/denial of expectations
Expository/conclusive
Statement/contrast
Repetition/variation
Equivalence/difference[18]
Expansion/contraction
Symmetry/asymmetry

These processes are manifest in the treatment of musical texture, gesture, harmony, voice-leading, and form, and will be engaged throughout my musical analyses. This category links up nicely with feminist readings of tonal narrative; for instance, McClary (1991) and Marcia Citron (1993) discuss examples of music in which a tonal conflict is interpreted as signifying a narrative in which one key "conquers" another. In this regard I avoid a priori assumptions and the attachment of fixed meanings to the individual values within the binary opposite pairing. For instance, in the evaluation of two keys, I do not believe in attaching an a priori value to the major and minor modes when I am considering the opposition of strong and weak. The attachment of *strong* to one or the other depends on the context of the music in question.

Structure and Structural Anomalies. With this interpretive category, I emphasize the importance of the musical structure; that is, formal, harmonic, and voice-leading structure. I also attach interpretive significance to those moments when a musical structure exposes a rupture, in order to relate this anomaly to some aspect of the lyrics. When I use the term *anomaly*, I do not wish to connote aberrance or deviance; indeed I would prefer a term with no pejorative connotations.[19] A deviation from convention has tremendous potential as an expressive musical device; for instance, the avoidance of a particular scale degree or expected harmony in the structural voice-leading design, or the avoidance of tonal closure when it has been expected.[20] In a traditional formalist interpretation, these moments might be viewed as problematic; there are even theoretical devices designed to smooth over such fractures, such as the "implied pitch" in a Schenkerian voice-leading structure. In my analyses, however, these moments will not be corrected in order to normalize the anomaly, but rather will be given analytical emphasis as strong signifiers.

Musical "Voice" and Dramatic Function. In any musical ensemble, the musical content is divided among the performers such that a given player will be responsible for the articulation of a particular element of the musical texture and structure. Middleton develops this idea to explore the association of a musical part or voice with a textual role or voice: "musical elements can be heard as representing particular social actors, whose identity can vary according to genre conventions and social context. An instrumental or vocal solo will usually be heard as an 'I'" (1990, 238). Cusick similarly develops the concept of musical "roles," exploring "the relationship among the parts as the place where [the] work's gender subject (and real drama) [lies]" (1994b, 13).[21] Lewin also explores the potential of a musical voice to bear (or to embody) a lyrical or dramatic meaning (Lewin 1982, 1992a, and 1992b), but he develops this further to allow any musical construct, not simply an instrumental or vocal part, to represent a dramatic function. For instance, he analyzes the harmonic or voice-leading patterns that are associated with the desires and motivations of different characters in an operatic scene (1992).

These authors advocate a kind of interpretive sensitivity that calls for an imaginative response to the music, as one's analytic perspective is shifted from a passive identification of events to an active engagement with the musical texture and its contrapuntal and harmonic design. I find such an analytic perspective to be invaluable for the interpretation of popular songs. Especially in the case of songwriting, the singer's voice in relation to the supporting musical texture can be an important site for the communication of tension or conflict. For instance, if the harmony and melody form a dissonant contrapuntal structure, I consider which musical voice articulates the dissonance and which the resolution. In this regard, one can invoke the concepts of musical *power*, *control*, and *freedom*: if the musical "voices" do not appear to be agreeing about the presentation of harmony and counterpoint, one can reflect on which voice is in control, and which voice is either subject to that control or resisting that control.[22]

Lyrical Meaning (in Relation to Music)

Subject/Object Perspective. All of the songs chosen for this study explore, expose, and criticize a conflict or tension within a social construct. Such tension is explicated by the lyrics, not only by means of the literal content, but through the mode of expression. In particular, within the genre of solo popular song, an important means of problematizing a conflict is how the singer's or subject's perspective is defined in relation to an Other (or Others). In the lyrics, this can be achieved through grammatical techniques, such as the subject's mode of self-reference, verb choices, verb forms, or the ascription of power; the analyst must be sensitive especially to how these techniques are handled in relation to the grammatical object as well as the subject. In the domain of music, it is very interesting to speculate how the music itself could explore or signify a subject/object relationship. Thus I will explore in my music analyses the following questions: How does the artist use musical constructs to invoke the kinds of perspectives engaged in the lyrics? What aspects of musical structure can signify the subject's relationship to the object?

Domination versus Subordination. Many of the songs that we have chosen to study explore themes of social, sometimes erotic, power. This power is distributed such that the subject and object are assigned dominant and subordinate roles, or vice versa. The distribution of power into a strong/weak contrast lends itself quite easily to a music-structural framework. (I have already discussed *contrasting values* as a theoretical category.) It is important to note that in the individual songs we have chosen to study, power distribution may not be fixed; indeed, these songs were chosen because of the ways in which they challenge traditional social norms. In addition to strong and weak values, other musical processes can be used to suggest the thematic concept of domination or containment: the use of devices such as repetition, harmonic stasis, or fixed registral boundaries.

Agency. In a song's lyrics, the subject will position herself within her particular social situation. Using a variety of lyrical means, she can explicitly invoke a broader social institution or establish an individual relationship that implicitly invokes a broader social construct. She can also indicate her position within that social construct either by participating in the system (suggesting conformity or self-discipline) or by resisting the confines that are placed upon her (suggesting freedom, liberation, or the rejection of systemic restraints). The concepts of convention (system) adherence or rejection can be nicely mapped onto music-theoretical constructs. Here, my musical interest in *code manipulation* offers great potential for theoretical and analytical elaboration.

Desire. This category has the potential to be an affirmative site for a feminist statement. From this perspective, I examine the ways in which the subject expresses or affirms her own desires and sense of self. Whereas the previous two categories, *domination/subordination* and *agency* suggest the subject's position in relation to an oppressive social institution, the present category exists to illuminate the ways in which a subject might affirm her unique position through innovative representations of desire. In the popular music repertoire that we are studying here, there are songs that invoke a dominant mode of discourse, but resist that social construct. In these examples, the dominant reference is ever apparent. However, there are also songs that allow patriarchal systems to recede into the background in order to offer something different in their places. It is a continuous feminist challenge that it is never possible to eliminate the dominant references, yet it is possible to deemphasize a patriarchal construct and substitute a feminist one. In this regard, the literary tasks of reform, rereading, and reinterpretation can be invaluable; in musical terms, these concepts can be explored through various creative strategies, including code manipulation and structural anomalies.

The critical-analytical work we have undertaken with this study requires the interpreter to possess not only the technical tools to describe musical content and the literary-critical tools and sociocultural perspectives to study the lyrical content, but also the methodological means by which these domains can be brought together. We believe that this collaboration, or coauthorship, offers a broad disciplinary base upon which to build such a methodology. In chapter 1, Mélisse provided a thorough explanation of her theoretical framework from the disciplines of feminist, literary, and cultural theory, and with this chapter, I have added the discipline of music theory to that theoretical framework. These individual disciplines have not been left to stand on their own, but rather, it has been my goal to illustrate the ways in which these interpretive domains can intersect. The interpretive method I have described provides a concrete analytic means by which one can view the "music itself" through the lens of lyrical and sociocultural meaning.

3

Tori Amos, "Crucify" (1991)

Yes, I do have a mission, to expose the dark side of Christianity.
—*Tori Amos, cited in S. Daly 1998, 39*

∽∽∽∽∽∽

THE PROBLEMS OF AGENCY AND RESISTANCE
IN TORI AMOS'S "CRUCIFY" (MÉLISSE LAFRANCE)

In an interview concerning the political sensibilities organizing her music, Tori Amos had this to say:

> These songs are not about make-ups and breakups. And they're not concerned about who is sleeping with whom. They're about the realization that you and the person you're with are talking different languages. They're about recognizing that an extreme kind of viciousness is being played out even as you exchange honeysuckle. They're about the things that go on in a woman's heart—the things that are expressed and *the things that have to remain hidden*. They're about the breaking down of the patriarchy within relationships and the idea of women claiming their own power. (Amos 1995, 2; emphasis added)

Discerning the overt and covert narratives structuring any creative work is always an archaeological endeavor inextricably linked to the cultural and discursive contexts from which it emerged. In the case of Tori Amos's "Crucify," the interpreter must go beyond what appears to be an author-centered testimony and excavate from a work so convincingly personal those vestiges of the radically cultural.

The archeological task in this case is especially formidable, as Amos herself declares that these songs are, first and foremost, about "the things that go on in a woman's heart...that have to remain hidden"

(1995, 2). Through her musical protagonists, Amos sometimes discloses those things. Most of the time, however, Amos's enigmatic linguistic style and complicated symbolic lyricism prohibit the listener from deducing much more than a semblance of authorial intention. The listener therefore enters Amos's music with only a loosely based interpretational schematic, and, as a result, often retrieves her own secrets, fantasies, pains, and terrors, rather than those of the author.[1] Indeed, Amos says of her own songs that "because the songs are complicated and not so literal, people get lots of room to move. And I think the songs can become little myths for people. All the myths are symbolic and representative of something" (Amos, cited in S. Daly 1998, 103). I would argue that "Crucify" is successful and intelligible to listeners, and especially female listeners (Evans 1994), not because its narrative is explicit and prescriptive, but because it expresses in both overt and covert ways those silent but immensely important experiences shared by many women in Western cultures.[2] Thus, my interpretation operates at levels both intrinsic and extrinsic to the text. It is intrinsic as it is interested in the text's structure and temporal organization, and the story it conveys. The analysis, however, is also extrinsic as it attempts to understand the various cultural and discursive fields out of which Amos's story grew.

In my view, "Crucify" is not only an articulation of one woman's personal traumas, but is rather an assertive and public interrogation of dominant religious and gender discourses. Amos's work is not, I would argue, merely a form of "self-therapy" (DeMain 1994, 1), nor is it subsumable by a "confessional" music genre (Reynolds and Press 1995). I reject exclusively personalized and "confessionalized" readings of Amos's work for two reasons. First, the tendency to view her music as self-therapy that "[confronts] some difficult *personal* subjects" (DeMain 1994, 1; emphasis added) is symptomatic of male supremacist readings that refuse to link the oppressions of one woman with the more widespread and profoundly systemic oppressions of all women. By constantly framing Amos's music as personal in nature, her critics irresponsibly ignore the social context from which her experiences emerged. The hyperpersonalization of her experiences depoliticizes these experiences and prohibits a systemic understanding of the male supremacist violence associated with them.

Second, I reject the application of a "confessional" musical categorization to this singer-songwriter. This organizing category is problematic due to its inevitable association with guilt, apology, and sin. It is also problematic as it appears to be reserved primarily for female artists, a reservation that implicitly reproduces Christian/male supremacist notions of woman-as-already-fallen. Simon Reynolds and Joy Press (1995), for example, contend that Amos's work is quintessentially confessional in nature. They justify this contention by stating that Amos's music attempts to speak the truth about "the traumas that shaped her" (268), and that it is "based around [sic] the idea of the talking cure, of finding one's voice... and turning suffering into a story" (267).[3] I would suggest that there is no essential causal relationship between (a) attempting to speak the truth about traumas that have shaped one's person and (b) a confessional genre. I also contend that there is no causal nexus between attempting to find one's voice, using that voice to articulate many of the traumas that remain silenced, and "confessing." Reynolds and Press have conflated Amos's attempt to unsilence the traumas that have shaped her with the act of confession, a conflation that effaces the courageous assertion of female subjectivity and replaces it with a female guilt leitmotif.

In my effort to move away from overly personalized and confessionalized interpretations of Amos's work, I propose the present critical reading of her text. Amos's discussion of concrete and metaphorical crucifixion both resists and disrupts some pivotal sites of discursive power. Drawing on feminist and cultural theory, my analysis will attempt to show how the spoken and unspoken narratives structuring Amos's work can be viewed as a manifestation of emergent gender consciousness, and as a "feminist" form of resistance in the domain of popular music.[4]

"Crucify," Verse 1: Self-Surveillance, Powerlessness, Discipline

The first verse is characterized by two narratives of self-surveillance and powerlessness; these narratives are linked causally by apprehended patriarchal disciplining.[5] Amos introduces "Crucify" with the following powerful statement: "Every finger in the room is pointing at me / I wanna spit in their faces then I get afraid of what that could bring." We see here that the protagonist is carefully regulating her behavior.[6] Although the anger expressed in "I wanna spit in their faces" connotes both agency and resistance, it is superseded by the more overwhelming sense of fear associated with the cultural implication of such an act. Whether Amos is describing a concrete or metaphorical phenomenon when she sings "every finger in the room is pointing at me" is insignificant. What is significant, however, is that this image seems to connote the protagonist's internalization of dominant modalities of self-surveillance. Consider the fact that it would be uncharacteristic and largely unacceptable for a young woman to speak out against voices of authority. Amos's protagonist does not speak out, presupposing the imminence of public scorn and discipline. In this instance, Amos's protagonist is policing her own gender; patriarchal influences need not interfere concretely.[7]

The protagonist goes on to explain, "I got a bowling ball in my stomach, I got a desert in my mouth." This phrase connotes the protagonist's feelings of powerlessness and paralysis. It sees the protagonist retracting, her anger expiring before it reaches a point of resolution. It can thus be seen here that her self-surveillance and subsequent powerlessness function to further articulate her passivity, docility, and conformity. The result of her inaction is, as she avows later in the chorus, continued crucifixion.

The protagonist's tendency to police her own anger out of fear of "what that could bring" is not an event specific to her. In fact, the protagonist's self-surveillance in "Crucify" is especially interesting to us as it is representative of what Sandra Lee Bartky (1993), using a Foucauldian perspective, considers a systemic and gendered phenomenon designed to maintain the bipolarization of gender and the primacy of patriarchal capitalist institutions. Numerous feminist philosophers (Balsamo 1996, Bartky 1993, Bordo 1993 and 1995, Cole 1996, Cole and Hribar 1995) have appropriated Foucault's conceptualization of surveillance and applied it directly to women's experiences as they relate to patriarchal power.[8] The protagonist's first declarations ("I wanna spit in their faces then I get afraid of what that could bring") are important precisely because they both crystallize the feelings of terror that a woman encounters when she feels that she might be seen as "doing her gender wrong" (Butler 1989, 255) and expose the point to which gender identity is dependent upon our active performance and renewal of it (Butler 1989 and 1990). Informed by a feminist-Foucauldian framework, one could argue that the protagonist in "Crucify" is portrayed as having been "explored," "rearranged," and "broken down" by patriarchal powers.[9] She need not, therefore, be repressed by others; she will actively (though perhaps not freely) choose to collaborate with the male supremacist project; she will, in a word, crucify herself.[10]

Women are disciplined by various male supremacist discourses and behaviors (both concrete and internalized), all of which can be situated in a continuum of violence against women (Edwards 1987, Kelly 1987). It is in patriarchal society's best interest to ensure that women are constantly aware of the threat of violence against them. It is these persistent social sanctions, real and imagined, that persuade women to self-survey and to discipline their thoughts, actions, and life choices.

In light of this, the protagonist's declaration "figures that my courage would choose to sell out now" is problematic on at least two counts.[11] First, Simone de Beauvoir ([1949] 1953) and Judith Butler (1989) argue that throughout the many processes of "becoming" a member of the feminine gender, girls and women are culturally constrained into becoming the Other. Butler posits, "As Other, women are not devoid of choice; rather they are constrained to choose against their own sense of agency, and so to distort and undermine the very meaning of choice" (256).[12] Since the notion of courage is dependent on the possibility of choice, it would seem that, for most women, possessing courage is incongruous with performing their gender well. Second, courage, by its very nature, is a phenomenon that comprises one's ability to surmount extremely challenging situations. If the protagonist's courage "sell(s) out" when she needs it, one could say that her actions are characterized by a lack of courage altogether (which would correspond with the protagonist performing her gender properly). What Amos is depicting, albeit indirectly and perhaps unwittingly, is the protagonist's failed courage and her state of powerlessness.

Thus, we understand the first verse as characterized, most importantly, by the explicitly gendered narratives of self-surveillance and powerlessness, and linked causally by apprehended patriarchal discipline. This fear of patriarchal discipline is articulated through the imminent threat of violence against the protagonist and the incongruity of courage with the culturally appropriate performance and renewal of dominant femininities.

"Crucify," Pre-chorus: The Dual Nature of Femininity
The pre-chorus reveals a great deal about Amos's rejection of both organized religion and the misogyny that works in tandem with it. When the protagonist declares, "I've been looking for a savior in these dirty streets / Looking for a savior beneath these dirty sheets," we see that the pro-

tagonist feels somehow contaminated by sin and impurity. Some theorists (Mary Daly 1973, Ruether 1974) would argue that this protagonist has internalized the gynocentered guilt and uncleanness pervasive in Christian doctrine. Sylvia Hale, citing Daly 1973, argues that religion is a powerful force "in the perpetuation of women's subordinate social status, by a conditioning process of sex-role socialization, in which the consent of the victims as well as the dominant sex is obtained" (Hale 1995, 146). This phenomenon of victim "consent" or "collusion," wherein women pursue existential projects that sustain their own domination, can also be mapped onto Daly's thesis on the internalization of misogynist beliefs (Daly 1973).[13]

In the next phrase, however, the protagonist is no longer the fallen woman but the martyr: "I've been raising up my hands drive another nail in." This phrase reveals the contradictory nature of dominant femininity. Indeed, Rosemary Radford Ruether (1974) argues that Christianity has a "dual view of women, represented by the Virgin Mary, who symbolizes sublimated spiritual femininity, and the Fallen Eve" (cited in Hale 1995, 147). In the pre-chorus, the protagonist plays with our notions of who she "is," who she "ought" to be, and how, within the rigid confines of Christian notions of Mary and Eve, she is inevitably, though always imperfectly, both. The last line of the pre-chorus, "Just what GOD needs one more victim," is obviously a rather ironic critique of androcentered organized religion, and an intimation that organized religion is no more than an illusory "victim recruitment agency." These sarcastic moments speak to the protagonist's forceful rejection of the misogyny of Christian faith. Amos holds this faith responsible for her socially constructed feminine duality as well as for her feelings of guilt and her state of social subordination.

"Crucify," Chorus: Disciplining the Feminine
The chorus takes the listener quite by surprise when it demands an answer to the question "Why do we crucify ourselves every day?" As discussed previously, the "we" of which Amos speaks seems to be qualified by its victimness and femaleness, as opposed to the "they," which seems to be qualified by its dominance and maleness.[14] The protagonist sings, "I crucify myself / Nothing I do is good enough for you." Because this fundamental statement could be interpreted in so many ways, I shall go outside the text to justify my analytic focus. As Lori will discuss, the video

production of "Crucify" dwells almost exclusively on women, their performance of various femininities (that is, prostitute, cheerleader, waitress), and how those femininities are bound up in a broader, oppressive context. We maintain, therefore, that it is both legitimate and meaningful to read "Crucify" as a critique of dominant femininities, of the compulsory performance of such femininities, and of the dominant groups that benefit from the constant renewal of such femininities.

With "why do we crucify ourselves" the reader understands that the protagonist finds the processes of feminine discipline questionable, and that this discovery in itself represents an act of resistance. In her interrogation of the process itself, the protagonist is affirming the theoretical possibility that what women do to themselves on a daily basis is not ontologically natural or given. This realization leads the protagonist to concede that she too takes part in this disciplining process (that is, she includes herself in the "we"), and that, despite her constant efforts to do her gender perfectly, no degree or kind of performance is ever sufficient for the male Other ("Nothing I do is good enough for you").

Women's sense of unpardonable inadequacy has been widely documented by feminist scholars of gender (Bartky 1993, Bordo 1993, Butler 1989, 1990, 1993a, and 1993b, Davis 1993), who posit that the strength of dominant femininities lies in the fact that they are impossible to master or perfect. But precisely because dominant femininities require the subject's constant and active renewal for their survival and consolidation, they also require rigid male supremacist sanctions in order for such renewal to appear imperative and inevitable.

The two most important ideas of the chorus are brought to light in the last couplet, wherein the protagonist openly declares her frustration with the process of crucifixion. The declaration "my heart is sick of being in chains" indicates that the protagonist sees the crucifixion as a disciplining process that leaves her bound and constrained. However, the preceding line, "I crucify myself," intimates that the protagonist owns the crucifixion and that she is the agent in the murderous process. It should seem curious, then, that she would voluntarily participate in a process of which she is "sick," a process that, as she herself declares, leaves her in chains. This is where it becomes important to look at the concept of crucifixion more closely.

Until now, the allegations animated by the chorus appear contradictory. It is only when we magnify the protagonists's choice of words and concepts that we understand the depth of implication in "Crucify." Consider the fact that crucifixion is, both biblically and colloquially, a radically involuntary act. The fact that Amos chooses to employ the concept of crucifixion, one that connotes radical coercion and unwillingness—as opposed to a host of other possible concepts (for instance, punishment or discipline) that would have accomplished similar narrative purposes—attests to the validity of a feminist framework wherein the renewal of dominant forms of femininity is conceptualized as an active, but unfree, reflexive process.[15] Therefore, when the protagonist declares that she is crucifying herself, this statement cannot connote unproblematic agency. What it more soundly connotes is the process we have been discussing throughout this chapter, a process described by Butler (1989 and 1990) as one wherein women, although agents in their own existential choices, are culturally constrained to choose against themselves.

"Crucify," Verse 2: Resistance

One could argue that Amos's declaration "got a kick for a dog beggin' for love" evokes impressions of incapacity and impotence. Imagery connoting impotence and dehabilitation recurs constantly in "Crucify" (for instance, recall from verse 1 "I got a bowling ball in my stomach I got a desert in my mouth"). Verse 2, however, is patterned differently. The second line, "I gotta have my suffering so I can have my cross," can be seen as an ironic and sarcastic critique of organized religion wherein the protagonist acerbically acknowledges the price she pays for her faith and "salvation." A similar use of sarcasm created a tone of resistance at the end of the pre-chorus. The third line of verse 2 continues the resistant tone: "I know a cat named Easter he says will you ever learn." This new personage, Easter, accomplishes two thematic functions.[16] First, he appears to be goading the protagonist into refusing organized religion, encouraging her to resist and warning her of the destructive consequences related to crucifixion. Second, the phrase "will you ever learn" insinuates that the protagonist has resisted before, that she has previously contemplated rejecting her membership to these cultural processes, but has, in the end, rescinded.

Although the sections that precede verse 2 (verse 1, pre-chorus, chorus) all connote some degree of subjective agency, they are equally characterized by their intimations of cultural constraint. The first verse is characterized primarily by narratives of self-surveillance, powerlessness, and fear of social discipline; the pre-chorus outlines the dual nature of femininity; and the chorus describes the disciplining process itself and its intrinsically involuntary nature. The second verse, however, seems to move from an anticipated powerlessness to unexpected resistance and expiation. Although the empowering and resistant potential of this verse is again frustrated by the crucifixion of the ensuing pre-chorus and chorus and the volatile style of the bridge, the resistance detected in this verse will nevertheless prove to be crucial in our overall understanding of how Amos's work figures into strategies of feminist resistance.

"Crucify," Bridge: The Problem of Resistance
"Please be save me I CRY." These six words constitute the bridge of Amos's "Crucify," six words that, at first glance, appear relatively trivial. And yet these six words are expressed at the most musically important, volatile, and distinctive segment of the work. The musical expression and structure of the bridge, as Lori will illustrate in her analysis, lead us to conclude that we cannot dismiss its accompanying lyrical content. What, in the context of gender narratives, could this lyrical segment be seen to represent? Amos sings these words in a way that distinguishes them from any other part of the song. Without pursuing a musical-technical analysis, one could reasonably argue that Amos's tone throughout the body of the song approximates a declaration or a stipulation. The bridge, however, is articulated differently. It appears to have been crafted to convey sentiments of weakness, such as crying, pleading, and/or suffering, rather than those of assertion and conviction. In our estimation, the bridge is the most emphatic articulation of Amos's cultural situation at the intersection of problematic agency, resistance, and oppression. "Please be save me" sees Amos's protagonist describing her perceived fallenness, impurity, and desperate need of salvation. With her statement "I CRY," the protagonist avows the pain caused by what could be called "discursive crucifixion."

Amos's acknowledgment of the suffering induced by her faith and "salvation" constitutes, in itself, an act of resistance. The bridge accomplishes a similar narrative function. The pained and desperate testimony offered by the protagonist in the bridge allows the reader to understand, above and beyond all else, the torment resulting from what women do to themselves in order to satisfy violent, sustained, and hegemonic cultural requirements. Our contention that "Crucify" is first and foremost a narrative about problematic female agency is confirmed in the bridge as the words *save me* prove that, although this crucifixion is a process in which the protagonist participates actively ("Why do we crucify ourselves"), it is not one in which she participates freely.

Interpretive Summary

My initial questions about Amos's "Crucify" were (a) how does Amos go about criticizing organized religion and oppressive modalities of gender; (b) what evidence, if any, exists in Amos's songs that there is an emergent gender consciousness in popular culture; and (c) is there important resistant potential in Amos's "Crucify"?

First, there are many narratives within "Crucify" that engage themes of organized religion and gender. The first verse depicts the protagonist's patterns of self-surveillance and consequent powerlessness, which are linked by the protagonist's fear of adverse cultural disciplining. I supported this contention with feminist scholarship (Bartky 1993, and Bordo 1993, 1995) informed by feminist and Foucauldian concepts of power, culture, and gender, paying special attention to Amos's use of the concept of courage. The pre-chorus reveals the oppressive dichotomies of femininity and depicts the ways in which the protagonist is culturally subordinated no matter which femininity she attempts to sustain; I supported this argument with feminist scholarship on religion and misogyny (Mary Daly 1968, 1973, and 1978, Ruether 1974). The chorus details the actual process of crucifixion; my use of selected feminist perspectives is validated by the understanding that crucifixion is a radically involuntary act. When the protagonist doubts the legitimacy of her actions, she offers a moment of resistance. Verse 2 continues to see acts of resistance and manifestations of problematic feminine agency, especially in the protagonist's acts of questioning and accusation, as well as in the cat Easter's encouragement of the protagonist's dissidence. The bridge is an emphatic crystallization of the torture involved in the protagonist's conformity. When one links these narratives, they yield a nuanced illustration of what one woman understands to be a most oppressive facet of her social existence.

Second, the fact that Amos has had enormous success within the realm of popular culture proves, at least to a limited extent, that there is increased gender consciousness in popular culture. In this study, I use gender consciousness to denote the increased visibility Amos brings to gynocentered social problems once considered private and individual. Although this visibility may accomplish some solidarity among women, it does not *essentially* lead to heightened feminist consciousness. It is my belief that Amos's work, though it does not make any overt denunciations or refusals, does resist. It excavates and unsilences much of what has been historically confined to the parameters of women's individual pain, contemplation, and trauma, so that while increased cultural gender consciousness does not have the subversive potential of increased cultural feminist consciousness, it nonetheless does bring initially personal and inevitably political gender oppressions into relief.

Third, I believe that Amos's message contains important resistant qualities. Certainly there are significant problems with Amos's work; the most significant one in "Crucify" is that she fails to explicitly responsibilize the male supremacist nature and cause of her crucifixion. Nevertheless, my analysis proves that the logical conclusion of her declarations does indeed reveal a male supremacist system. But as regards the internal structure of "Crucify," Amos is, in my opinion, overly cautious. Nevertheless, the very fact that "Crucify" destabilizes and denaturalizes that which is implicated in the production and re-production of femininity constitutes a resistant narrative strategy as well as a raising of gender consciousness.

MUSICAL AGENCY: STRATEGIES OF CONTAINMENT AND RESISTANCE IN "CRUCIFY" (LORI BURNS)

Mélisse has explored the thematic and narrative content of "Crucify." I would like to underscore an issue in her commentary that has influenced me in my own analysis: the protagonist's agency within an oppressive social context. The term *agency* is critical here in its ability to connote the protagonist's own responsibility within the system, including her ability to participate as well as to resist. My goal is to investigate how these constructs are represented, not only in the lyrics, but in the video and the music as well. The video is itself a complex commentary on the lyrics and music, and, as Mélisse has suggested, its content has influenced our interpretation of the song.

The Video of "Crucify"

As is the case in many of her videos, Tori Amos is the only actor in the film of "Crucify." We do not explicitly see her in relation to others, yet a variety of techniques are used to express the issue of agency within a context of societal control. Specifically, this larger issue is raised primarily through a critique of dominant modalities of femininity. The filmic techniques that play an important part in the communication include the different "images" of the subject (her manner of dress and her positioning), the "actions" of the subject (the roles she plays, the functions associated with her image), and the "gaze" (that is, the way in which these images and actions are viewed by the camera).

The video begins with a dark couch centered in a dark background. Amos enters wearing a white sheet or towel and high-heeled shoes, her hair loose and wet. She sits in the center of the couch while the camera holds the centered framing. The music begins and she sings the first line, "Every finger in the room is pointing at me." The perspective of the camera invokes the text reference to the gaze she senses upon her; she is conscious of herself and of being watched. The camera moves closer as she begins to invoke her own perspective. We are invited to observe her angry and fearful response to this uncomfortable situation. The camera's gaze creates a feeling of discomfort and alienation, a tension between the perspectives of the spectator and the spectacle, the subject and the object. Are we meant to identify with her, or are we in fact a part of the oppression?

Feminist film theorist Laura Mulvey explores two contradictory aspects of looking in the following remarks from her article "Visual Pleasure and Narrative Cinema":

> The first, scopophilic, arises from pleasure in using another person as an object of sexual stimulation through sight. The second, developed through narcissism and the constitution of the ego, comes from identification with the image seen. Thus, one implies a separation of the erotic identity of the subject from the object on the screen (active scopophilia), the other demands identification of the ego with the object on the screen through the spectator's fascination with and recognition of his like. (1975, 365)

The images accompanying the second verse are filmed in a similar way (dark background, centered framing): we see a nineteenth-century prostitute, with her hair drawn back, wearing dark satin clothing with a low neckline, shawl, and wide black choker. The camera perspective is again scopophilic and voyeuristic; she is very still, poised, posed for our scrutiny.[17] The image and gaze here clearly invoke the male spectator as subject and the female spectacle as object. However, there is once again an uneasiness to this voyeurism. Geraldine Finn explores the tension in the subject-object relationship in prostitution and in pornography. First, she establishes that "[the] pornographic woman is simultaneously produced as an object of male desire and is addressed to the male spectator precisely to solicit from him some sort of sexual response. She is in fact produced as both idol and idolizer. For her desire is constituted as his desire for her" (1985, 85). Finn then goes on to identify a conflict in the male reaction to a prostitute:

> [It is] difficult for a man to maintain his illusory belief in the objectivity of Woman when he is actually engaged in some sort of sexual activity with a real one.... This threat of encountering the Other as subject... can be circumvented in pornography; which substitutes an image of an unreal prostitute for an interaction with a real one. (85)

I am interested in Finn's formulation here because she engages the notion of male discomfort with facing the prostitute head-on, and I believe that Amos also wishes her audience to feel that anxiety. In another scene of the video, the prostitute is viewed in fragmented form through a narrow window; in this scene, the prostitute's body is nothing but a series of fetishized parts, an "unreal prostitute." This grants the male spectator greater control, defining him clearly as subject to the female object. Thus, the complete image of the prostitute, although still objectified for the male gaze, is *relatively* a greater cause of male anxiety than the fragmented and fetishized body parts.

The discomfort and tension of the verse are seen in direct contrast to the pre-chorus. For the first statement of the pre-chorus, the setting is a simple white backdrop with Amos sitting at a black piano, adopting the stance and manner of dress that is typical for her concerts: legs straddling the piano bench, hair falling loosely, wearing a halter top, pants, and medium-heeled shoes.[18] The camera now moves quickly, changing direction, not lingering on any part of her in particular, but rather moving from distant shots to close-ups of her face in an imitation of how one's own gaze and focus might change very naturally. It swings over the piano and then back, moves so that her face is centered in the frame, and then uncentered. Amos meets the eye of the camera with confidence; she conveys a sense of security, comfort, power. We see her playing the piano and singing in a virtuosic style of music that she has composed herself. In the context of the system of images that comprise this video, the image-action-gaze complement of this particular scene stands out for its efforts to portray Amos as an empowered woman.

I would modify this as "relative" power because, although I would like to do so, it is impossible to assert that Amos is not being in any way objectified in this scene. Although the image-action-gaze scenario creates a marked contrast to that of the verse, there remains a kind of discomfort between the spectator and the spectacle, subject and object. Indeed, perhaps this scene brings home the depth of the problem: What does it mean for Amos to choose her manner of dress and the style of video address? The way she has carved out her own image is ultimately responsive to societal definitions of her gender, as well as those of the female popular artist.

The lyrics of the chorus ask the question "Why do we crucify ourselves?" The video establishes unequivocally here that the issue behind this question is that of gender performance, as the images explicitly address definitions of femininity as negotiated through the manner of dress and the gaze of the camera. During the first statement of the chorus, the screen is framed as if we are looking through a narrow window; that is, a dark border on either side of the screen frames the light from a window. This perspective invokes two possible venues: a confessional booth, but also the peep-show window. Through the window we see fragments of Amos as the prostitute, and her apparel: a high-heeled shoe, a black choker, parts of her body dressed in dark satin. This particular filmic technique suggests scopophilia and voyeurism as well as fetishism: the hidden viewer receives erotic gratification by watching Amos, who is not seen as a whole being, but rather as a series of fetishized body parts and of the ornaments with which she is adorned— specifically, ornaments that are quintessential symbols of female constraint, such as the choker and the high heels.[19] Mulvey remarks on the purposeful construction of the female image as an object for male viewing: "The determining male gaze projects its fantasy onto the female figure, which is styled accordingly. In their traditional exhibitionist role women are simultaneously looked at and displayed, with their appearance coded for strong visual and erotic impact so that they can be said to connote *to-be-looked-at-ness*" (1975, 373). As Mulvey's theoretical formulation asserts, the relationship here between male subject and female object also suggests exhibitionism: Amos is performing for this peep show, after all. However, a feminist interpreter would ask how she negotiates this role of exhibitionist. Does she derive pleasure from it, or is the performance contrived, ironic? It is necessary to consider the entire context of the video in order to answer this question.

The lyrics of the chorus engage women as a group ("Why do *we* crucify ourselves?"), demonstrating that the protagonist is addressing a generalized problem. The oppressive "others" are invoked in an accusatory style, and the ultimate statement is one of reflection. The chorus thus offers some opportunity for empowerment and resistance. Given the images of this video, one wonders how resistance might be conveyed. The peep-show gaze represents in fact an explicit kind of female objectification. Although the final line, "my heart is sick of being in chains," returns us to the image of Amos at the piano, the greater part of the chorus does not treat Amos as a subject, but rather as an object.

The second statement of the chorus offers a new image. With a white background, the screen is split to accommodate two images of Amos, who is wearing the same clothing but moving slightly out of sync so that we see her images as clones, not as the same individual simply duplicated. The message here is one of conformity: these two women conform in image and function to a stereotype defined by society. The costume this time is that of a waitress, someone who serves. She wears a short blue satin dress, sleeveless, with a white collar and white apron. A red slip hangs down beneath the dress. She wears high-heeled shoes, and a narrow choker and an arm band. Once again, the issue of conformity begs the question of interpretation: Is she agreeing to conform? The final line of the chorus offers some relief from the negative impression of conformity. At "nothing I do is good enough for you," we see the positive image of Amos at the piano; however, we return to the waitress? at "my heart is sick of being in chains."

The images accompanying the bridge develop the visual narrative further. Accompanying the unusual shift in text perspective ("Please be save me") is a startling shift in scene; for the first time, the object of the viewing is something other than Amos. A white bathtub is centered in a black background; a large quantity of water falls into the tub from above. The "prostitute" enters from the left and walks resolutely toward the tub. She steps in, and then immediately the camera shifts to focus on specific parts of the prostitute's body immersed in the tub.[20] The religious connotations of the bathing are clear: the prostitute is being cleansed of her sins. As the immersion and bathing begin, we hear the pre-chorus, which creates a new context for that part of the text. The pre-chorus lyrics refer to the misogyny of the institution of religion and allow her the opportunity to reflect on her own participation in that institution. The explicit connection of that text with the bathing of the prostitute represents symbolically the themes of misogyny in the Christian tradition and problematizes Amos's involvement with the institution of religion.

The final chorus begins with a white background. Amos enters wearing the prostitute's dress and gloves, but she has removed the choker and the shawl and her hair is now loose and wet. Her attitude seems both liberated and defiant; her dancing is aggressively rhythmic, her overall expression strong. The camera gradually moves in so that by the time she articulates "chains," we see only Amos's face; her attire is no longer visible. She thus sheds the role of prostitute (object) and assumes the role of subject.

This image of the prostitute after the bathing ritual raises the question of what is accomplished by the bathing. I would like to suggest that there is an inversion of the expected meaning. The bathing ritual implies that the prostitute is being spiritually cleansed; however, Amos does not emerge with the attitude of a chastened woman. In addition, the water is used as a vehicle for drowning the symbols of constraint; we see the water nozzle and the high heels being immersed. During the first statement of the chorus, in which Amos performed at the piano, the immersed chains and high heels also appeared, then without any explanation. Now their purpose is clear: the chorus is concerned with the drowning or rejection of such symbols of constraint.

The chorus moves into the coda, which comprises a repetition of lines from the chorus. For this passage, the waitress figure returns, now cloned several times. These clones assume a kind of cheerleader stance; the high heels are gone and the women move across the screen in a cheerleader routine. Although they appear as clones of each other, symbolically representing women's conformity to feminine gender "programming," the last one refuses to conform. As the music fades, she faces the camera head-on, folds her arms across her chest, and refuses to run through the routine.

When I reflect on the narrative of this video, I am struck by a temporal contradiction.[21] The opening scene of the video shows Amos with wet hair, wearing a towel. In retrospect, we understand that this opening scene occurs, in real time, *after* the bathing ritual. How does this manipulation of the temporal narrative affect our interpretation of the final outcome? I have interpreted the ending of the video as a statement of resistance. But that ending is not the last *temporal* event that we see: rather, the beginning, where she has taken off all of the costumes and wears nothing but a white sheet, is the final image in the time continuum. What does this mean for the narrative of resistance? In that opening scene, although we may in retrospect understand that the *image* is a rejection of the stereotypes, the *lyrics* place her back in the situation of failed courage. Ultimately, I believe that this is Amos's theme: the message is one of resistance, but it is an ongoing kind of resistance within a problem of institutionalized proportions.

I shall now consider how Amos uses musical style and convention to explore the perspectives evident in the video and lyrics of the verse. What aspects of musical convention could Amos manipulate to signify the problem of *agency* within societal control, the tension between subject and object? Similarly, how could she signify her *resistance* to authority and control? What constitutes the "gaze" in music, and what, for my purposes, might constitute a tension in that gaze, a tension between spectator and spectacle? How might she demonstrate in musical terms the problem described by Mélisse as "active but not free participation"?

"Crucify": Verse

As I discuss the lyrics and music of the verse, I would like to remind the reader that the perspective of the camera in the video for this section invokes the text reference to the oppressive gaze that the protagonist senses is upon her. The scene features the centered image of Amos in a towel, sitting on a couch. In the lyrics of the first verse, the protagonist explores a profound tension between subject and object. Her first two lines ("Every finger in the room is pointing at me / I wanna spit in their faces then I get afraid of what that could bring") establish a conflict between the self and others in very clear terms by means of the content as well as the grammatical construction. In these two lines she establishes her subjective perspective, her reaction to others, and the tension in the subject-object relationship. The subject of the first line is "every finger"; these are fingers that obviously belong to others, fingers that are "pointing," a verb that suggests an object, the protagonist herself ("at me"). This first line thus represents, using the metaphor of pointing fingers, the social forces acting upon her. In this first line, she is the object. In the second line, she is the subject ("I"), and the verb and object construction expresses what she wishes to do in reaction to these forces ("spit in their faces"), but she polices her behavior. The fear and anxiety are confirmed in the third and fourth lines, when she describes how it feels to be the object of this scrutiny.

In the music of the verse, the reverberation of the voice is quite dry, creating a "room effect" in keeping with the text reference to the room she is in.[22] The texture of the first verse is sparse; we hear open fifths in the bass guitar, accompanied by strong attacks on beats two and four on the kick drum, with quiet subdivided pulse attacks on the high hat. As Amos sings about her discomfort within the room, her voice, with a nervous edge, is heard above the hollow-sounding fifths. The voice seems to be holding back: words at phrase endings stop in her throat until, at the last word of the verse, the reverberation increases to create a "stage" or "hall" effect, anticipating what is about to happen in the pre-chorus. The combined effect of these different features makes up the "sound" or style of this verse, and projects the kind of tension that I have attributed to the lyrics and video.

The phrase design and harmonic patterning of the verse are repetitive, but carefully manipulated to create a sense of contrapuntal tension. The form comprises four phrases; that is, two phrases that then repeat with some minor modifications. The harmonic pattern that recurs, shown in a reductive style of notation in figure 3.1, is a kind of neighboring construction that circles around the modal tonic, G♯ Dorian.[23] The progression derives its tension from a movement away from tonic, up to ii, then down to VII, before returning to tonic. In the first phrase this movement is complete or closed, in the second it is incomplete or open, ending on VII. The harmonic effect of the stop on VII is comparable to a half cadence; it is a dissonance that requires resolution. These two phrases form a closed-then-open design (the opposite of a typical period structure).[24] The third and fourth phrases move through the same closed-

FIGURE 3.1 "Crucify," Voice-Leading Graph (Verse 1)

then-open pattern. The vocal line is determined by the harmonic progression, in that it merely moves in parallel with the bass, a fifth above. The bass guitar actually articulates these parallel fifths in a performance technique that is quite unusual for rock. Thus the vocal line simply mirrors what is already being heard.

How do I evaluate the *conventional meaning* of the musical strategies used in the verse? My immediate response to the particular use of mode, harmony, and formal structure is to use the classification of stasis or containment, but I would like to interrogate that response. The referential harmonic pattern is indeed cyclic in nature, and thus connotes the idea of containment: there is movement away from the tonic to the harmony a step above, followed by the movement to the harmony a step below, followed by the return. That this pattern provides the basis for four entire phrases contributes further to the sense that movement is being contained. In addition, the voice does not function as an independent contrapuntal line; rather, the singer's line follows the harmonic progression at the fifth above. Amos does manipulate this contrapuntal relationship, as I shall discuss below, but at the level of structure (that is, the abstract relation of her vocal part to the bass), her line is determined, or contained, by the harmonic progression. Thus, the specific handling of harmony and voice-leading within the context of cyclic repetition and phrase design justifies my interpretation of the harmonic *conventions and codes* as "static" or "contained," and thereby also justifies that associative meaning in relation to the textual message of the song.

Within this system of containment, however, there is space for resistance. Amos's voice interacts in a very interesting way with the bass progression, and I shall consider this interaction from the perspective of my interpretive category *musical "voice" and dramatic function*. As with most popular music vocal performance, Amos's pitches do not always line up with the vertical harmonies to which they belong. That is, she uses various devices to offset the melody and harmony; for instance, she might anticipate her next vocal pitch before its harmony has arrived in the other instruments, or she might suspend a pitch from the previous harmony, resolving only after the new harmony has arrived. Although one might argue that this offsetting technique is simply a feature of the performance style, there are moments when it creates a striking dramatic effect. Given the context of the vocal line as a doubling of the upper fifth in the guitar's parallel fifth progression, it is possible to identify what the singer "ought" to be doing at any point. To say so is perhaps contentious, yet it is precisely this notion of deviation from convention that I mean to engage. Certain of Amos's deviations from the established norm are remarkable. For instance, in the very first phrase, the E♯ on the third beat (at "room") is the harmonic pitch in relation to the bass; however, it is sung as a brief sixteenth note, moving immediately down to D♯. The D♯ is actually a dissonant passing tone (moving on to the next harmonic pitch, C♯), yet it receives the emphasis. The effect is that the harmonic pitch, E♯, sounds more like a neighbor note than a harmonic note. Each time this gesture is heard at the beginning of each of the four phrases in the verse (although varied), the D♯ is emphasized in some way. Indeed, in the third and fourth phrases (for the words "stomach" and "courage"), the D♯ actually receives the accent on the beat, relegating E♯ to a secondary status.

This detailed description of the voice-leading is not intended to create an objective theoretical distance from the musical events; rather, I mean to demonstrate in specific theoretical terms that the discomfort or tension felt at these moments in the song ("room," "faces," "stomach," "courage") is in part created by a dramatic tension between the singer and her accompaniment. Although I would not explicitly map the roles of subject and object onto the voice and guitar (especially since the subject/object roles were not absolute or stationary in the text), I do feel that the dramatic tension between the two is a musical depiction of the conceptual problem. As I ask myself how Amos might signify in musical terms her *agency*, or her "active but not free participation" in the oppressive social system, as well as her *resistance* to control, I believe it is important to consider this kind of deliberate manipulation of musical conventions or narratives.

Another dissonant moment occurs at the end of phrase 2 of the verse. Here the bass holds the VII harmony and avoids the resolution to the tonic, creating the open harmonic ending of the phrase. The voice, however, does not stop with the C♯, the note that is part of the VII chord, but rather continues on to the note that would create the tonic resolution; that is, the fifth of the tonic, D♯. So although the harmonic movement is open, the vocal line attempts to close. The effect is not one of closure, but rather one of strong *contextual* dissonance, occurring precisely at the word "bring" in the expression "then I get afraid of what that could bring." At the end of the fourth phrase (the comparable place in the form), the bass moves again to the VII harmony, and this time the voice appears to be in line, taking the C♯ and treating the D♯ as a simple upper neighbor. This resolving vocal gesture occurs at the line "sell out now," possibly signifying her complicity within the system. However, the voice plunges immediately into the pre-chorus, moving back up to the D♯ as it begins. The VII harmony at the end of the verse is reinterpreted as a dominant harmony in B major, and the pre-chorus begins in that key. The verse and pre-chorus are thus linked harmonically at the moment when the vocal reverberation begins to give the voice a warmer sound. As the music shifts from the verse to the pre-chorus, many parameters change; thus, the section shift is a site for the theoretical category of *contrasting values*.[25]

"Crucify": Pre-chorus

The pre-chorus contrasts the directly oppressive situation of the verse by providing a larger social context. The lyrics suggest a possible identity for the oppressive social force: organized religion. They also speak to the protagonist's motivation for participating in the system; her actions represent her efforts to search for self-definition within that social institution. The protagonist describes continuing actions ("I've been looking for a savior" and "I've been raising up my hands"), suggesting a certain degree of optimism that they will yield positive results. The remark "drive another nail in" and the final ironic line demonstrate the futility of her efforts. The tension that exists now arises from her own ability to comment ironically on the situation, ascribing to her some degree of strength or power. This "power" is problematic, because she is still engaging an oppressive force, but she demonstrates some resistance to that force.

In the video, the pre-chorus shifts from the verse's sense of discomfort with the spectator-spectacle relationship to a more "natural" gaze and natural appearance of Amos performing at the piano, once again providing her with an opportunity for self-reflection and commentary. The musical shift between verse and pre-chorus is articulated by many parameters: the striking mode shift from G♯ Dorian to B major (or Ionian); the voice's D♯ shifts in function from the "hollow" fifth (*conventional meaning*) above the bass G♯ to the "warmer" major third above B; at the same time, the "room" vocal reverberation of the verse changes to the "hall" reverberation; the sparse texture of the verse is expanded to include a very active piano part; the bass guitar that had moved in the repetitive open fifth progression now articulates a more melodic bass line; the drum accent that had been on beats two and four, syncopated with the harmonic changes, is now on beats one and three, in time with the harmonic changes; and, finally, the repetitive harmonic progression and phrase structure are replaced by a strongly directional harmonic progression and a more complex formal design.

In the verse, the vocal line was derived structurally from the bass accompaniment. Now, in the pre-chorus, the vocal line is not dependent on the bass for its line, but instead its contrapuntal relation to the bass is more varied. In addition, whereas the verse melody was predictable because of its repeated neighbor-note construction, the pre-chorus melody is not locked into a pattern of repetition. The pre-chorus melody works with the notion of linear and harmonic expectations, thus in a sense with tonal "predictability"; however, these expectations result from Amos's manipulation of a conventional phrase design that requires a longer span (two full four-measure phrases), a studied manipulation of harmonic and voice-leading conventions, and a contrapuntally complex relationship between voice and bass.

The form comprises two phrases that have an interesting harmonic relationship (figure 3.2). The first phrase is a straightforward harmonic progression from tonic to dominant, with a half cadence. The movement from tonic to dominant is immediate, and then the harmony hovers around the dominant, F$\sharp$, with the bass line moving to its upper and lower neighbors G$\sharp$ and E (harmonies vi and IV) before cadencing on F$\sharp$ (V). The second begins similarly, suggesting a parallel period structure and a continuation that will this time be closed; that is, after the V–vi–IV–V progression of the antecedent, one would expect a clear tonic resolution in the consequent, thus diffusing the tension created by the antecedent's dominant prolongation. However, the harmony takes a sudden shift when the bass moves to the chromatic E$\sharp$, the leading tone to the dominant, harmonized by a secondary dominant function (viio$_7$ of V). This chord is first heard as a chromatic intensification of the earlier progression; instead of the antecedent's diatonic V–vi–IV–V, one might expect the progression now to be V–vi–viio$_7$/V–V, before finally moving on to I. It is not an unusual tactic for an antecedent phrase to up the stakes like this; that is, to intensify the movement to V through a chromatic shift. However, the E$\sharp$ does not resolve to F$\sharp$ as expected, but rather continues on to E and the harmony of IV, where the phrase closes; there is neither a return to V nor an ultimate resolution of V to I.

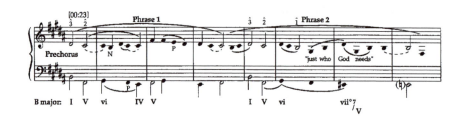

FIGURE 3.2 "Crucify," Voice-Leading Graph (Pre-chorus)

The voice and its contrapuntal relation to the bass have an important role in the creation of expectations in the antecedent and denial of these expectations in the consequent. The antecedent establishes the conventional melodic progression that moves down from scale degree 3 to 2 (D♯ to C♯); the "implied" continuation of this progression would be to scale degree 1 (B). This descent occurs immediately in the first two measures of the antecedent phrase, but with the "wrong" bass support; that is, the B in the voice is supported by the deceptive G♯ (vi). The bass has avoided the expected continuation, so now the voice has to set up the potential progression for another attempt. The ensuing melodic movement is therefore concerned with the linear connection from 3 to 2. The antecedent phrase occupies itself so much with the 3–2 movement in the voice that it creates an expectation that this movement will be answered in the consequent by a complete linear progression 3–2–1, harmonized by I–V–I.

However, the consequent phrase denies these expectations. The phrase begins with the same 3–2–1 movement over the deceptive bass progression I–V–vi, but this time, when the harmony digresses, the melodic line gives up its efforts to create closure and similarly digresses. In response to the bass's deceptive turn to vi, the voice outlines a G♯ minor triad, precisely at the moment of ironic self-reflection, "just what God needs." The bass supports this G♯ minor arpeggiation with the chromatic E♯ discussed earlier. As the harmony cadences on the surprising harmony of E major, the voice comes to rest on B (at "victim"), but then leaps down to a dissonant and unresolved F♯.

This consequent phrase thus creates in musical terms an ironic expression (a *structural anomaly*), matching the ironic commentary in the text. The musical irony is created by a number of details that combine to disrupt the expected narrative of the harmony and voice-leading (*codes, conventions*). I have already commented on the harmonic turn to E major, which avoids the resolution of the chromatic E♯ and supplants the expected perfect cadential progression. In addition, the vocal B for the cadence is the pitch we were expecting at the conclusion of the phrase, but certainly not with this particular harmonization (E major), and not with this particular approach (G♯ minor arpeggiation as opposed to a clear 3–2–1 descent). Our surprise at the cadence is not just based on immediate musical events from one measure into another measure; rather, we hear the disruption at a larger level. That is, our expectations for a particular harmonic or voice-leading event are based on the antecedent-consequent phrase design. In addition, we hear the disruption at the level of the relationship between the verse and pre-chorus; out of the static modal progression in G♯ Aeolian emerges a strongly directional B-major progression that surely will offer us a satisfying resolution. However, these expectations dissolve (textually and musically) into ironic reflection at the end of the pre-chorus.[26]

"Crucify": Chorus

The chorus divides into what I shall refer to as the "crucify" and "heart" sections; the devices and techniques that create sectional division at this important juncture (the chorus and namesake of the song) contribute greatly to the song's meaning and message. I would like to emphasize the importance of contrast in the lyrics and music as a strategy for the succinct expression of the song's thematic concerns in this culminating moment of the chorus. As Mélisse has suggested, the "crucify" theme elevates to the level of religious metaphor the problem of the female disciplining process; the verse and pre-chorus explore this process in what might be understood as more descriptive or narrative terms and thus create a context in which we can understand the more enigmatic question "why do we crucify ourselves" when it occurs in the chorus. The question is repeated in a rather emphatic style, without further narrative development. The "heart" section, by contrast, returns to a more personal style of expression and represents Amos's resistance, or strengthening of resolve, even as the nature of her resistance and her agency remains problematic. The video images confirm the division of the chorus into two sections. In the first statement of the chorus, the "crucify" section is accompanied by fragmented images of the prostitute through the confessional booth window (thus confirming that the issue behind the question "why do we crucify ourselves" is that of gender performance, negotiated through the strictures of organized religion); for the "heart" or resistant section, the more "natural" image of Amos at the piano returns (as she was seen during the pre-chorus). I am placing interpretive significance on the division of the chorus into these two different modes of expression because, through this division or contrast, the chorus signifies the essential thematic content of the song. The other sections of the song are vital in the communication, but here in the chorus we are presented with the central problem of the song's text; that is, the problem of *agency* and *resistance* within an oppressive system.

How does the music for the chorus participate in this communication and connote the disciplining process ("crucify" section) as well as the protagonist's efforts to resist ("heart" section)? The "crucify" section is very repetitive: the vocal melody and bass line pattern repeat every two measures, and we hear repetitive percussion articulation with a strong accent in the kick drum on beats one and three, an even stronger attack on beats two and four on the floor tom (recorded with a huge reverberation effect), and a constant shaking of maracas at the subdivided pulse. The drum attacks overwhelm the texture; this section of the song places percussion in the foreground of the mix. The piano part is now restricted to a very narrow range, essentially functioning as simple "chording."

Harmonically, the chorus (graphed in figure 3.3) returns us to the style of the verse. The mode is now G$\sharp$ Aeolian, and the voice-leading simply moves from the open fifth on G$\sharp$ to the open fifth on F$\sharp$ (i to VII). In the verse, that harmonic progression was articulated in such a way as to contribute to a clear phrase structure, and the functions of G$\sharp$ and F$\sharp$ as i and VII were clear. In the chorus, however, the melodic and bass patterning are organized so as to confuse form and function. The harmonic movement between i and VII, then VII and i, is mediated by C$\sharp$ (iv). The harmonic progression seems simple, yet an interpretive problem arises from this scenario: given the cyclical nature of the pattern repetition, it is very difficult to sort out the phrase structure. That is, one statement of the pattern runs into the next in the manner of an elision. The pattern begins on "why do we," harmonized by G$\sharp$; "crucify ourselves" is heard to the falling fifth progression C$\sharp$–F$\sharp$, perhaps creating a kind of resolution into F$\sharp$; however, "every day" is set to a progression from C$\sharp$ to G$\sharp$, returning us to the place where we started. From that G$\sharp$, which may sound like an ending, we really do begin again as the whole pattern repeats. There are three complete statements of this material, in the course of which we are lost in the repetition of the cyclic pattern, not knowing if F$\sharp$ (VII) or G$\sharp$ (i) represents the harmonic goal. Indeed, it is not possible to identify a phrase ending (that is, a cadence) throughout this entire passage. The drum attacks on beats one and three (relatively strong) and beats two and four (very strong) do not help matters, as we are constantly thrown by the syncopation. The voice does not help either, because it simply

FIGURE 3.3 "Crucify," Voice-Leading Graph (Chorus)

oscillates between D♯ and C♯. The musical devices of cyclic repetition, ambiguous harmonic center, and nondirectionality in the context of the same mode and harmonic framework that was earlier (that is, during the verse) associated with the protagonist's feelings of constraint are surely meant to connote the problem of her continuing agency and participation in the disciplining process of crucifixion.

After the "crucify" section, the voice initiates change with an intonation pattern for "my heart is sick of being"; the intonation is then repeated, which contributes to the enunciatory style of the moment. The instruments also announce a shift by holding back; the maracas drop out, the bass guitar avoids the earlier repetitive pattern and changes harmony only once per measure. As the "heart" section announces this change, the harmony breaks the pattern: we hear the progression G♯–C♯–F♯–C♯, as before, but it stops on the C♯ (iv) for an entire measure when the voice announces "my heart is sick of being," then moves on to a new harmony (E, or VI) for a repetition of the announcement. This announcement leads into the setting of "chains," for which the voice assumes the greatest level of activity thus far in the song. The voice is accompanied by piano, mandolin, and ukelele, as well as bass guitar, and is released from its previous emphasis throughout the song on the middle register (especially the pitches D♯ and C♯). The musical irony here is that the voice is liberated at the same time that the protagonist is decrying the "chains" that hold her. The voice is now in a higher register (G♯ and B) and the vocal line is more elaborate. The harmony also breaks free from its oscillation between G♯ and F♯ to confirm G♯ minor. The bass is still repetitive, but now the progression features mediant relationships in G♯: i–III–VI–iv, repeated. The rising movement from i to III, especially in the context of the liberated vocal line, contributes to the sense of musical *freedom* at this point in the chorus. The shift into this more liberated style of expression is a fitting depiction of the protagonist's efforts to resist; however, it is a clever musical device that this passage is still written within the mode of G♯, the modal center that has been strongly linked with the containment of the verse and the disciplining nature of the crucifixion in the first part of the chorus.

Musically, then, the chorus signifies the two opposing constructs in the text: the *containment* of the "crucify" section and the *resistance* or efforts to be liberated in the "heart" section. The chorus is distinguished from the verse and pre-chorus by its strategy of internal contrast. In general, I would identify both the verse and pre-chorus as having an internally unified thematic and musical content; these sections present a particular musical phrase and harmonic structure, and then work within that structure. The chorus, however, makes a clear division in the musical content. Out of the repetitive, cyclic pattern of the "crucify" section, we are witness to the protagonist's resistance with the "heart" and "chains" material.

"Crucify": Bridge and Overall Narrative

The song moves through two complete statements of verse, pre-chorus, and chorus; thereafter, there is a single statement of a bridge that leads into the final pre-chorus and chorus statements, followed by the coda. As Mélisse mentioned, this bridge is lyrically, visually, and musically unique, and thus rivets our attention. The video images associated with the bridge are the bathtub and the immersion ritual; the use of inserted images of immersion throughout the entire video indicates the importance of this image for the narrative. Similarly, in the domains of lyrics and music, the bridge is a defining moment in the song's structure. I find myself incapable of analyzing the bridge outside of its context; that is, without reference to the whole song. Therefore, as I discuss the internal content of the bridge, I will also begin to offer my conclusions concerning the overall narrative of the song.

The text utterance of the bridge is simple: "Please be save me I CRY." Such a declamation represents a marked shift in poetic style and perspective. It is a plea, an appeal. Mélisse underscored the bridge text as the moment when the protagonist avows the pain of her participation in the "discursive" crucifixion. Musically, the bridge launches us into a different sound-world: the voice has an ecstatic, melismatic line, accompanied by the back-up vocals an octave higher, recorded with a "cathedral effect" reverberation. The plea, or prayer, invoked by the lyrics is illuminated by this rich vocal sound. For the music theorist, the harmony and voice-leading of the bridge are also of strategic importance. Thus far, the song has established the two harmonic or modal regions of G♯ and B. I have not yet posited any particular associative meaning for these key areas, but with the content of the bridge, I believe Amos offers a context from which to draw interpretive conclusions. Although it is not the last musical section we hear, it is the last presentation of new material, and thus is the last piece of the puzzle for our interpretation.

FIGURE 3.4 "Crucify," Voice-Leading Graph (Bridge)

Throughout the bridge (graphed in figure 3.4), the bass line repeats the pattern G♯–A♯–B–F♯. The pattern begins on G♯, thus possibly ascribes to it a referential function. However, as the pattern is repeated, we hear the succession from F♯ to B (starting with the last note of the pattern, F♯), which the tonal analyst will hear as a dominant–tonic succession in B major. Thus, the simple bass riff manages to suggest two potential tonal centers, depending on how the analyst parses the pattern. And the listener who has followed the harmonic narrative presented thus far in the song will hear, within this bass line, references to the emphasis on G♯ from the verse and chorus, as well as the F♯–B patterning of the pre-chorus. The rhythmic presentation of the bass also contributes to the ambiguity of harmonic function. The harmonic changes (G♯–A♯–B–F♯) occur on beats one and four, while the kick drum is attacking beats two and four. The vocal part has a critical role in defining the tonal focus of the bridge; that is, in projecting the governing harmony for the ambiguous bass progression. The voice and the back-up vocals emphasize B♯; as is indicated in the voice-leading analysis, the voice moves through a repetition of the pattern B♯–D♯–C♯ against the bass G♯–B–F♯. It is not possible to interpret this contrapuntal structure as a prolongation of B major: the cross-relation of B♯ in the voice against B in the bass disrupts any effort to hear B as stable. In addition, as the pattern begins to repeat, the voice-leading resolves into the G♯–B♯ tonic third. That is, the specific voice-leading within the cyclic repetition of the pattern creates the effect of an elision: the end of one statement is directed into the beginning of the next. My interpretation of the harmonic pattern is thus I–III–VII in G♯, which then returns to I as the pattern repeats.

Amos's choice of a G♯ center for the bridge is significant for the overall context of key relations in the song. G♯ is the mode of the verse and the chorus; in opposition to G♯ stands the functionally tonal B-major material of the pre-chorus. One could spin any number of interpretive tales to account for this G♯–B tonal conflict. When I consider this tonal contrast, I perceive it in relation to the protagonist's perspective. G♯ Dorian is heard when we are witness to her feelings of constraint in the verse, and G♯ Aeolian in the chorus when she interrogates her own role in the crucifixion process. B major enters when she identifies and explores, with a tone of ironic critique, the source of her oppression: organized religion and its definitions of femininity. In this comparative context, G♯ signifies her oppression, while B major signifies a degree of empowerment. The bridge acknowledges the tonal conflict between G♯ and B, but ultimately favors a G♯ modal center, thus reinscribing the protagonist's position within the system of oppression.

This interpretation of the tonal narrative suggests that the bridge ultimately decides the conflict between B and G♯ in favor of the latter, thus in favor of the tonal center that symbolizes her oppression and her crucifixion. However, the bridge is not the final section of the song. It moves immediately into a statement of the pre-chorus, returning us to the key of B major and then on to the chorus in G♯, which is extended into a coda. The effect is that the process begins all over again, but this time avoids the final resolution. But perhaps this is a crucial aspect of Amos's message: she does not choose to conclude with the message of the bridge.

It is useful to recall here that the video concludes not with the oppressive image of the bathing ritual (bridge), but rather with resistant images: the prostitute image and waitress/cheerleader images are utlimately rejected. I do not mean to suggest that the ultimate message of the song is one of successful resistance, or a resolution of the societal problem. Amos remains in the costume of the waitress, she remains in the mode of G♯. Indeed, as Mélisse has also shown, resistance is never unproblematic. Amos's song can be read as a resistance against particular social constructs and institutions, but she does not attain or even explicitly define an ultimate goal of knocking down those barriers; rather, she simply illustrates a degree of resistance to the systems and structures she invokes.

4

Courtney Love (Hole),
Live through This (1994)

CULTURES OF INJURY: COURTNEY LOVE ON VIOLENCE AGAINST WOMEN AND THE PATRIARCHAL AESTHETIC (MÉLISSE LAFRANCE)

> The dish swirling about Courtney Love has only increased as our lady of the swollen red lips and glossy covers becomes ever more iconic: speculation about her drug use, her ruthless drive to "make it," who she's screwing, how she's mothering. Love occupies a great deal of psychic space, especially among women I know, less for reasons of hype and Kurt association than the fact that she's the first female rock star with whom many of us truly identify: a well-read former chubette who lets her seams show and is fearless about dispensing sardonic, bitter wisdoms. Hole's *Live Through This* (DGC) is our fierce feminist manifesto, laden with girlcentric insights about bodies, sex, pain and power so acute that every song produces a wince of recognition. (Dieckmann 1995, JA3)

Situating Courtney Love and Hole in the Late-Twentieth-Century Popular Imaginary

In 1995, *Rolling Stone* magazine published a feature article entitled "Hole Is a Band, Courtney Love Is a Soap Opera" (Jason Cohen 1995). In a sense, *Rolling Stone* could not have described the perceived divide between this alternative rock group and its lead singer with more accuracy. For when journalists and fans discuss "Hole," they tend to discuss a popular musical phenomenon: a fearless and gritty mid-nineties band whose 1994 album *Live through This* topped every music critic's poll and went platinum shortly thereafter. Yet when these same individuals appraise Courtney Love in particular, their conversations tend to pertain not so much to musicianship as to Love's relationship with the late Kurt Cobain, her physical appearance, her alleged drug overdoses, and her supposedly shrill and uncontrollable behavior. Reading Hole and Courtney Love as discrete and divisible popular cultural formations appears to constitute the prevailing strategy in the mainstream press.

I would argue that when the mainstream press read Hole and Love as discrete popular cultural formations, they do not do so innocently. The popular media's portrayal of Hole as a serious and accomplished alternative rock group and of Courtney Love as a confused and hysterical woman allows the press not only to elaborate Love as radically distinct from the creative work of her group, but to oppose Hole and Love in a vertically dichotomous relationship of "good" and "bad." In my view, when the press read Hole and Love as separate phenomena, they enable themselves to both *recognize* Hole as a significant and successful popular musical presence (which is empirically undeniable and, if not acknowledged, would be seen by most as a conspicuous case of poor and biased music journalism) and to simultaneously *deride* Courtney Love as hysterical, dangerous, and generally ridiculous.

If my argument appears overwrought with complexity, then it is useful to consider a number of particularly salient and revealing citations from the popular press. In these quotations, one sees a clear instance of Love's creative contributions being left out of descriptions of Hole's success. Moreover, some of these citations make special reference to the only male in the band, which, it could be argued, constitutes a concomitant effacement of the group's gynocentered themes and investment of the group with phallocentered "grunge" prestige and authority.

> With Eric Erlandson's lupine guitar their *mainstay,* Hole is a band whose savage attack never wavers. (*Rolling Stone* 1994–95), 190; emphasis added)

> Love flayed the melody with suicidal anguish in front of Erlandson's industrial-strength guitar snort. (*Rolling Stone* 1994, 83–84)

Hole, when discussed *without* intimate or personal reference to Love, is presented as an earnest and proficient musical presence. When discussed *with* reference to Love, however, reflections on the music become little more than a forum for speculative popular psychological analyses of Love's purported history and mania:

> On "Doll Parts" from Hole's second and most recent album *Live Through This* (DGC), Ms. Love sings, "I want to be the girl with the most cake." It is this need for more attention and more approval than those around her get that has dogged Ms. Love her whole life.... Though she is one of the most gifted performers in rock music, she continues to be a near mythomaniac, driven by a need to belong. (Strauss 1995, L14)

> Even before she ascended to celebrity spousehood, Love was the scarred beauty queen of underground-rock society, a fearless confessor and feedback addict whose sinister charisma—part ravaged baby doll, part avenging kamikaze angel—suggested the dazed, enraged, illegitimate daughter of Patti Smith. (*Rolling Stone* 1994, 83–84)

> Band members quickly learned to sidestep thrashing limbs as Courtney hit the boards with the speed and flexibility of a riled swamp gator.... Love seems stagily committed to her PMS-queen rep. And loyal fans are hip to the truth behind Love's cranky, oft-quoted lyric, "I fake it so real, I am beyond fake." (Hirshey 1997, 88–89)

Above and beyond the depoliticized pop psychology that suffuses "analyses" of Courtney Love's creative output, there is an entire genre of Love journalism that might be seen as outright slanderous.[1] From what I can gather, this journalism neither pretends to be based on empirical evidence (as opposed to periodicals such as *Billboard* and *Rolling Stone*) nor expects to be read as a truthful rendering of the subject at hand. While the amount of trash-tabloid coverage of Love is too abundant to scrutinize completely here, it is worth examining a number of fairly representative excerpts. When reading these reviews, I suggest that one be particularly sensitive to the devices through which the members of the press represent Love as hysterical, lurid, ugly, and unruly:

> Turning up onstage at London's Dominion Theatre two hours late, clutching a bottle of whiskey, her face smeared with mascara, she antagonized an already restive audience by drawling, "What the f*** YOU lookin' at?" She then struggled to adjust the height of her microphone stand. When the compeer of the event...offered to help her, she smashed him about the side of the head, knocking his glasses off and shouted, "F***in' condescend to ME, you f***ing MAN, huh?" (*Melody Maker* 1995, 26)

Looking drawn and emotional, her troubled day began early when she came down to the elderly women wearing twin set and pearls, eating from a pot of jam. Concluding from this that the woman was a Pearl Jam fan, she flung herself upon her, tearing at her hair, shouting "F*** you, Eddie Vedder!" (*Melody Maker* 1995, 38)

[Column juxtaposed with a large and unflattering picture of Courtney Love] There are just two types of female making pop music today—those blessed with good looks [girls], and those who would perhaps be better served by a undercover visit to the local plastic surgeon [women]. [Women rockers] are just indulging in ugly wimmin bleating (see: Babes in Toyland, Hole, L7). When ugly wimmin get left by some scrawny, spotty failed musician at 2am morning in some miserable hovel in Seattle or Southwark, they blame the whole world but you couldn't give a shit because they sound so f***ing whiningly horrible. (Lester 1992, 45)

Feminists have reason to be concerned about these articles—and the periodicals in which such articles appear—for a number of reasons. First, their critiques of Courtney Love seem to be premised on a fairly explicit antifeminism (see first citation). Moreover, they present Love (and women in general) as desperate and pathetic (see second and third citations). Finally, all of these reviews rely on normative notions of femininity and dominant stereotypes of typical feminine behavior in order to, in the end, make Love (and other feminist musicians) appear responsible for their own ill treatment at the hands of the media. Within the context of a highly sexist mediascape, this last is not terribly surprising. What makes it particularly offensive in this case, however, is the fact that Love writes and sings against precisely the forms of gendered, antifeminist representation of which she is the undeniable object. Potential Love enthusiasts who read both the more serious periodicals and the tabloids would never know that Love writes intelligent feminist polemics, because such intelligent political redaction is read right out of her work.

If I might digress briefly, it is interesting to note that Love herself openly, and indeed frequently, alludes to what she perceives to be a sexed (or sexist) double standard in popular music criticism. She declares that while male musicians are often considered serious musicians, or musicians whose talent merits discussion and from whom aspiring musicians can learn, female musicians are interesting to the press (and, one can infer, to society in general) primarily because their bodies, their femininities, and their love lives can be commodified and (re)formulated to meet the demands of an admittedly androcentric consumer culture.[2] Love elucidates this problem through a discussion of why being featured in a strictly musical magazine is so significant for female musicians:

> This is the thing with women, this is the issue: We all want to be in [the magazine] *Musician*. It's a common thing, you know why? Because, like, all the grungy guys are like "why would you want to be in that fucking fascist magazine?" And it's because there is some kind of weird validation in the question "what kind of bass strings do you use?" (Love, quoted in Udovitch 1994, 96)

Reading Courtney Love: Discourse and Power

It is important to consider the discursive effects of the prevailing representations of Courtney Love. What do these reading strategies say about the media who exploit them? What do they communicate to those consuming them? And how do they intervene in and/or shape the listening process? In my view, the fact that the mainstream press often choose to read Hole and Love as separate phenomena, the former as "musical" and the latter as "trash-tabloid queen," reveals to me a fervent unwillingness to engage with Love as a musician proper. Rather than understanding Love as a musician who happens to have a difficult personal life, Love is read as exactly the opposite: a difficult woman who happens to be a musician.

Ultimately, refusing to engage with Love as a proper musical presence while insisting on reading (and thus writing) her as an incarnation of hysterical femininity functions to discredit the insurgent feminism of Love's lyricism. I am not suggesting that the primary agents of mainstream media devised a plan to disgrace Courtney Love in order to subdue the countercultural impulses of her songwriting; what I am suggesting, however, is that regardless of the media's intentions, they accomplished exactly that. Whether the press carefully calculated the persistent and systematic damage done to Love's reputation has little bearing on the overall plausibility of my analysis. Michel Foucault explains why:

> Power relations are both intentional and nonsubjective. If in fact they are intelligible, this is not because they are the effect of another instance that "explains" them, but rather because they are imbued, through and through, with calculation: there is no power that is exercised without a series of aims

101

and objectives. But this does not mean that it results from the choice or decision of an individual subject; let us not look for the headquarters that presides over its rationality; . . . the rationality of power is characterized by tactics . . . which, becoming connected to one another, attracting and propagating one another, but finding their base of support and their condition elsewhere, end by forming comprehensive systems: the logic is perfectly clear, the aims decipherable, and yet it is often the case that no one is there to have invented them. ([1976] 1990)

The media's treatment of Love produced a number of fairly coherent effects, and those effects manifested themselves through the indisputable devaluation and depoliticization of Love's lyrical radicalism. Indeed, both the relentless scrutiny to which Love has been and continues to be subjected and the ensuing tomes of crude and derogatory "criticism" in which she figures must be seen as tactics of a polymorphous patriarchal power mobilized with the aim of arresting the subversive potential of Love's creative work.[3]

THE POLITICS OF FEMALE CORPOREALITY: FEMINIST THEORY, VIOLENCE AGAINST WOMEN, AND BEAUTY CULTURE

I have divided my analysis of Hole's work into two thematic categories: those pertaining to violence against women, and those pertaining to what I have termed the "patriarchal beauty aesthetic." Admittedly, both themes essentially pertain to women's experiences of violence in contemporary culture. Yet I have divided my analyses of these songs into two categories so that I may draw from two related but distinct theoretical formations. This section will be confined mainly to a discussion of feminist theories of violence against women and end-of-century beauty culture. I will highlight those theoretical positions that bring into relief the broadly ideological positions from which Love appears to be working in her songwriting.

Feminist Perspectives on Violence against Women

A sociological definition of violence needs to include both the use of force and its threat to both compel or constrain women to behave or not to behave in given ways. (Hanmer and Maynard 1987, 6)

[Dominant] images of sexuality, heterosexuality and the interconnection between sex and violence reflect and reinforce masculinity, male power, and the depersonalization, objectification and degradation of women. In this process aggressive male sexuality and the dominance of men is legitimated and women are portrayed as creatures for whom "sex is essentially masochistic, humiliation pleasurable, physical abuse erotic." (Edwards 1987, 25)

The late 1960s and the 1970s might be seen as somewhat of an epochal cornerstone as regards theorizing on violence against women in Western cultures. According to Jalna Hanmer and Mary Maynard (1987), it was through the process of consciousness raising that many women came to the realization that sexual assault was not simply an individual or isolated incident but that it was, as both an event and an ideological issue, a powerful means of understanding the psychological and political matrices of oppression. In other words, violence against women in contemporary society was beginning to be conceptualized as not only a concrete act, but also an embodiment of abstract and even invisible networks of masculinist modalities of power and coercion. For the first time, the analysis of violence against women was being seen as a potential master key to unlocking the elusive inner workings of patriarchy. However, in her now classic text *Sexual Politics*, Kate Millett reminds us that gendered forms of violence are not only the *products* of a patriarchal and misogynistic society; they are also the *conditions* in and through which patriarchal societies sustain themselves. Millett writes,

just as under other total ideologies... control in patriarchal society would be imperfect, even inoperable, unless it had the rule of force to rely upon, both in emergencies and as an ever-present instrument of intimidation. (1970, 43)

As the 1970s progressed, feminists began broadening formulations of violence against women. Throughout this process of theoretical construction, feminists began focusing on the less immediately visible forms of woman-related abuse. The feminist etiology of patriarchal violence thus grew to encompass not only physical coercion but also routine and seemingly "ordinary" forms of masculinist intimidation, humiliation, and exploitation. This new analytic orientation involved a thorough investigation of women's physical and psychological health, their sexuality, their fertility and reproductivity, their mothering, their intellectual and educational development, their participation and treatment in the paid workforce, and, perhaps most importantly for the purposes of the present discussion, their presentation of self and their interpersonal relationships. Feminists quickly learned that a holistic consideration of these factors yielded new and powerful insights—insights that would enable theorists to render intelligible the intricacy of patriarchal power's machinations. Anne Edwards states,

> A significant development in feminist work...is the attempt to formulate a perspective which can encompass several or all of the various forms of male violence, abuse and exploitation of women and to link them all to the underlying struggle by men to retain and reinforce their dominant position as a group over women in society. (1987, 23–24)

Although it was never explicitly formalized as such, this development in feminist thinking constituted one of the first moments in what would later become an explicitly feminist politics of corporeality.[4]

Since the 1970s and 1980s, many broad and far-reaching perspectives have been developed by feminists from a number of different disciplinary positions. While these perspectives may disagree regarding the definition of *violence* and how to eliminate it, they tend to cohere when it comes to seeing the sex/gender order as a social, economic, and cultural system that functions to regulate and normalize women and their bodies.

Liz Kelly (1987) elaborates a particularly persuasive framework for understanding the manifold violences women suffer at the hands of a masculinist society. According to Kelly, violence against women must be seen not as a series of discrete acts, but as unfolding along a sort of continuum. The *Oxford English Dictionary* defines *continuum* as both "a basic common character that underlies many different events" and "a continuous series of elements or events that pass into one another and cannot be readily distinguished" (cited in Kelly 1987, 48). Viewing violence against women as operating along a continuum is particularly fruitful for feminist analysis, as it allows for both an apprehension and understanding of how extreme forms of male violence (such as rape, murder, and aggravated assault) are in some fundamental way related to the more common, everyday experiences of, say, sexist jokes and insults, unwanted touching, and catcalling.

The concept of a continuum of violence against women may appear somewhat simple, but when one explores its implications, one finds that Kelly's model is actually quite radical. This model derives it radicalism from its two central implications. First, Kelly's model—when drawn to its logical conclusion—implies that most women experience sexual violence at some point in their lives. Hence, this model allows one to understand the everyday experiences of fear, intimidation, and humiliation as systemically related to the less common, yet more violent events, labeled as "crimes." Second, the notion of a continuum undermines any unquestionable distinction between "victims" and "other women." Kelly elaborates on this point:

> The fact that some women only experience violence at the more common, everyday end of the continuum is a difference in degree not in kind. The use of the term "victim" in order to separate one group of women from other women's lives and experiences must be questioned. (59)

In the new millenium, a large corpus of feminist research now attests that women's fear of violence limits women's freedom of movement. One can thus surmise that both the reality and the threat of violence against women function as forms of social control: the threat of violence against women restricts what women do, the life choices they make, and where they go and with whom.

Feminist Theories of Patriarchal Beauty Culture

> The body is not only a text of culture... it is also a direct locus of social control. Culture is made body. (Bordo 1993, 13)

If the late 1960s to the early 1980s constituted a pivotal period in the production of theory on violence against women, then the 1980s and 1990s constituted a near explosion of theoretical inquiries related to gender, beauty culture, and personal aesthetics. The politics of the body—that is, what culture does to the body and what the body does to culture—might be seen as the central issue of this more recent development in feminist theorizing.

In her important piece "Material Girl," Susan Bordo asserts, "popular culture does not apply any brakes to... fantasies of rearrangement and self-transformation" (1995, 67). If anything, it might be said that late twentieth-century popular culture is supersaturated with discourses of bodily mastery and self-determination, rhetorics of image choice and selection, and narratives of satisfied weight-loss clinic customers. This ensemble of discourses, however, is both pernicious and paradoxical. On the one hand, these discourses instruct all individuals whose body types do not conform to dominant bodily ideals to use each and every means at their disposal to bring their body in line with such ideals. On the other hand, these discourses are in fact deceitful. Popular media do not genuinely subscribe to an ethos of bodily choice. If bodily choice were truly a viable and valorized option in contemporary culture, a much wider range of body types would be deemed beautiful and desirable. On this point, Bordo adds,

> [The] rhetoric of choice and self-determination and the breezy analogies comparing cosmetic surgery to fashion accessorizing are deeply mystifying. They efface, not only the inequalities of privilege, money and time that prohibit most people from indulging in these practices, but the desperation that characterizes the lives of those who do. (67)[5]

Bordo's remark begs the question of who suffers most at the hands of these discourses of bodily self-mastery. As Naomi Wolf ([1990] 1997) explicates with precision and persuasion, these kinds of discourses, rhetorics, and narratives are targeted primarily at girls and women. Consequently, girls and women tend to be well acquainted with the pain, frustration, anger, and desperation associated with unsuccessful attempts at corporeal transformation. According to Bordo, "the dark underside of the practices of body transformation and rearrangement reveals botched and sometimes fatal operations, exercise addictions, eating disorders" (1995, 67) — all of which affect women far more than they do men. Women, as constrained but active subjects, are literally dying to be "beautiful." Courtney Love communicates the desperation involved in the quest for bodily perfection as well as the torment caused by such a quest.

Sandra Lee Bartky (1993), Susan Bordo (1993), Susan Brownmiller (1984), and Naomi Wolf ([1990] 1997) have worked extensively on the cultural and economic capital tied up in the "beauty" industry and have concluded that while this industry is in no way gender-neutral, it is an industry devoted to the thorough colonization of female bodies. While many may prefer to view the techniques of femininity (such as hair styling and hair depilation, cosmetic application, and careful wardrobe selection) as "free play" or innocuous forms of self-enhancement, then why do so many women feel anxiously compelled to be fully "made-up" before going to the corner store, the café, or the mailbox? While women's feelings of compulsion as regards personal aesthetics might be seen to undermine the "free play" hypothesis, such feelings of compulsion are more often than not attributed to an essential feminine hysteria and/or sexual nature.

If women are dissatisfied with the way they look, popular mores have it, it is because they are biologically predisposed to fussiness and dissatisfaction, not because they have been relentlessly instructed by the powers of mass media to look different (indeed, "better") than they do. In her songs, Love denaturalizes women's dissatisfaction regarding their presentations of self. With painful lucidity, Love depicts the strength and sway of patriarchal beauty ideologies as well as their intrinsically cultural nature. Love succeeds in bringing into relief the veritable cultural grip she feels on her body, simultaneously showing that she is an agent of these forces. While she reveals that she reproduces patriarchal aesthetics, she does so by means of anger and frustrated rage: she realizes that what is required to sustain a "proper" modality of femininity is injurious to the point that it makes her sick and desperate.

The following statement in many ways summarizes my position on mass beauty culture and its impact on women's corporeal practices:

> Through the pursuit of an ever-changing, homogenizing, elusive ideal of femininity—a pursuit without a terminus, a resting point, requiring that women constantly attend to minute and often whimsical changes in fashion—female bodies become what Foucault calls "docile bodies"—bodies whose forces and energies are habituated to external regulation, subjection, transformation, "improvement."... Through these disciplines, we continue to memorize on our bodies the feel and conviction of lack, insufficiency, of never being good enough. *At the farthest extremes, the practices of femininity may lead us to utter demoralization, debilitation and death.* (Bordo 1993, 14; emphasis added)

Bordo's statement underscores why Love's album is so incisively feminist. In my view, Love's lyrical strategies are especially powerful because they bring the listener to the furthest extremes of feminine practices. The listener is quite literally forced to experience the extremes of her culture's violences and psychoses by hearing Love recount her protagonist's experiences of physical, sexual, and psychological abuse. Through both embodied and discursive demonstration, Love indicts the ideals and practices of dominant femininity by enacting them to the point where their destructive potential is revealed for all to see.

Selected Readings of Hole's Live through This

"Violet." A cursory reading of the lyrics to the song "Violet" reveals that it describes sexual violence.[6] Indeed, the word "Violet" gains importance when one considers that its sound and structure are unmistakably similar to the word that best describes the song's subject matter: violence. Moreover, when one considers that the song is about sexual violence—and the title of it is represented by the name of a flower, the violet—then it seems reasonable to associate this song title with the event of an aggressive and nonconsensual "deflowering."

The first verse begins with the following lines: "And the sky was made of amethyst / And all the stars look just like little fish / You should learn when to go / You should learn how to say no." In the first two lines of this verse, Love sets the landscape in which its narrative will unfold: a place where "the sky was made of amethyst." Amethyst is a stone with a violet or purple color. The amethyst sky must be a particularly dark shade of violet, because in the second line this amethyst sky is described as strewn with stars. Because stars appear only in evening darkness, we can assume that Love's protagonist is describing a dark, probably late-night sky. Thus, we can also deduce that in the context of this song, amethyst—or violet—comes to represent darkness.

The simile "all the stars look just like little fish" further complicates the narrative landscape of "Violet." Certainly it is worth asking why Love chose to compare the stars to "little fish." To arrive at an answer, we need to place this image in its context. Initially, I know that this song is set in darkness. For now, all I can say about this darkness is that it pertains to a night sky barren of light (although it is probably not unreasonable to presume that this darkness also refers to something more sinister). I also know that this song is about sexual violence against women. Lines three and four of the first verse feature narrative fragments undisputedly reminiscent of warning language used in date-rape awareness campaigns ("you should know when to go, you should know how to say no"). Thus, I can be fairly certain that up to now this song pertains to darkness and sexual violence against women. What could a landscape saturated with "little fish" represent in a seemingly sexual context? I am of the opinion that the little fish represent sperm; and if the little fish (always already cast in darkness) represent sperm, and the sperm represent men, then Love's story unfolds within a context of masculine sexual dominance.

Equally interesting is what appears to be a shift in narrative voice. In the first two lines, the narrator is merely describing a context of masculine sexual power. The second pair of lines, however, appear to indict women who prove unable to distinguish between trustworthy and dangerous men (and this indictment is intensified through the vocal and instrumental strategies exploited simultaneously). When articulating this indictment, I suspect that the narrator is assuming the persona of the male oppressor in order to underscore the irrationality of blaming victims of rape for the violence done to them in a context so overwhelmingly overdetermined by masculinist modes of sexuality. In lines three and four of this verse, the protagonist could also be expressing the guilt she feels for not having halted an undesirable act. Either way, these two phrases underscore—with impressive complexity—the many states of affect and consciousness that surround a rape: guilt, inadequacy, pain.

In the second half of verse 1 ("Might last a day / Mine is forever"), the narrator appears to be illustrating the fact that the emotive repercussions of rape vary significantly for men and women. For male perpetrators of sexual violence, affective states of guilt and remorse may only "last a day." Yet for female victims and survivors of sexual violence, feelings of guilt, pain, shame, and disgust may very well last "forever." Moreover, this verse is brilliantly litotic; the narrator understates the affective dynamics in question (for example, "Might last a day / Mine is forever") and as a result emphasizes their importance and effects.

The pre-chorus repeats the phrase "when they get what they want, they never want it again." If one accepts that the overall subject of the song "Violet" is sexual violence against women, then the pre-chorus seems to be fairly straightforward. What the narrator appears to be describing is the way in which women often feel, and indeed are, viewed and used by men for sexual gratification only. That is, once men "get what they want" from women, they have no desire to pursue any extrasexual interaction with them. This section of the song could also be alluding to the notion that, for men, women become sexually uninteresting after the initial sexual act.

In the chorus, the narrator's haunting and repetitive, albeit incisively sarcastic request "go on take everything, take everything, I want you to" can be interpreted as an articulation of the rapacious quality of sexual violence, illustrating that when a woman is raped she is robbed of "everything." Through her use of sarcasm and irony, Love brings into relief the nonsensical nature of the belief that female victims of sexual violence "want it," by showing that a woman who wants to be raped is about as likely as a woman who wants to be stripped of her selfhood. This verse could also be read as a communication, on the protagonist's part, of being so overpowered and worn down by the male in question that she feels that it would be a lot easier to consent to sex she does not want than to attempt to fight him off. To fight him off would be to risk graver and more violent consequences for the victim and/or public humiliation at the hands of the unsatisfied male. Indeed, one might link the themes of psychic torment and death evinced in this piece with those evinced in the song "Asking for It."

The second verse begins with the lines "And the sky was all violet / I want it again, but violet, more violet / And I'm the one with no soul / One above and one below." While in the first verse the narrator states that "the sky was made of amethyst," in this second verse the narrator states that "the sky was all violet." The shift from the word *amethyst* to *violet* is not unimportant. In the first verse, the narrator's violence-imbued sexual landscape was described in metaphorical terms. That is, it was only through deductive interpretative strategies that one could grasp the violent nature of the sexual context. In this verse, the narrator is more explicit. The sexual landscape is no longer simply linked to violence through the metaphor of amethyst. The landscape is, in this instance, "all violet" and by extension "all violence." This assertion is for the most part confirmed by Love's pronunciation of the word "violet" (the lyric notated in her published songsheet) with an ultimate sibilant to suggest the word "violence," thus creating an overt equivalency between the concepts *violet* and *violence*.

The following line, "and I'm the one with no soul," once again sees the narrator exploiting sarcastic and ironic devices in order to show how absurd it is to accuse the victim of impurity and sin when it is the male perpetrator who has committed the violent acts. "One above and one below" can be taken as a simple illustration of dominance in sexually violent situations. However, when one reads "and I'm the one with no soul" in combination with "one above and one below" one realizes that

the author could be making biblical references. That is, the protagonist—despite the fact that she is the victim—is made to feel that she is
the devil, the temptress, the fallen woman. In essence, then, she is made
to feel like an incarnation of evil. Yet the man is let off the hook, as it
were. In this sense, Love is satirizing the fact that he is the one who is
seen to be "above" (holy, pure) and she the one "below" (evil, sullied).

The final statement of the pre-chorus ("I told you from the start just
how this would end / When I get what I want, well I never want it again")
could represent one of two things when read from a feminist perspective. On the one hand, it can be read as an emancipatory and redemptive,
albeit not unproblematic moment for the narrator. In this lyrical instance
she becomes stronger than the violence done to her and thus enabled to
inflict it on others. On the other hand, however, it can be read as the final
articulation of the abuser who vows that he will commit his acts of violence again.

"Asking for It."

> Women's experiences of heterosexual sex are not either consenting or rape,
> but exist on a continuum moving from choice to pressure to coercion to force.
> (Kelly 1987, 58)

Immediately foregrounded in the two first lines of "Asking for It"
("Every time that I sell myself to you / I feel a little bit cheaper than I
need to") are imbalances of sexual power and will. The protagonist
couches the communication of her sexual experience with the (male)
Other in terms reminiscent of prostitution. Interestingly, however, she
appears resistant to feeling guilty about the way in which she "sells herself" to the man. This resistance complicates and indeed renders
ambiguous the relationship the protagonist shares with the male Other.
In effect, it leads the reader/listener to question the extent to which the
protagonist is in fact autonomous and agential within the context of this
relationship.

The second pair of lines in the first verse ("I will tear the petals off
of you / Rose red I will make you tell the truth") are more metaphorical.
Indeed, the act of tearing the petals off another bears a striking resem-
blance to the notion of deflowering a young (presumably female) virgin.
Through a severe reversal of this notion, this passage could be construed

as a vow by the protagonist to effect some sort of vengeful violence on the male Other (who, it would seem, has wronged the protagonist) by means of an aggressive sexual act. This vengeful act (and the dominant sexual position it implies) would enable the protagonist to learn from the violent male Other the true nature of their sexual relations.

The ominous chorus consists of the following questions: "Was she asking for it? / Was she asking nice? / If she was asking for it / Did she ask you twice?" This interrogative sequence can be understood as the series of questions the protagonist intends to pose the male Other when he is completely subjugated to her. The protagonist would "make [him] tell the truth" about whether she did in fact ask for and/or desire the sexual relations she ultimately "participated" in. This interrogative sequence is particularly powerful in that it exploits a well-known expression employed by men who force women to engage in nonconsensual sexual relations. This sequence is also rendered particularly incisive through its sarcastic and ironic tone: it quite literally mocks sexually violent men and their pathetic rationales for having sexually violated women. Interestingly, this use of irony is similar to that utilized in the song "Violet," wherein the protagonist screams "go on take everything" in a similar vein.

The passage that opens the second verse ("Every time that I stare into the sun / Angel dust and my dress just comes undone") can be read as a deeply metaphorical representation of the rape-in-process. The notion of "staring into the sun" presupposes that the protagonist is looking up, toward the sky. This knowledge of the protagonist's position, in combination with the information provided in the subsequent phrase, "and my dress just comes undone"—which suggests that the protagonist is not involved in undoing her clothing—can be read as describing the protagonist's powerlessness during the sexual act.

The words "angel dust" in this context gain particular pertinence because they are placed directly before "and my dress just comes undone." Generally, the words "angel dust" in this context condense and metaphorize a kind of psychic departure from the body. Whether this departure is to be read literally or metaphorically, however, is another question. The words "angel dust" could suggest that the protagonist was high when the sexual assault took place and that she does not recall how it began. They could also suggest that rape or nonconsensual sexual relations are so traumatic that they produce effects comparable to hallu-cinogenic substances. That is, in order to cope with the violence transpir-ing, the victim psychically divorces herself from the realities of her corporeal situation. Finally, these words could suggest that the noncon-sensual sexual relations were habitual, and that the protagonist con-sumed angel dust prior to them in order to make them more bearable. It is worth noting, as well, that with the persistence of religious imagery in Love's lyrics, it is probably not incidental that the particular drug dis-cussed in this passage is "angel" dust. Lines three and four of verse 2 ("Every time that I stare into the sun /Be a model or just look like one") are interesting because they make a direct link between patriarchal beauty norms and violence against women.

The bridge of the song is particularly elusive ("If you live through this with me / I swear that I will die for you"). It is important, however, for a number of reasons. First, it hosts the album title, *Live through This*, and thus must hold some sort of special significance. Second, the musical structure that animates this text changes dramatically here. Musically, this moment in the song is presented almost as an epiphany. Perhaps the protagonist is speaking to her abuser. In this dialogue, the protagonist could be positing that only one of them will emerge from the abuse "alive." That is, if the abuser lives, and continues the abuse, she will die (either physically and/or psychically). But the bridge could also be con-strued as an abstract call to female solidarity: urging other women to join her in the struggle against male oppression. Either way, the protagonist is positioned as "dying"; the question is whether she is dying as a martyr or as a nameless casualty of violence against women.

"Jennifer's Body."

> Breasts, thighs, buttocks, bellies; the most sexually central parts of women, whose "ugliness" therefore becomes an obsession. Those are the parts most often battered by abusive men. The parts that sex murderers most often mutilate. The parts most often defiled by violent pornography. (Wolf [1990] 1997, 150)

> The body... is a powerful symbolic form, a surface on which the central rules, hierarchies, and even metaphysical commitments of a culture are inscribed and thus reinforced through the concrete language of the body. (Bordo 1993, 13)

The first verse of this song opens with "I know it, I can feel it / Well I know it enough to believe it / And I know it, I can't see it / But I know it enough to believe it." Within the context of this song—a song featuring gendered forms of violence—one could surmise that the protagonist is expressing the fact that while she does not "feel" or "see" the threat of violence against her, she still "knows" that it is omnipresent. This threat of violence may circulate formlessly and amorphously, but it is nonetheless firmly rooted within her.

The pre-chorus, "To better you and better me, my bitter half has bitten me / To better you and better me, I'm sleeping with my enemy, myself, myself," is particularly charged. The line "my bitter half has bitten me" appears to allude to the protagonist's spouse (whom one might normally or commonly refer to as one's "better half") and an act of violence that he has committed (coded as "biting"). The phrase "sleeping with my enemy myself," however, is not quite as straightforward. On the one hand, this phrase could be expressing the protagonist's feeling that she is collaborating with, or at the very least existing nonconfrontationally alongside, her oppressor, her "bitter half," her "enemy." If the phrase were understood in this sense, it would read "sleeping with my enemy, myself." On the other hand, this phrase could also mean that the protagonist feels as though she is her own enemy, and that the patriarchal norms she has internalized have spawned an agent of male dominance within the sphere of her own consciousness. If the phrase is understood in this sense, it would read "sleeping with my enemy: myself."

The chorus consists of the following ominous phrases: "He found pieces of Jennifer's body / Just relax, just relax, just go to sleep." The sordidly repetitious "he found pieces of Jennifer's body" reverberates with meaning. First, it introduces a new figure in the song: Jennifer. Jennifer is, in my view, not necessarily the protagonist in particular, but every woman in general. Because "Jennifer" is such a common female name in the United States, it can be used to signify the universal or generic woman's experience.

The fact that Jennifer's body is in "pieces" poses yet another set of complex interpretative questions. For instance, should the interpreter treat this description of Jennifer's body in literal or metaphorical terms? I would argue that in a song with a chorus that consists of phrases such as "he found pieces of Jennifer's body," it would be difficult for a listener not to conjure some sort of image of a mutilated female body.[7] Hence, in view of the violence that saturates the song's tone and texture, it would be plausible to consider the depicted state of her body in literal terms. Jennifer's body, then, could quite literally be understood as having been mutilated and dismembered—perhaps by the protagonist's "bitter half."

Considering this phrase in metaphorical terms, however, one comes up with an equally if not more compelling reading. Jennifer's body in pieces evokes notions of corporeal fragmentation. Feminist theorists have remarked that often the female body is admired not in its totality, but piecemeal in objectified parts. That is, a woman is valued not for her embodied subjectivity, but for her breasts, her legs, her lips, and so on. I believe that the male Other—who is only interested in her for one or several of her bodily components—has dismembered Jennifer metaphorically. This notion of the fragmentation of women's bodies is also wholly congruent with the one evinced in "Doll Parts."

The chorus ends with the eerie chant "just relax, just go to sleep." Here the narrative voice shifts, with the protagonist assuming the role of the male Other. In this role, the protagonist imitates attempts by sexually exploitative men to lull a woman to sleep in the hopes of sexually dominating her.

In the second verse ("You're hungry but I'm starving / He cuts you down from the tree / He keeps you in a box by the bed / Alive, but just barely"), the trope of starvation is introduced in a manner similar to its introduction in the songs "Plump" and "Miss World." The protagonist—who has gone back to her original female role—is presented as starving, while the male Other is presented as merely hungry. Moreover, while it seems clear (especially in view of the remainder of the verse) that the protagonist is starving for food, it is not at all clear whether the male Other is hungry for food or for something else, such as sex.

The line "he cuts you down from the tree" is more ambiguous. In a lyrical context overwhelmed by images of hunger, and on an album characterized by frequent allusions to biblical tropes, however, it seems reasonable to assume that the "you" in this line refers to a fruit of some sort. In that this passage is also imbued with sexual connotations, the fruit in question is most likely an apple (a forbidden fruit representing sin). Thus the apple is a metaphor for the female protagonist as seen by the male Other. That is, the protagonist—like the forbidden fruit—represents to the male Other decadent and indeed prohibited sexual pleasure. Moreover, by using the apple as a stand-in for the protagonist, the reader/listener is able to appreciate the object-status to which the male Other has reduced the protagonist.

"He keeps you in a box by the bed / Alive but just barely" evokes images of a woman held captive in a boxlike prison. The fact that this box is kept by the bed is significant, in that "the bed" alludes to a site of sexual activity. Thus the woman is held prisoner by the bed for purposes of sexual exploitation, and, like a prisoner, she is given only enough sustenance to maintain her physical existence. Furthermore, the fruit metaphor is, in this instance, particularly brilliant: one can visualize a box of decaying fruit by the bed.

The final verse is as baffling as it is compelling. In it, Love writes, "He said, 'I'm your lover, I'm your friend / I'm purity, hit me again' / With a bullet, number one / Kill the family, save the son; himself, himself." The first two lines see the abusive male captor claiming that he is good to the protagonist while simultaneously hitting and perhaps even shooting her. The rest of the verse is difficult to understand in that the reader is unable to identify the son's relationship to the drama unfolding in the rest of the song. The verse does suggest, however, that the sexual abuse taking place has the effect of either literally or metaphorically destroying an entire family. Again, the relationship of the family to the protagonist is unclear.

"Miss World."

> Men look at women. Women watch themselves being looked at. (Berger 1988, 9)

> So even those women who take men's beauty pornography to heart and try, and even succeed, in looking like it, are doomed to disappointment. Men who read it don't do so because they want women who look like that. The attraction of what they are holding is that it is *not* a woman, but a two-dimensional woman-shaped blank. The appeal of the material is not the fantasy that the model will come to life; it is precisely that she will not, ever. Her coming to life would ruin the vision. It is not about life. (Wolf [1990] 1997, 176)

This song begins with "I am the girl you know can't look you in the eye," which might be seen as an immediate thematic foregrounding that will come to characterize the entire song. This thematic structure involves, first and foremost, the paradoxical identification of the female protagonist as coveted and valorized by those around her ("I am the girl you know") while simultaneously submitted to them ("can't look you in the eye"). Moreover, the title of the song ("Miss World") enables the reader to presume that this paradoxical identification is mediated by the social status invested in the protagonist's physical appearance.

In the next phrase, "I am the girl you know, so sick I cannot try," the leitmotif of sickness—and an acutely gendered sickness at that—is manifest. Indeed, the theme of sickness is stated repeatedly not only in this song, but in many of the other ones, such as "Plump." Again, the protagonist is represented as well known and presumably esteemed by those around her ("I am the girl you know"), but this esteem is abruptly undermined by her concomitant representation as sick, weak, and powerless ("so sick I cannot try").

The next phrase ("I am the one you want, can't look you in the eye") reinforces these themes, with one notable difference. Changing the word "know" to "want" introduces the idea that, despite her illness and powerlessness, the female protagonist is the one that the (presumably male) Other wants. Thus, it is made clear that the protagonist's prestige and widespread recognition are bound up in radically unequal relations of (hetero)sexual desire.

The phrase "I am the girl you know, I lie and lie and lie" suggests that the protagonist's prestige is maintained at the expense of honesty with herself and others. This dishonesty is probably quite complex and related to the multitudinous stories women tell themselves (and are told) in order to sustain the stereotypical (and largely unattainable) norms of dominant femininity.

The pre-chorus ("I'm Miss World, somebody kill me / Kill me pills. No one cares my friend, my friend") shows that—in enacting the Miss World persona—the protagonist literally involves "death-tempting" acts and habits. The phrase "somebody kill me" suggests that she views her performance as akin to asking to be killed. It is interesting to note, however, that the protagonist does not express this desire in suicidal terms; she conflates the enactment of Miss World with murder, not suicide. This conflation is significant because it sees the protagonist making others responsible for her suffering rather than just herself. The trope of sickness is reintroduced, this time through the allusion to "kill me pills." This can reasonably be seen as an allusion to either diet pills or even tranquilizers/antidepressants, which arguably abrogate an individual's personality and which are disproportionately prescribed to women.

The phrase "no one cares my friend, my friend" introduces another interesting theme into the piece. Not only is the protagonist describing the scandalous insensitivity toward and marginalization of those women who suffer through the traumas posed by conforming to dominant modalities of ideal femininity, but she underscores that not even her friends appear to be concerned. Because of the way in which the song is framed, the reader already expects that male Others will be indifferent to the protagonist's suffering. The reader, however, does not expect the protagonist's female friends to be presented as similarly indifferent. This introduces the problems of internecine violence, competition, and acrimony among women, and the way in which these problems remain both a symptom and product of patriarchal regimes of gender. (I am alluding to the notion elaborated by movement feminists that male supremacist societies are maintained and strengthened through the "dividing and conquering" of female communities, and through the pitting of woman against woman in the pursuit of seamless personal aesthetics and, by extension, the affection of ideal male partners. The maintenance of a divided community of women and consequently the preclusion of gyno-centered forms of solidarity ensures the stability of patriarchal norms.[8]

In the following verse ("I'm Miss World, watch me break and watch me burn / No one is listening my friends"), the protagonist reiterates the relationship between her enactment of Miss World on the one hand, and psychic and physical states of injury ("break," "burn") and isolation ("no one is listening") on the other. The choice of the word "burn" when describing the protagonist's gendered torment is an interesting one. Might this be an allusion to the burning of women during the witch trials? It is worth considering, in that Love explicitly makes reference to the witch trials in the following song, "Plump." The witch-trial metaphor is a powerful and indeed suitable one in that it evokes many of the same themes already discussed in this text, such as internecine violence and surveillance among women as well as norms and sanctions related to the pursuit of ideal femininity. it could be argued that the protagonist views the cult of Miss World and beauty pageants in general as akin to a modern-day witch trial. Consider the fact that the structure of a beauty pageant is quite similar to a trial: women are trotted out onto a stage and cross-examined about their female talents and abilities. This process allegedly provides the (male) prosecutors with special insight into just how womanly these women truly are. Beauty culture and pageantry uphold the notion that men have the right to judge, rate, and consume beautiful female bodies, and this is powerfully conveyed by Love's lyrical work.

In the chorus ("I made my bed I'll lie in it / I made my bed I'll die in it"), Love takes a hackneyed cliché related to the ethics of responsibility and transforms it into a rather macabre description of the consequences of pursuing dominant modalities of femininity. These consequences are quite obviously related to death ("I made my bed I'll die in it") and its trappings (her bed is figured as coffinlike).

In the third verse ("Kill girls watch, I eat ether / Suck me under, maybe forever, my friend"), the female torment produced through beauty pageants is figured as a spectacle ("kill girls watch"). Further, the line "I eat ether" is connotatively charged. Ether is a pleasant-smelling liquid often used as an anesthetic; one could argue that the protagonist is comparing participation in the cult of Miss World to being rendered unconscious. It is also worth noting that the protagonist's troubled relationship to food is being reintroduced here. That is, she does not eat healthy, life-sustaining matter but poisonous and noxious matter that will—at least in her view—improve her chances for success in the Miss World pageant. The fact that ether is pleasant-smelling but ultimately harmful is, it could be argued, comparable to the enactment of Miss World and the body tyranny it promotes—apparently pleasant but ultimately harmful. Indeed, Love's comparison between becoming Miss World and becoming etherized is strikingly reminiscent of this comment by Naomi Wolf: "A healthy body's reflexes lead it to avoid pain. But beauty thinking is an anesthetic, with the ability to make women more like objects by cauterizing sensation" ([1990] 1997, 249).

The phrase "suck me under, maybe forever" connotes the irresistibility of conforming to ideal modes of femininity as well as the difficulties of recovering from this injurious conformity. Recalling the earlier image of eating ether, the words "suck me under" are fairly similar to "being put under," which is the ultimate effect of ether. Moreover, the notion that Miss World sucks the protagonist under "maybe forever" can also be mapped onto the potentially fatal effects of ether. That is, it is entirely possible that one, in consuming ether, will be "put under" forever.

"Plump."

> Fat is portrayed in the literature of the [beauty] myth as expendable female filth; virtually cancerous matter, an inert or treacherous infiltration into the body of nauseating bulk waste. The demonic characterizations of a simple body substance do not arise from its physical properties but from old-fashioned misogyny, for above all fat is female; it is the medium and regulator of female sexual characteristics. (Wolf [1990] 1997, 191–92)

> The continuum between female disorder and "normal" feminine practice is sharply revealed through a close reading of those disorders to which women have been particularly vulnerable. These, of course, have varied historically: neurasthenia and hysteria in the second half of the nineteenth century; agoraphobia and, most dramatically, anorexia nervosa and bulimia in the second half of the twentieth century. (Bordo 1993, 16)

The title of this song, "Plump" (presumably referring to the protagonist's actual or feared body type), immediately evokes the sorts of problems reflected upon in the songs "Miss World" and "Jennifer's Body." However, in the first verse ("He shakes his death rattle, spittle on his bib / And I don't do dishes, I throw them in the crib"), Love tackles yet another set of gynocentered thematics. Not only is it an apparent rejection of dominant ideologies relating to motherhood, it is also strongly associated with food imagery. "Spittle on his bib" depicts the physical rejection of food, and "I don't do the dishes" also depicts the refusal to clean up after eating.

The chorus ("I'm eating you / I'm overfed / Your milk's in my mouth / It makes me sick") connotes a particularly troubled and complicated relationship to alimentation. First, it communicates the protagonist's disgust with the eating process and particularly with the feeling of being overfed. The disgust with the sensation of being "full" could be conceptualized in this context as acutely gendered. It recalls the guilt women feel when they have eaten "too much," as well as the taboo ascribed to those women with big appetites. This disgust produced by the protagonist's overeating foreshadows the events of the next verse.

This chorus also seems to allude to what the protagonist considers a grotesque sexual act (fellatio) and its consequences. It could be argued that for the protagonist, consuming men is commensurate with consuming the ideological constraints they place on women. That is, the patriarchal norms associated with women, corporeality, and alimentation quite literally make the protagonist sick. In addition, this passage sets up a complex yet correlative relationship between the politics of sex and food.

The second verse ("I have stumbled here, failed to make it mine / They say I'm plump, but I throw up all the time") is, again, connotatively charged. Here the protagonist's tormented relationships to both food and her body are rendered explicit. The protagonist feels sick because she feels as though she has eaten too much. The phrase "they say I'm plump, but I throw up all the time" communicates yet another, albeit more violent, physical rejection of food. It also signals the protagonist's frustration with her body's refusal to comply with her desire to be thin.

In the lines of the bridge ("Do you fake it for me like I?"), the dynamic between sex, the body, and gender is conveyed once again. This passage could be read as both a reference to the protagonist's unfulfilled sexual needs (that is, faking an orgasm) and a reflection on whether her male sexual partner "fakes" his enjoyment of sex in the same way she does. However, the bridge could also be read more metaphorically. The protagonist could be indirectly stating that she fakes her entire presentation of self, and that her embodied subjectivity is the site of far more insecurity than she openly avows. In my view, Love dramatically underscores the disparate nature of women's relationships to their sexed bodies in relation to men's by posing this question, which would be (truthfully) answered by an unequivocal "no" by most men.

The final lines of verse 3 ("Like a liar at a witch trial, you look good for your age") are crucial to both the song's and the album's thematics. I suspect that at this lyrical moment, the protagonist has assumed the voice of the male oppressor. Viewed this way, these lines become a dialogue between the protagonist and herself. The protagonist says that she is a "liar at a witch trial" who "looks good for [her] age." In other words, the protagonist is "faking" her presentation of self and her self-concept—she's a liar—within the context of severe patriarchal corporeal regulation: a witchtrial. With the line "you look good for your age," the

121

protagonist is admitting that she looks better than she normally would at her age if she weren't faking her appearance.

⌒⌒⌒⌒⌒

MUSICAL FORCE: VIOLENCE AND RESISTANCE IN "VIOLET" (LORI BURNS)

Mélisse has explored several interrelated themes that recur throughout the album, including sex, gender, violence, and body politics. I have chosen to conduct a close reading of the first song on the album, "Violet," a song that explores the subject of violence against women. My analysis will illustrate how Courtney Love musically represents the sociolyrical themes of violence and oppression, demonstrating how she not only invokes violence, but also creates a narrative of resistance to that force. This song is about pushing: being pushed and pushing back. As a result, the shifting and unstable relations of domination and subordination are the subject of the music. The music-analytical challenge exists in finding the means to illuminate not only the force, but also her resistance.

Hole's alternative (grunge) musical style provides an effective musical means to amplify Love's lyrics. Just as the lyrics are sometimes offered as an assault, the music is aggressive, and explores the extreme limits of expression through the use of power chords, guitar distortion and feedback, and hard-edged vocal strategies. This is a musical style usually associated with male performers and the connotations of anger and alienation; to hear a female voice working within this style elevates the expressive stakes. Indeed, there is a great deal at stake here.

Anger is an important element in this music, but equally important is the role of irony in the communication of the stories that Love chooses to tell. In order to relate and to disrupt these stories, she assumes many voices, roles, and stances throughout the album—participant, victim, perpetrator, judge—with the result that the listener is often left to question meaning and lyrical intentions. The importance of the music itself for the communication of her messages cannot be overstated.

General Stylistic Features of "Violet"

Structure. The song presents two statements of a verse–pre-chorus–chorus sequence, followed by an altered version of the pre-chorus–chorus, then by a concluding sequence of bridge–chorus–coda. The verse section is long, subdividing into two sections, almost in the manner of a verse–chorus unit. Love's songs are based on simple and repetitive harmonic patterns, four-measure harmonic units that repeat to form larger phrases or sections. The harmony is treated to repetition as opposed to development. However, the potential exists for the repeated material to take on new meaning through a change in textual context or association, or through the use of different sound strategies. The harmony is clearly articulated by the guitars, with a functional bass line and chord harmonization. The harmonic changes occur very strongly on downbeats, and there is a hypermetric regularity to the pattern repetition, as well as a clear distinction between verse, pre-chorus, and chorus sections through changes of harmonic pattern. Against this harmonic framework the vocalist sings her part, sometimes as "singable" four-measure melodic lines, sometimes as simple half-measure fragments. Repetition and emphasis are the primary melodic procedures, but there are strategically placed developments or transformations of a previous idea. In other words, the vocal melody is very restricted, but this has the effect of drawing attention to the moments when it does "move." The melodies tend to be static, with no obvious directional resolution, yet there still exists contrapuntal tension within a clearly established modal context. The voice's contrapuntal relationship to the bass and harmony and its role in phrase creation are two important ways that the musical structure supports the lyrical message.

Sound Strategies. Love uses guitar distortion and grating vocal techniques at strategic moments in the song. There is a range of guitar effects, from clear acoustic guitars to fully distorted power chords and feedback. It is hard to imagine a stronger musical expression than the distortion and volume that is attained in certain sections. To match this range of guitar expression, Love uses different vocal strategies, from a quiet, gentle vocal sound in the low register to a high-volume, harsh vocal sound in the upper register. Through the use of contrasting performance techniques, Love creates a musical narrative that is intricately tied to the narrative of the lyrics.

"Violet": Verse

Each section of the verse comprises four lines of text (see appendix 1). In the first section, the first couplet establishes a physical setting, in the past tense: something has happened under the amethyst sky and stars. As Mélisse has demonstrated, the overarching thematic context of the song (and album) suggests that this physical setting is the scene of a rape. The second couplet is a directive in the imperative: "You should learn when to go / You should learn how to say no." These lines use popular expressions that refer to negative attitudes toward sexual promiscuity and the subject's self-chastisement for being sexually active. In the second section of the verse, the mood is more speculative: "Might last a day / Mine is forever." Given the context of the rape, the paradox of a day versus forever signifies the potential that this single act will have continuing consequences for the victim.

A transcription of the first four measures is given in figure 4.1. In the music of the verse, the first section features a repeated four-measure harmonic pattern (heard four times), with the voice entering in measures 3–4 of each statement. The guitars introduce the harmonic pattern in a clear, undistorted sound, and the voice enters toward the end of the pattern in a low register and with a hushed quality. The "hall effect" reverberation and the vocal placement in the center of the mix establish a storytelling context. There is also a mysterious effect here: because we have to wait for the voice to enter with each line, there is great anticipation of what she will say.

A voice-leading reduction of the entire verse is given in figure 4.2, in which each four-measure unit is indicated with a single bar line. The melodic content contributes to the effect of story communication: the fragments are internally repetitive, and as one melodic statement moves to the next, there is a gradual climb in register, until the fourth statement, at which point the register dramatically shifts to the upper octave. This registral shift is accentuated by a change from a hushed sound to a rough, loud, distorted vocal quality.

Throughout the verse, the bass and voice share a dramatic harmonic/contrapuntal relationship: the bass *controls* the harmonic pattern while the voice works within the confines of that pattern. The harmonic gesture used throughout the opening section is E–C_7–G; this could be interpreted as VI (#3)–IV_7–I in G Ionian. The basic harmonic movement is from E to G, with G receiving the emphasis of duration (two measures) as well as being the goal of the progression. Once the harmony has arrived on G, the voice *can* enter, but the G is sustained as a pedal beneath her statement. The voice climbs from the low G, through B (and

FIGURE 4.1 "Violet," Transcription, mm. 1–4

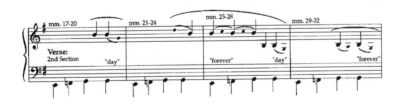

FIGURE 4.2 "Violet," Voice-Leading Graph (Verse)

B♭), to D, outlining a G triad in keeping with the bass support. The voice is restricted in terms of harmonic orientation, and hypermetric placement within the phrase. Within these confines, the voice's ability to work expressively is severely limited, yet the restrictions are disrupted at some strategic places in the song. The first such disruption is the melodic bend to B♭ in the second and third vocal statements (at "little fish" and "when to go"). The B♭ is a blue note, invoking a mode quality change from G major to minor. Within the context of the major-quality triads (E–C–G), the minor third above G is a modal contrapuntal strategy that the voice can use to disrupt the controlling harmony. Not only is the quality of G affected, but also as the B♭ lingers in the ear, the harmonic return to E major creates a dissonant clash. The second disruption occurs in the fourth vocal statement, when the voice sings "you should learn how to say no" in the upper register, with a harsh quality. The intensity with which the voice proclaims this line is matched by the accompanying guitars as they begin to use distortion, power chords, and greater volume. As the voice shrieks this line, we hear an ascending glissando in one of the guitars, the beginning of the distortion, and a drum roll anticipating the downbeat of the second section of the verse. The two primary forces here—harsh voice and distorted guitars—create a competitive sound, a musical representation of the violence and anger that is invoked by the lyrics.

In the second section of the verse, the harmonic pattern changes to E–F–G (VI#–VII–I in G Mixolydian), with the same design of four measures per statement, the voice entering in the third measure. The harmony is still directed toward G, the vocal statements heard above that harmony. In this section, the guitar distortion and harsh vocal production that were established at the end of the first section are sustained. The voice remains in the upper register until the end of the section, at which point it returns to its initial low registral position.

It is during this second section of the verse that a third and potentially more striking instance of vocal disruption occurs. This time, as the voice enters with "mine is forever," it extends the normal vocal statement to continue through to the next harmonic phrase. Love sustains her musical expression here, and in an admittedly simple melodic gesture with a powerful musical effect: she begins on the high D^5 and skips down to B^4; instead of stopping there, while the new harmonic statement begins on E, she embellishes her B^4 with its upper neighbor, C^5. She holds on to this pattern until the moment when her next statement entry would occur, thus joining two statements together. The "hall reverb" that has been used since the beginning of the song is now put to greatest effect for the voice: in the neighbor pattern B–C–B–C, she sustains the high Bs for the longest note values heard thus far in the voice (three beats), allowing her voice to truly ring. Following this outburst of expression, she collapses back to the low-register B^3 for the second statement of the line "might last a day." The final vocal entry for the verse occurs in its normative patterning of controlled, restricted entry in the third measure of the harmonic statement.

The voice-leading graph illustrates the voice's role in the contrapuntal structure: we can trace the narrative of her restricted movement and the moments when she breaks free of registral and temporal confines. The registral shifts and the expanded vocal phrase are especially visible in that graph. Another feature that emerges is the vocal emphasis on the pitch B, both in the lower and higher registers, and in both forms, B and B♭. The vocal emphasis on B is particularly strong in the second section of the verse, where she invokes her own pain: "Mine is forever." (I will have more to say about the note B when I analyze the chorus.)

"Violet": Pre-chorus

The pre-chorus is relatively brief (eight measures), especially following the lengthy verse (thirty-two measures). The lyrics comprise one direct thought, a popular cliché concerning men's desire for sexual gratification and disdain for commitment: "When they get what they want, they never want it again." This is sung with a kind of falsely sweet vocal style, with a sparse instrumental texture, allowing back-up vocals to be heard on warm thirds at the line "never want it again." The rhythmic content of the vocal line is more lively, more dancelike; this is a melody with which listeners would want to sing along. There is a message of conformity here, a message that male sexual gratification is privileged and women have nothing to do but go along with it, to sing about it in unison. But there is also a quality of ironic derision here: the text is a bitter statement of sexual inequity that is heard in ironic opposition to the liveliness of this musical phrase and Love's apparent conformity. This is an excellent example of an *oppositional reading* (defined in chapter 2).

The concept of "ironic conformity" is apparent also in the harmonic and contrapuntal organization of the pre-chorus (see figure 4.3 for a

FIGURE 4.3 "Violet," Voice-Leading Graph (Pre-chorus)

voice-leading graph). The harmony begins as the verse did, with a movement from E to C, but continues differently, moving on to D and then A major. The A-major harmonic goal is a full step higher than the G-major goal of the verse, creating a very "bright" harmonic effect. The vocal melody begins on E, and then moves to C, in octaves with the bass; the voice also moves at the same time with the bass, whereas in the verse the vocal entry was delayed. Thus for the line "when they get what they want," the voice is in rhythmic and pitch agreement with the bass. This agreement is disrupted slightly as the phrase continues, "they never want it again." Here the voice overshoots the D that would be in octaves with the bass and leaps to E instead, but does then immediately move on to D. As the harmony cadences on A, the voice steps from D down to C♯, breaking the octave duplication in order to create a bright major third above the A. The brightness of that third is felt, not only because C♯ is a chromatic pitch for the overall mode of G, but also because the vocal line for this phrase moves first from E down to C, and then from E down to C♯. Just as the voice played on the chromatic identity of the third B (or B♭) of G in the verse, here it plays on the chromatic identity of the third C (or C♯) of A. In the verse, the lowering of the third B had the effect of disrupting the expected harmony and creating chromatic tension; the minor third B♭ contributed to the mysterious and disturbing quality of the night scene described in the lyrics. In the pre-chorus, the C♯ creates a different kind of chromatic tension, the kind of tension felt from false security. Irony is Love's desired effect: she may be singing in unison (in agreement) with the bass, and she may be examining the problem of sexual conformity, but she is certainly not advocating that action.

"Violet": Chorus

The music of the chorus expresses the intense anger behind the lyrics "go on take everything, take everything, I want you to." High volume, distortion, and harsh vocal production are all engaged to hurl the accusation with bitter irony. Figure 4.4 graphs the counterpoint of the chorus. The chorus continues the harmonic pattern of the pre-chorus, thus binding these two sections together. The harmony we hear for this angry chorus was thus associated with the ironic conformity of the pre-chorus; there was, however, a sarcastic levity to the musical presentation in the pre-chorus that is replaced by a heavy display of power and anger in the chorus. In addition, the vocal melody of the chorus begins with a refer-

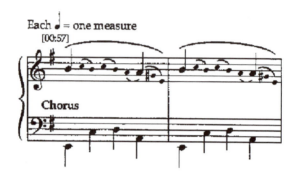

FIGURE 4.4 "Violet," Voice-Leading Graph (Chorus)

ence back to the verse by returning to the higher register, to the high B and distorted vocal presentation that was associated with "you should learn how to say no." The melodic pattern that Love sings (alternating from B^4 to C^5) recalls the passage "mine is forever," which I singled out as a significant moment of discursive disruption in the verse. She thus makes a musical association between the line "go on take everything" and the negative implications of rape trauma as a continuous ("forever") state of suffering. The fact that we make this contradictory association at the same time that we are also hearing the "conformity" harmony from the pre-chorus juxtaposes all three problematic concepts in a single musical phrase that is imbued with an incredible contextual tension.

Although the chorus represents the culmination of the song's narrative, a later development of the pre-chorus section offers one more opportunity for resistance. After two statements of the verse–pre-chorus–chorus sequence, we hear an additional pre-chorus–chorus before the music moves into its final segment. In that additional pre-chorus, Love makes a remarkable change to the lyrics and musical content. She replaces the first line with a phrase that shifts the textual perspective, invoking a direct personal communication: "I told you from the start just how this would end." The vocal line abandons the earlier pre-chorus vocal outline that was in octaves with the bass (figure 4.3), and instead skips down from the initial E to a low B, then descends to low A. The darker low register creates a reference back to the mysterious opening scene of the rape; the voice's denial of the "conformity" melodic line (octaves) is a deliberate act of musical resistance to the normative pattern that was established. This is a very thoughtful moment in the song's narrative. Following this line, Love returns to the "conformity" melodic line of the old pre-chorus; however, she alters the text with the pronoun shift from the third person ("when *they* get") to the first person: "when *I* get what I want, then I never want it again." Here she assumes the voice of the perpetrator. Mélisse interpreted this moment as Love's appropriation of men's sexual control and disregard for women. We hear Love returning punishment in the context of retribution. Women are traditionally denied access to that form of anger or aggression, but this song moves toward a moment of female appropriation. When the song then ends with the repetition of the chorus's "go on take everything," it is with this resistant context in mind.

5

Me'Shell Ndegéocello, "Mary Magdalene" (1996)

The just-over-five-foot Ndegéocello is a commanding presence while simply stand-
ing at her mike or noodling at the keyboards, but when she finally strapped on her
bass (which is almost larger than she is) for "If That's Your Boyfriend (He Wasn't
Last Night)," she officially owned the place.
—*Bohager's, Baltimore, May 8, 1997*

∽∽∽∽∽∽
TEXTUAL SUBVERSIONS: THE NARRATIVE SABOTAGE OF RACE,
GENDER, AND DESIRE IN THE MUSIC OF ME'SHELL
NDEGÉOCELLO (MÉLISSE LAFRANCE)

The popular music industry has long been considered a preserve of het-
eromasculine privilege (Kearney 1997, McClary 1994). Even genres considered most specific to the African-American experience, such as rap
and hip-hop, have been criticized for their sometimes violent and misogynistic lyrical proclivities (hooks 1994). This seemingly hostile musical
context, however, has recently seen the emergence of a number of subversive and arguably feminist hip-hop sensations. One of the most compelling among these disruptive presences in hip-hop music is Me'Shell
Ndegéocello, an unabashed spokesperson for African-American, feminist, and queer politics.

Ndegéocello's 1996 release *Peace beyond Passion* discloses a fierce
and critical reflection on postmodern America.[1] Despite the vast implications of both her music and her widespread recognition, few scholars of

popular culture have endeavored to critically interrogate and/or culturally situate Ndegéocello's work.[2] This chapter, therefore, is devoted to assessing the subversive potential of Ndegéocello's music by discussing her lyrical deployments of gender, race, and desire. Drawing on literary criticism as well as on feminist, queer, and cultural theory, I will argue that Ndegéocello's compositional strategies subvert and displace many operative sites of both white and masculine supremacy.

The analytic component of this investigation consists of a "reading" (or a textual analysis) of Ndegéocello's song "Mary Magdalene." While chapter 1 discussed the myriad questions that enshroud hermeneutics, a number of additional comments are necessary, as Ndegéocello explicitly evokes the intricacies of meaning and interpretation in "Mary Magdalene." Hence, this section will briefly explicate some of the theoretical sensibilities that inform and organize my analytic approach.

Poststructuralism and Textuality: Reading as Writing

According to Chris Weedon, "all forms of poststructuralism assume that meaning is constituted within language and is not guaranteed by the subject which speaks it" (1997, 22). The poststructuralist exposition of language is conceptually indebted to structuralist theorists (for example, Althusser 1969, Barthes [1970] 1974, Jakobson 1990, Lévi-Strauss [1971] 1981, Saussure 1974), who pioneered the notion that "individual signs do not have intrinsic meaning but acquire meaning through the language chain and their difference within it" (Weedon 1997, 23). It was the structuralist insistence on pregiven, fixed linguistic structures, however, that would be subsequently questioned by poststructuralist contentions. Poststructuralists like Jacques Derrida (1976) disrupted the supposed fixed and coherent conception of linguistic structures by focusing not on the stasis of the sign but on the instability and plurality of both the signifier and the signified. These theorists showed how the signified changes constantly depending on the historical and/or cultural discursive context. Derrida's concept of *différance* (that is, the dual production of meaning through *difference* and *deferral*) thus becomes instructive, as it reveals how texts and the meanings they appear to generate are essentially open to rereading and reinterpretation.

Viewed in this way, the instability of meaning invariably connotes the radical incompleteness and indeed inevitable instability of textual interpretations. Moreover, such a conceptual scheme undermines any singular and/or unified interpretation of any text and therefore necessitates a disruption of conventional literary binaries (for example, author/reader, truth/fiction, correct interpretation/incorrect interpretation). Such an understanding of meaning has important implications for any discussion of narrative potential.

Resistance through Rereading
The poststructuralist conception of textuality as inherently unstable and essentially open to constant rereading is particularly instructive to those attempting to "make sense," albeit provisionally, of Ndegéocello's work. Indeed, Ndegéocello's music consistently rereads, reinterprets, and reconfigures dominant cultural texts while acutely resisting the oppressive meanings generally attributed to marginalized groups through such texts.

"Mary Magdalene" sees Ndegéocello rereading and rewriting the biblical "story" of Jesus and Mary Magdalene.[3] To do so, Ndegéocello writes herself, a black and openly bisexual woman, into a cultural text whose interpretations are frequently used to legitimatize sexism, misogyny, racism, homophobia, heterosexism, and the derision of bodies materialized and conditioned by norms of femininity. Indeed, Ndegéocello unabashedly positions herself as Magdalene's only true love and repositions the male characters as Magdalene's "unworthy burdens." The following sections will explore further the implications of Ndegéocello's rereading for norms of race, gender, and desire. For now, however, suffice it to say that in reclaiming one of the most important biblical stories, Ndegéocello has appropriated a traditionally oppressive text and subverted its traditionally oppressive effects.

In "Cultural Studies and the Culture of Everyday Life," John Fiske conceptualizes strategies of resistance in conditions of oppression and constraint. Despite his reductionistic treatment of oppression, Fiske nevertheless elucidates the resistant possibilities produced through the (re)appropriation and rereading of cultural texts—especially as they pertain to the culturally marginalized. He writes,

> The social order constrains and oppresses the people, but at the same time offers them resources to fight against those constraints. The constraints are, in the first instance, material, economic ones which determine in an oppres-

sive way the limits of the social experience of the poor.... *Yet the everyday culture of the oppressed takes the signs of that which oppresses them and uses them for its own purposes.* (1992, 157; emphasis added)

While Fiske's discussion pertains primarily to the subversion of economic oppression, his reflection on the appropriation of "contaminated resources" by the culturally marginalized could be seen to articulate the strategies employed by Ndegéocello in much of her music. Indeed, by virtue of her blackness, femaleness, and bisexuality, Ndegéocello is doubtless marginalized by dominant discourses of race, gender, and sexuality—discourses that often efface or pathologize her. Yet through the reappropriation and subversive rereading of a dominant cultural text (that is, the Bible), Ndegéocello "takes the signs of that which oppresses [her] and uses them for [her] own purposes."

Consistent with other authors who have examined resistance in conditions of constraint (for example, Beausoleil 1994, Fisher and Davis 1993, Fiske 1992), I do not intend to dismiss the oppressive effects of dominant and structural regimes. However, I do understand culturally marginalized individuals as both "subjects-in-discourse" and "subjects-at-work" who are "actively involved in all aspects of the production of the social order" (Beausoleil 1994, 36).

Ndegéocello's project of rereading/rewriting biblical narratives that have typically produced and/or sustained the subordination of, for instance, women, people of color, and homosexuals is most certainly not straightforward. Indeed, it could be posited that any subversive value gained by a rereading of the biblical stories is undermined by the fact that the Bible is, in modern Western society at least, bound to a particularly broad and hegemonic apparatus of power. Following Michel Foucault ([1976] 1990), however, I would argue that this position is untenable, and that its untenability is rooted primarily in the fact that no act of resistance or subversion can transpire outside the complex matrix of power relations. Relations of power are not "outside" other types of relations—be they intersubjective, economic, or cultural—but are instead "immanent" in these relations. In Foucault's words, "relations of power are not in superstructural positions, with merely a role of prohibition or accompaniment; they have a directly productive role, wherever they come into play" (94).

If one subscribes to the Foucauldian view, then one must consider any act of subversion or resistance as invariably imbedded in and mediated by an all-encompassing matrix of power. No text is in a position of exteriority to power, just as no reading of any text escapes power's interception. Resisting *accepted* readings of dominant texts by producing *subversive* readings of them can never completely transcend contemporary relations of power, and as such is necessarily "a difficult labor of forging a future from resources inevitably impure" (Butler 1993a, 241). I see Ndegéocello as involved in forging this future. Working boldly from "resources inevitably impure," Ndegéocello allows the listener to understand the story of Mary Magdalene as a tale of same-sex love, interracial harmony, and female empowerment rather than one of fallen women, mighty men, and racially coded slavery.

Biblical Interpretations of Mary Magdalene

The dominant or patriarchal story of Mary Magdalene's encounter with Jesus sees Mary as a vain and decadent prostitute.[4] In this story, Mary commits many impious acts, not the least of which consists in performing "deeds of lust in the Arbor" such that the sun is made to "blush" (Robinson 1899, 25). Mary's impiety eventually becomes too formidable to bear. She becomes ridden with guilt and anxiety. It is on the day that Mary realizes she can no longer cope with her sinful existence that "conscience winds herself [*sic*] into Mary's heart, and asks her how she can escape God's eye." Desperately overcome by her grief and tormented by her conscience, Mary "returns to her lust." Her lust, though, cannot deliver her from the "cave of melancholy" into which she is increasingly drawn. All of Magdalene's pleasures have now turned to sadness. Nemesis, and other spirits, have overcome her and are slowly committing her to Hell (27–32).

Christ, in his travels, sees Mary. Mary is so overcome that "the spirits in her cast her at his feet." Christ bids the spirits quit Mary and she is "rescued." She collapses. Christ reaches out to her and comforts her. Christ guides Mary to the palace of Wisdom, where she will be cleansed and purified by her tears. Here, Magdalene will avow "the vanity of pleasure" and wish "she could recall her ill-spent days" when her "smiles tempted the onlooker." Although she is "unclean," Magdalene returns to see Jesus. Upon arrival, she "washes Christ's feet: wipes them with her hair and kisses them." How "happy she [is] to touch and kiss her savior's body" (43–63).

Some feminist scholars (for example, Schottroff 1996, Troost 1996) have begun questioning the mainstream, patriarchal Christian conception of Mary Magdalene. In fact, these scholars are challenging the fundamental legitimacy of such interpretations. For instance, Luise Schottroff asserts:

> It is correct to say that Luke 7.38 describes an erotic scene. In this narrative, the only actors are the woman and God. The rest is commentary. The woman tells Jesus of her reverence for him, her pain, and her capacity for uncensored love. Jesus accepts this gift in mutuality. *By reinterpreting the story to make it the tale of the whore's repentance, it was made to function within the context of the oppression of all women*: the separation of whores from "normal" women and discrimination against female eroticism is thereby perfected....Jesus, in fact, does not distance himself from the woman's erotic actions or from her real existence as a prostitute....For him the woman has loved in the fullest sense of the word—in spite of her being misused. (1996, 340)

Although feminist readings can underscore the radical masculine bias inherent in dominant interpretations of the Bible, the cultural impact of patriarchal biblical readings remains flagrant and undeniable. Western culture has been profoundly marked by dominant patriarchal interpretations of Mary Magdalene. Derivatives of this patriarchal interpretation continue to manifest themselves in contemporary conceptions of femininity. Indeed, feminist scholars of religion and gender have convincingly argued that operative patriarchal Christian constituents of femininity, such as uncleanness, impurity, temptation, and decadence, continue to define and naturalize the patriarchal gender relations of the late twentieth century (Mary Daly 1968 and 1978, Griffin 1981, Reuther 1974).

Writing Blackness In
Natalie Beausoleil (1996) reflects on how dominant culture produces simple and pejorative representations and definitions of Others in order to justify their social and economic subordination. These strategies, both material and discursive, are constituted and compelled by socially constructed racial categories (for example, "visible minority," "woman of

color") that function to pathologize the nonwhite body and further normalize the supremacy and centrality of the white body (Beausoleil 1996, Carty and Brand 1993). Whites, explains Beausoleil, continuously construct their "normality" through the reification of the cultural belief in the "raceless" character of the white body.

White culture's processes of autonormalization, however, are also sustained through the "distancing" of racial Others. For Toni Morrison (1992), this distance was achieved in the New World primarily through the exclusion of African-American experiences from the national literature. Consolidated by the idealization of canonical literary forms—many of which are either based on or inspired by biblical tales—the marginalization of African-American texts was intimately involved in the production and manipulation of racial identities in the United States. When blacks were integrated into the national literature, they were only integrated insofar as they fulfilled the roles of rapist, promiscuous savage, and/or irrational animal. For Morrison, this "[constructed] Africanism, deployed as rawness and savagery," not only maintained the distance between white Americans and African Others, but also "provided the staging ground and arena for the elaboration of the quintessential American identity" (44). By means of culturally privileged texts, then, American racial cohesion was maintained through both the distancing of the African-American Other and the performative pathologization of that Other.

Many authors (for example, Butler 1993a, Cole 1998, Cole and Hribar 1995, hooks 1994, Lafrance 1998, Lafrance and Rail 1998, Snead 1994) have argued that postmodern America's culturally privileged texts (for example, popular music, television shows, Hollywood movies, and commercial advertisements) continue to distance and pathologize African Americans. Movie sensations such as *Hoop Dreams* and *Paris Is Burning*, as well as consumer crazes initiated by transnational corporations such as Nike, persistently spectacularize the destitution and misery of many African-American communities (Butler 1993a, Cole 1998, Cole and Hribar 1995, hooks 1992, Lafrance 1998, Lafrance and Rail 1998). This spectacularization is thinly veiled as a sympathetic attempt to confront "real social problems" through the consumption of mass-mediated texts. Neither the mainstream cinema nor the corporate initiatives, however, locate the cause of African-American oppression in structural relations of inequality from which white middle- and upper-class citizens benefit. In other words, dominant groups are never made responsible for their role in systems of oppression and privilege. In fact, the success of popular cultures of consumption could not be sustained without the support of society's dominant groups. Therefore, for society's dominant groups to continue subsidizing these cultural texts, it is essential that they reinforce and consolidate their privilege as dominant groups.

Cheryl Cole and Amy Hribar's (1995) Foucauldian analysis of the modern production of deviance and pathology is instructive when considering America's obsession with spectacles of African-American destitution. They write,

> The normal and the abnormal must be understood as both contingent and mutually implicated and dependent categories: The border that marks the self is continuously generated through a social process of producing and policing the other. Although the techniques and strategies of modern power are masked, the productivity of power is rendered visible in its effects: the deviant, the pathological, and delinquent. (355)

Dominant culture's appropriation and exploitation of African-American oppression, therefore, invites "status quo readers to imagine that they too can consume images of difference, participate in the [practices] depicted, and yet remain untouched—unchanged" (hooks 1994, 15). From the Bible and canonical literature to Nike advertisements, dominant groups producing and regulating culturally privileged texts have been invested in the simultaneous diffusion of white supremacist fantasies. While white authors have typically dominated the expression of fantasies through textual media, artists like Ndegéocello appear to be challenging this state of affairs.

Rereading Jesus, Rewriting Salvation
As previously mentioned, Morrison (1992) contends that the authors of the literary canon not only imagined American racial identities, but also constituted and compelled them. Morrison's discussion therefore conceptualizes texts as performative in nature. Performativity, in Butler's (1993a, 1993b) conceptualization, refers to dominant discourses that have the ability to produce what they name. With the performative nature of discourse in mind, Ndegéocello's subversion and reconfigura-

tion of the biblical text and its discourses can arguably be seen as a disruptive event.

Patriarchal interpretations of the biblical character Mary Magdalene differ quite substantively from those put forth by Ndegéocello in her song "Mary Magdalene." In this composition, Ndegéocello sees Magdalene as trapped in a degrading occupation, everywhere surrounded by unseemly men who appropriate her body for themselves. Magdalene is positioned as the exotic one, the one who "entices" Ndegéocello. Right from the outset, then, Ndegéocello resists positioning herself as the black "exotic other," and instead positions the white Magdalene as the "enticing" yet untouchable object of desire.

With respect to race, the most important lyrics of this song occur at the beginning of verse 2.[5] Ndegéocello writes, "Come and I'll set you free / into an endless valley of fruits both sweet and sour / and whatever displeases your palate my kisses will wash away." If, in biblical accounts, Magdalene was both physically and spiritually saved by Jesus, then Ndegéocello's self-attribution of saviorlike powers has considerable implications. Ndegéocello seems to have usurped Jesus' role as savior, and written herself into his place. Ndegéocello contends that she has the will and the capacity to set Magdalene free "into an endless valley of fruits." This "valley of fruits" has both positive and negative elements, a considerable departure from the dominant biblical understandings of certain fruit—particularly the apple—as inherently sinful.

Writing oneself into the Bible is a disruptive, some might even say sacrilegious, act. However, recasting oneself as Jesus when one is black, female, and bisexual is especially subversive. It would be quite difficult for many individuals to genuinely envisage a biblical story within which black characters assumed important narrative functions. For many, the presence of blacks within biblical stories would be both unimaginable and untenable. The difficulties related to conceptualizing blacks in biblical stories are quite obviously related to dominant discourses of whiteness at once sustained and produced by privileged interpretations of texts like the Bible. Many authors (for example, Frankenberg 1993, Morrison 1992, Snead 1994) have reflected on how such discourses of whiteness are culturally accomplished and sustained. James Snead (1994) discusses many strategies through which whiteness is textually consolidated, two of which are particularly pertinent to this discussion.

The first strategy, omission, is perhaps the most relevant to this discussion, as blacks appear nowhere in the Bible except as "miserable slaves" in the Old Testament.[6] As regards omission, Snead comments:

> Omission and exclusion are perhaps the most widespread tactics of racial stereotyping but are also the most difficult to prove because their manifestation is precisely absence itself. The repetition of black absence from locations of autonomy and importance creates the presence of the idea that blacks belong in positions of obscurity and dependence. (6)

The second strategy that consolidates white privilege, marking, was superficially discussed at the beginning of this section. Snead elaborates on marking:

> We seem to find the color black repeatedly overdetermined, marked redundantly, almost as if to force the viewer to register the image's difference from white images.... Marking is necessary because the reality of blackness or of being "colored" cannot always, either in films or in real life, be determined. The racial terms "black" and "white" refer to a wide range of hues that cannot be positively described—by being this or that—but only by negative contrast: black is not "white" (where "white" itself is a difficult term to fix). (5)

Such marking is strategic. The color black is frequently used to encode impurity and evil in Western cultures; the color white, on the other hand, is deployed to encode absolute purity and goodness (Frankenberg 1993, Snead 1994). So although marking is frequently discussed with reference to the black body (that is, the black body is marked so as to display the proximity of black people to impurity and evil), I want to argue that visual representations of biblical figures are also marked—but for opposite purposes. Visual representations of Jesus and the Virgin Mary, for example, have been exceedingly whitened so as to avoid any association with impurity (that is, blackness equals impurity). Indeed, the whitening of these biblical figures reinforces the relationship between goodness and whiteness, therefore making absolute "goodness" an unattainable goal for nonwhites.

This analysis is in no way far-fetched when applied to the work of Ndegéocello. Although the question of the symbolic value of color binaries is more implicit in "Mary Magdalene," Ndegéocello's song "The Way" explicitly reflects on that question. This racial "consciousness" is made manifest in the following passage:

They say you're the way the light
the light is so blinding
Your followers condemn me
your words used to enslave me
I am so ashamed on bended knees
prayin' to my pretty white Jesus
Mother Mary full of grace
I'm so confused by her pale white face

The writing of a black woman into biblical texts exposes the extent to which the biblical stories supposedly representing purity and goodness are predicated on subtle but insidious ideologies of whiteness. Ndegéocello's writing of herself into the Bible disrupts these ideologies of whiteness, exposing the far from raceless character of biblical characters and stories.

Denaturalizing Sex/Destabilizing Desire

Ndegéocello's desire for Magdalene is rendered lyrically explicit in "Mary Magdalene." The song begins with the declaration "I often watch you the way you whore yourself / You're so beautiful, you flirt and tease / enviously, I wish you'd flirt with me." This wishing is transformed into sexual fantasy when, in the next line, Ndegéocello expresses, "I imagine us jumpin' the broom foolish I know / 'Cause that's not the life you live." Interestingly, the previous phrase seems to connote a frustration of Ndegéocello and Magdalene's sexual possibilities due to Magdalene's life of heterosexual prostitution. Although Ndegéocello is aware of the "forbidden" nature of her desire for Magdalene, she continues to assert such desire with confidence and vigor. Ndegéocello affirms,

Spend one night with me
satisfy me for free
and I'll love you endlessly.
You always tell them you'll give them what they want
So give me what I want

These statements are especially interesting because they see Ndegéocello challenging Magdalene to spend a night with her (presumably for reasons of a sexual nature). In extending such a challenge, Ndegéocello seems most confident that Magdalene will be profoundly changed by the sexual experience—so changed, in fact, that it might prompt Magdalene to leave her life of prostitution and pursue a life with Ndegéocello. It could be argued that the previous claim is validated by the chorus: "Tell me I'm the only one.../I want to marry you / Tell me I'm the only one." Once again, Ndegéocello positions herself as the agent of salvation in Magdalene's trajectory.

Some may argue that Ndegéocello's fantasies of Magdalene are not completely unlike typical heterosexual male fantasies. Certainly such fantasies, which position a man as proverbially saving a sexually mis-used and unfulfilled woman, are neither original nor particularly pro-gressive. I argue, however, that because Ndegéocello's fantasies are accomplished through discourses of same-sex desire and against dis-courses of heterosexual desire, Ndegéocello's fantasies must be under-stood as fundamentally disruptive to heteronormative regimes. I also contend, as does Judith Butler (1990), that it is precisely the queering of allegedly "natural" heterosexual acts that both exposes their radically constructed character and generates, through the sexually transgressive nature of such queering, the erotic significance. Butler posits,

> Within lesbian contexts, the identification with masculinity that appears as butch identity is not a simple assimilation of lesbianism back into the terms of heterosexuality.... It is precisely this dissonant juxtaposition and the sex-ual tension that its transgression generates that constitute the object of desire. In other words, the object [and clearly there is not just one] of lesbian-femme desire is neither some decontextualized female body nor a discrete yet superimposed masculine identity, but the destabilization of both terms as they come into erotic interplay... the idea that butch and femme are in some senses "replicas" or "copies" of heterosexual exchange underestimates the erotic significance of these identities as internally dissonant and complex in their resignification of the hegemonic categories by which they are enabled. (1990, 123)

Certainly Ndegéocello's mobilization of love affairs predicated on monogamy and marriage (that is, "tell me I'm the only one...I want to marry you") recalls a dominantly heterosexual modality of sexuality in particular and conjugal existence in general. Nevertheless, the recupera-tion and subsequent superimposition of such heterosexual vestiges onto a same-sex love affair inevitably call into question the "very notion of an original or natural" (Butler 1990, 123) heterosexual identity.

The fantasies evidenced in this composition are rendered even more subversive through Ndegéocello's conceptualization of Mary Magdalene and the fact of Magdalene's prostitution. In patriarchal formulations, the prostitute is seen as impure, fallen, and thus unworthy of just and respectable treatment. Concerning patriarchal formulations of women's sexuality, Schottroff (1996) posits,

> The separation of women into honorable "normal" women and whores, and the discrimination against whores, are instruments of domination. By this means women are forced apart, and they are robbed of their eroticism. Female eroticism appears as something dirty or else as something to be reserved for the marital bedroom. (1996, 339–40)

In Ndegéocello's formulation, however, Magdalene is viewed as in some way trapped by the men she serves. In fact, Ndegéocello positions these men as unworthy of Magdalene altogether. Consider Ndegéocello's positive descriptions of Magdalene and relatively negative descriptions of the men who visit her:

> I often watch you the way you whore yourself,
> *You're so beautiful* . . .
> In a harlot's dress you wear the smile of a *child*
> with the *faith* of Mary Magdalene.
> Yet you wash the feet of unworthy men. (emphasis added)

The author resists conventional representations of prostitution by attributing to Magdalene qualities of beauty, innocence, and faith. Moreover, by choosing not to efface Magdalene's subjectivity—by, in fact, revealing Magdalene as entrapped and capable of envisaging other modalities of sexuality—Ndegéocello destabilizes the dichotomously organized subject positions of virgin/whore available to women in patriarchal cultures (Schottroff 1996). Finally, by framing the men who use Magdalene as unworthy and burdensome, Ndegéocello undermines codes of hegemonic masculinity that continually assert men's natural entitlement and constant access to the bodies and sexualities of women (Guillaumin 1981 and 1983). It also connotes an especially powerful critique of Christianity, in that the feet washed by Magdalene most likely belong to Jesus.

This interpretation points to an intimate relationship between the body and various forms of cultural regulation and/or conflict. Many feminist scholars have explained the importance of the body as a site of both discursive domination and surveillance (for example, Bartky 1993, Bordo 1993) and of struggle and resistance (for example, Beausoleil 1994, Fisher and Davis 1993). By making sexuality the organizing theme of the song "Mary Magdalene," Ndegéocello is profiling the potential union of two discursively pathologized bodies: the whore body and the black bisexual body. This compositional act not only destabilizes binary oppositions by constructing the narrative around two Othered bodies (as opposed to one deviant and one normal body), but also explicitly confronts dominant discourses of race, gender, and sexuality by using the sexual body as a critical site of subversion and contestation. This is supported by Fiske's assessment of the centrality of the body in social struggle:

> The body and its specific behavior is where the power system stops being abstract and becomes material. The body is where it succeeds and fails, where it is acceded to or struggled against. The struggle for control, top-down vs. bottom-up, is waged on the material terrain of the body and its immediate context. (1992, 162)

Ndegéocello's textual strategies denaturalize heterosexual modalities of gender and desire through the "replication of heterosexual constructs in non-heterosexual frames," which has the effect of bringing "into relief the utterly constructed status of the so-called heterosexual original" (Butler 1990, 31). Ndegéocello's explicit love and desire for a prostitute whom she considers beautiful, innocent, and faithful undermines the patriarchal-Christian view of prostitutes (and women in general) as impure and fallen. Ndegéocello's view of Magdalene's clients as "unworthy men" (within which group Jesus is included) undermines the patriarchal belief that men have the right to appropriate and regulate women's sexuality. Finally, by profiling the sexual union of two discursively pathologized bodies, Ndegéocello once again resists binary oppositions and wages narrative war against power regimes of race, gender, and desire through the textualized materiality of her own body.

Me'Shell Ndegéocello: "Critically Queer"
In *Gender Trouble*, Butler asks, "Which possibilities of doing gender repeat and displace through hyperbole, dissonance, internal confusion, and proliferation the very constructs by which they are mobilized?"

(1990, 31). By writing herself into a text that has been deployed to naturalize the categories of gender, race, and desire, I believe that Ndegéocello has at least partially "repeated and displaced" the constructs by which such categories are mobilized. Ndegéocello's subversive critique of power regimes seems almost impeccable in the breadth of its conceptual scope: "Mary Magdalene" simultaneously criticizes dominant discourses of race, gender, and desire, without marginalizing one critique for the sake of another.

Ndegéocello has fulfilled many of the criteria queer theorists now deem necessary for truly "queer" theorizing and activism. As Ruth Goldman (1996) explains, queerness, ideally, involves resisting regimes of the normal and creating a space for diverse discourses that challenge heteronormativity and the systems that sustain it. Queerness, if it accomplishes what it was devised for should not only challenge and confuse our understanding and uses of sexual and gender categories but should also provide a theoretical and practical framework within which one can challenge racist, ageist, and classist norms. Through my exposition of Ndegéocello's compositional strategies, I have shown that she challenges many regimes of the normal. By writing herself into the Bible, she challenges myths of purity premised on racist ideologies of whiteness. By structuring her song around her desire for another woman, she displaces and renders incoherent allegedly "natural" heterosexual categories. By professing her love and desire for a prostitute, whom she considers beautiful, she destabilizes rigid patriarchal norms of femininity that polarize the sexual subject positions available to women. Moreover, her narrative strategies constantly resist the hierarchization of oppressions and/or the establishment of binary oppositions. In short, Ndegéocello's music

> articulates a cultural and political struggle over sexual relations: a struggle that is directed against the objectification of female sexuality within a patriarchal order but which also tries to reclaim women's bodies as the sexual and sensuous objects of women's song. (Carby cited in Sanjek 1997, 142)

REVISING THE SEXUAL "GAZE": MUSICAL ATTRIBUTIONS OF POWER IN "MARY MAGDALENE" (LORI BURNS)

With her critical analysis, Mélisse has discussed how Ndegéocello creates a contemporary feminist narrative with a historical biblical subject.

147

As Ndegéocello rewrites the old story, she develops new perspectives on the original themes of sexual agency and sexual desire, allowing her to explore racial, gender, and sexual identity. Ndegéocello uses a conventional musical form (ground bass) as a fitting musical setting for her story, but her treatment of that form within a contemporary hip-hop style similarly offers new perspectives and modes of expression.

As Mélisse has shown, Ndegéocello "simultaneously criticizes dominant discourses of race, gender, and desire, without marginalizing one critique for the sake of another." The breadth of conceptual scope and the complexity of the narrative in "Mary Magdalene" offer a challenge to the music analyst, since the question of narrative privilege naturally arises in any close reading of lyrics and music. As I respond to Mélisse's thematic reading, I must find a route into my musical reading that will not privilege one particular theme to the detriment of the others, but that will rather encourage a comparable breadth of conceptual scope and complexity of narrative in the musical domain. With that goal in mind, I will begin by reviewing briefly the interpretive categories from my analytic method that are most applicable to this particular song; the reader is reminded that these categories are intended to permit a malleable interpretive method.

Lyrical Meaning

In the interpretation of this song, it will be valuable to consider the *subject/object perspective*. Ndegéocello as subject is watching Mary, defining her as an object of desire. Yet, as Mélisse has argued, the subject's gaze is not simply a copy of the male gaze; rather, because the fantasy is developed through a discourse of same-sex desire, it must be understood as disruptive, as a revision of the heterosexual male gaze. Ndegéocello assumes a voyeuristic position, but her desire does not hold negative potential consequences for the object. In my musical analysis, I will explore this concept of a revised subject creating and adopting a revised "gaze."[7]

Mary's and the singer's own *agency* will be considered as the story explicitly engages the themes of conformity versus resistance to a dominant discourse. In this context, I will consider the ways in which the singer and Mary are ascribed power within the lyrical and musical narratives. The music draws upon particular conventions that admit the potential for variation; the characters' representation through the variation strategies can signify power (virtuosity, musical control) and resistance (code manipulation).

The song is undeniably an exploration and expression of Ndegéocello's *desire*. During the narrative presentation of the lyrics, there are many expressions of desire, occurring in the form of descriptions of Mary and appeals for her attention, as well as the more cerebral desire for commitment. The music represents these forms of desire by means of compositional strategies that suggest feelings of movement, urgency, and intensity.

Musical Meaning

"Mary Magdalene" is based on a formal convention (a ground bass) that is manipulated by Ndegéocello to create a set of variations. In that regard, the most meaningful of my theoretical categories will be *codes, conventions, styles* (and their manipulation), and *structure* (and structural anomalies).

The song features a single-measure ground-bass pattern that runs through all verse and chorus statements. (It is not heard during the two contrasting bridge sections.) The backdrop of a simple musical pattern, with its potential for repetition and subtle variation, allows the complex textual narrative to emerge. The ground-bass pattern bears its own particular musical meaning that creates expectations (harmonic, melodic, rhythmic); these expectations can be manipulated to be fulfilled or thwarted in a variety of ways. The listener is asked to hear and interpret the music at different levels, from the meaning of the individual moment, to its comparison against an established context, to the grouping of several statements into a phrase or section of the music, to the larger conception of the entire musical form. Thus, although seemingly simple, the ground-bass form can be a powerful musical strategy.

Over this ground bass, the voice alternates between spoken and sung lyrics, an alternation that is conventional to the hip-hop style. These two vocal strategies allow the story to be told with different effects and degrees of intensity. Ndegéocello's choice of when to speak and when to sing is significant to the narrative. In addition, the contrasting vocal strategies are heard against the regulated ground bass, the meaning of which is varied and manipulated. The melodic material that Ndegéocello sings is derived from the ground-bass progression, but is subjected to a variety of transformations that have great potential for lyrical intersections. The degree to which the original bass pattern is maintained or transformed is of interest, as are the moments when the melodic material lies completely outside the ground-bass pattern, thus creating an anomaly within the existing structure.

Ndegéocello articulates a regular rhythmic and metric structure on the bass guitar, creating a strong pulse of four beats per measure with a triplet subdivision (12/8). The immediate metric pulse is then developed into a hypermetric structure, such that each section of the song functions as a clear hypermetric grouping (four-measure introduction, eight-measure verse, and so on). This larger metric organization, like the ground bass at its smaller (one-measure) level, creates musical expectations that can be either realized or thwarted, and therein lies another opportunity for the expression of the lyrical narrative.

"Mary Magdalene": Introduction

A brief introduction establishes the ground-bass pattern and metric organization of the song. We hear four statements (that is, four measures) of the ground-bass pattern. The downbeat of measure 5 arrives as the beginning of the verse, establishing a structural division and a clear hypermetric design.

The ground-bass pattern is illustrated in figure 5.1. The bass attacks D on the downbeat, moves to E on the second pulse, and arrives at A on beat three. In some statements of the pattern, the A is held through beat four, and in some it is embellished; nevertheless, the underlying structure is a sustained A through beats three and four. The details of the pattern's harmonization are varied as the song proceeds, but as a basic progression, the harmony moves from a D-major chord, through the bass E with no triadic change, to an A-minor chord with added dissonance. Figure 5.1 provides a harmonization of the progression that could be considered the normative model, as it emerges quite strongly through the course of the song. In this harmonization, the D-major triad has an added dissonance (the ninth, E). When the bass moves on to E, the harmony does not really change, as the D-major triad carries over. The bass A supports a minor-seventh harmony.

The tonality or modality of the ground-bass progression is best understood as D Mixolydian, with an emphasis on the tonic D in the first half of the measure and on the Mixolydian minor dominant A in the sec-

FIGURE 5.1 Harmonized Ground-Bass Pattern

ond half of the measure. The D is accented not only because it occurs on the downbeat, but also because it is the lowest pitch in register. At the beginning of each measure we hear the A from the preceding statement fall to the low D. The A, however, is also a strong referential pitch, as it is sustained for two beats and is approached by its fifth, E. In the musical texture, it is made to sound as an arrival, as the synthesized strings begin a swell on A on the second beat and release into the third beat when the bass attacks the A. The sense of A as an arrival might suggest a tonic function, with a IV-V-I progression in A Dorian for the ground bass as opposed to the I-II-V in D Mixolydian. Whether it is a polarity of mode or simply a polarity of degrees within one mode, a tension between D and A seems to be the harmonic intention.

With this simple modal progression, Ndegéocello establishes a harmonic framework that has great potential for manipulation. There are certain moments when the downbeat D is articulated as an emphatic tonic arrival; similarly, there are certain moments when the sustained A is intensified as a dominant prolongation. She does not treat each statement of the ground bass in the same way, but rather makes some arrivals stronger than others in order to create a structural design that will shape her song lyrics.

"Mary Magdalene": Verse Lyrics

The verse lyrics comprise fourteen prose lines of irregular lengths (see appendix 1). The only repetition occurs at the end of the verse, with the text "you'll give them what they want / So give me what I want." She sets the lengthy verse within a brief musical timespan (eight measures) through the use of quickly uttered spoken text, as well as sung text with syllabic declamation in small rhythmic subdivisions (the sung lines are italicized in the quotations that follow). The long passage of text also covers an expanse of conceptual and thematic ground, as Mélisse has revealed in her critical reading. For my lyric and music interpretation, it is useful to parse this lengthy and thematically complex verse into four sections, and then to examine how these lyrical subdivisions are articulated musically.

The first section establishes the subject watching the object. The perspective of the narrative here is voyeuristic: the subject watches her object of desire, interprets her actions as sexually provocative, and then projects herself into a relationship with her. In the first line, the singer is the grammatical subject of the phrase ("I ... watch ... you"); in the second line, the Other becomes the grammatical subject ("you're ... beautiful"), attributing to her a degree of power; in the third line, the singer is once again the subject ("I wish"), but she is now a subject who would like to be the object of the Other's attention ("I wish you'd flirt with me"). "I often watch the way you whore yourself / You're so beautiful, you flirt and tease / enviously, I wish you'd flirt with me." These lines, therefore, comprise an exploration of subjective power in which that power is at first assumed by the singer, then transferred to the Other.

I would like to comment briefly on the use of spoken versus sung text in connection with this transferal of power. The first line, in which the subject is watching the Other, is spoken. The second and third lines, which begin to illuminate the Other's power, are sung. This contrast between spoken and sung lyrics can be interpreted as a means of distinguishing the two personas (the subject and Mary), and thereby as a means of creating a stronger presence for Mary as a true subject in her own right. One could argue that there is a value of strength, or power, to both modes of musical expression: the subject speaks in hushed, metrically emphasized, low-register tones (D^3), offering a lengthy passage of text within a short span of musical time, while Mary is invoked (still through the eyes of the subject) by means of melodic (sung) gestures that are musically complex (to be illustrated presently).

The subject continues to consider the Other in the second section, but from a perspective that is now more speculative. The subject admits that her fascination may derive from an interpretation of the Other's sociosexual role. She speculates about the woman's role as a prostitute and confesses that her attraction for her may be based in some response (sympathy, empathy, or sexual desire) to that social construct as an abstract phenomenon. She invokes the sexual life of the Other and imagines how that woman feels, which we understand to be only speculation and not an actual account of her real experiences. The third and fourth lines of this section, words that explicitly engage the Other's life, are sung:

Perhaps I'm enticed by what you are
I imagine us jumpin' the broom foolish I know
Cause that's not the life you live
You live alone in a crowded bed
never remembering faces, conversations
just a body for the lonely.

The third section comprises an appeal in which she expresses her desire. It is a more direct statement, with an internal rhyming scheme ("me," "free," "endlessly") that contributes to a sense of urgency and sexual desire. It is also a promise, a personal investment, a commitment that this relationship would not be a temporary one; in other words, the Other would not be treated as a prostitute. With this sincere expression, we understand that she values the Other, who is not merely a material object of desire. The appeal is important for the narrative of this song because it sheds an unexpected light on the voyeuristic gaze and the conventional roles of subject and object, representing a challenge to the patriarchal norm of power distribution. This entire appeal is sung, with no spoken text: "Spend one night with me / satisfy me for free / and I'll love you endlessly."

The fourth and final section of the text constitutes a demand. Here the subject places herself alongside the prostitute's clients, for she wants what they receive. With "give me" and "I want," the subject expresses her own desire in no uncertain terms. It is not a gentle appeal, but rather an order; significantly, it is performed as spoken text: "You always tell them you'll give them what they want / So give me what I want."

The lyrics of the verse move from voyeuristic observation of the Other, through speculation about the life she leads, to a direct appeal and an expression of desire, and finally to a sexual demand. This creates a lyrical narrative of increasing intensity as the subject positions herself in relation to the Other. She starts from a distance, but moves metaphorically closer, building from an abstract consideration of the Other's life to the direct sexual claim. In this particular narrative, the dramatic movement belongs to the subject, and is directed at an object who occupies a "fixed" position. However, at the same time, the musical presentation lends the Other her own potential for dramatic "movement." The subject's reflections are presented in spoken form, while the Other is presented in an elaborated melodic form. The Other is, in that context, not in a "fixed" position after all. This second conception of the Other (imbued with the power of movement) might be understood as a contradiction of the former image (in a "fixed" position). However, I would prefer to privilege neither one, but rather to explore the potential of each and to celebrate the equal distribution of dramatic-musical power between subject and object that results. I believe that this is a musical representation of the revised conception of the sexual "gaze" discussed earlier. In my analysis of the music, I shall trace both the narrative of metaphorical movement in the lyrics as well as the musical presentation of spoken versus sung lyrics, and demonstrate how these two interpretive paths intersect.

"Mary Magdalene": Verse Music

Given the context of a repetitive ground-bass pattern, how could Ndegéocello achieve a feeling of dramatic movement or directionality in the music? At a very immediate level, she achieves it with the ground-bass pattern itself; as I discussed the song's introduction, I identified a harmonic tension in the pattern's fifth-relation between D and A. Over the course of the entire verse (the larger span of eight measures), she achieves a feeling of movement by means of the interplay between the ground-bass statements and the vocal phrasing.

The vocal phrasing is best explained through reference to the ground-bass pattern. Figure 5.1 gave a normative harmonization of the ground bass with the soprano A^4–D^5–C^5. I will argue that the vocal line throughout the entire song can be understood as a series of variations on that pattern. Figure 5.2 reproduces two prominent motivic patterns from the vocal line. The first (a) is the melodic pattern that derives from the normative progression of the ground bass. The second (b) is an elaborated form of that normative pattern in which the second note of the model, D, is embellished first by an upper neighbor E♭, and then by a complete lower neighbor C. The stepwise descent from D down to C, which was part of the original pattern, is interrupted by a leap down to A. This elaborated form of the pattern is used frequently throughout the song, but in different contrapuntal relationships to the bass.

The contrapuntal relationship between voice and bass is indeed significant, and offers the opportunity for unusual manipulations and contrapuntal anomalies. It is not the case, as one might expect, that each measure's vocal melody presents the underlying gesture in keeping with the bass's rhythmic pattern (quarter note–quarter note–half note). Rather, the vocal elaborations on the pattern work out of phase with the bass, moving at a much faster rate of articulation than the bass. In a given measure, one might hear three statements of the soprano pattern in elaborated form against a single statement of the ground bass. The contrapuntal tension that results is a musical requisite if the music is to have a sense of directionality; ground-bass repetition could result in

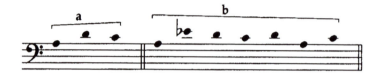

FIGURE 5.2 Vocal Line Motives

"squareness" of musical form. However, Ndegéocello allows the ground-bass pattern to coincide with the melodic pattern only at strategic points in the song.

Figure 5.3 transcribes the bass, vocal line, and lyrics for the first verse. I have labeled each of the four sections of text with a simple caption: "voyeurism," "speculation," "appeal," "demand." These captions are reductive in nature, but they should allow the reader to recall my earlier commentary on each section of text. I have also labeled the motivic content of the vocal line, maintaining the labels a and b from figure 5.2.

Ndegéocello begins verse 1 in measure 5 with spoken text, uttered at the pitch level of D^3, in keeping with the tonic D that initiates the ground-bass pattern. As she exclaims "you're so beautiful," she switches to sung melody, singing a form of the motive that begins on the elaborative pitch G but then immediately follows the primary motivic path A–D–C. In relation to the ground-bass pattern, this melodic statement begins late and is heard over the last note of the progression (A). As a result, the G that initiates the line is elaborative, as a dissonant neighbor to A, and the melodic D is also dissonant, as a neighbor to the C that forms a third against the bass A. Ndegéocello thus achieves contrapuntal dissonance by offsetting the rhythmic presentation of the soprano and bass in the normative pattern.

The next melodic statement is given another rhythmic/contrapuntal variation. Ndegéocello begins in measure 6 with the melodic A just after its consonant bass support D, but then sustains the A as the bass moves on to E, delaying the melodic leap to D (the contrapuntal "norm" for the progression). The third beat is spoken on the low D, interrupting the melodic passage that invoked the Other and offering an opportunity for self-reflection with the word "enviously." She then returns to her singing voice on the fourth beat of the measure for the continuation of the motive in an elaborated form (b). The high E♭ is dissonant against the supporting A in the bass. The dissonance and tension of that harmony are resolved at the beginning of measure 7 as the voice and bass both resolve to D, but the resolution is momentary; as the bass D is held, the voice continues on from D through A to C, a dissonant seventh against the supporting D. Contrapuntal tension is also created by the effect of overlapping; the vocal pattern begins at the end of one ground-bass statement (end of measure 6) and concludes at the beginning of the next statement (measure 7), creating a dissonant sort of "cadence" that gives a

FIGURE 5.3 "Mary Magdalene" (Verse)

sense of nonresolution. The sung passages in this first section of the verse are musically tentative in their weak (that is, out-of-phase) relationship to the ground bass. The tentative nature of this presentation is in keeping with the subject's own feelings of distance from the Other; these are the first moments when the Other is ascribed a dramatic presence. At this stage, the subject is only wishing for flirtation, but the desire becomes more intense later on.

The second section of the verse ("speculation") begins on beat two of measure 7, in the middle of a ground-bass statement. Here Ndegéocello speaks (again on the pitch D^3) for an extensive span of lyrics, allowing the words to become prominent against the backdrop of the ground bass. Although these lyrics are not sung, Ndegéocello does articulate her words with strong rhythm and accent: "enticed" arrives on beat three of measure 7, "I imagine" on beat four of measure 7, "broom" on beat one of measure 8, and "foolish" on beat two of measure 8. She switches to sung melody at the end of measure 8 with three statements of the motive in different forms. During this passage, the presence of the melodic motive gains momentum as compared with its presentation in the first section. The momentum derives from a sense of contrapuntal urgency created by the compression of these three statements into one and a half measures. The first statement is an elaborated form of the motive. The contrapuntal arrangement of bass and melody on the downbeat of measure 9 is comparable to that on the downbeat of measure 7, but in measure 9 it is not allowed to be a cadence, as the lyrics continue with some urgency. As the bass proceeds to the E of beat two, the voice presents its basic motive again (A–D–C), arriving on the C when the bass arrives on A. This marks the first moment in the song when the melodic C is heard in time with its structural bass according to the normative model. The sense of alignment is momentary, however, as the voice moves back up to D on beat four (dissonant with the bass A), and then skips down to an A and then a dissonant G at the end of the bar. The voice returns to spoken text (measure 10), ending that section without a melodic cadence. The overall form of this section is an arch: the phrase begins with a self-reflective spoken text, moves through an elaborative melodic line that offers several moments of contrapuntal dissonance, and then returns to spoken text.

The third section ("appeal") is entirely sung and presents the strongest melodic phrase of the first verse. The melodic line comprises two direct (that is, unelaborated) statements of the motive (measure 11), followed by an embellished statement leading to the cadence. These direct statements have a forceful musical effect, not only because of the pitch content but also because of the immediate repetition; the quick presentation of three statements of the melodic pattern in immediate succession has a hurried, determined effect. During the first two direct statements, the determination is intense, but it is softened by the third statement, which is more melodically elaborated and rhythmically extended to occupy two full beats. This elaboration underscores the text "I'll love you endlessly." The musical power I have attributed to this section stems implicitly from the Other (or at least from the subject's desire for the Other), thus the momentum for her continues and reaches its strongest point.

In direct contrast to the sung third section, the fourth section ("demand") is offered completely in spoken text. Whereas the third section featured melodic elaboration, this section's musical power derives from the forceful demand of the lyrics and the rhythmic emphasis. There is a rhythmic accent on the word "give" (of "give them") on beat four of measure 12, and again on "give" (of "give me") on beat one of measure 13, and on "I" (of "I want") on beat two of measure 13. The subject has reached her strongest moment of self-expression in this section, just as the Other was strongly projected in the previous section. The subject's musical power is confirmed through the most resolute cadence (the verse ending) thus far in the song. The text "so give me what I want" is presented in the first part of measure 13, serving as the cadence or close of the verse. Musically, it is not a melodic cadence, but it is nevertheless powerful as a tonic close; she utters her text here on tonic pitch D.

By cadencing at the beginning of measure 13, Ndegéocello creates an anomaly within the hypermetric design. The first two beats of measure 13 serve a double purpose: the ground bass is beginning the statement that "belongs" to the hypermetric unit of the chorus that is about to begin, while the lyrics "belong" with the preceding verse. This creates an overlapping effect in the formal structure at precisely the point in the text that constitutes the strongest and most direct statement of the subject to the Other: "So give me what I want." One of the results of this overlapping is that the chorus seemingly begins in the second half of the measure and, therefore, in the middle of the ground-bass pattern. The chorus thus begins on an upbeat, which is the first signal that it will have an unusual rhythmic/metric character.

"Mary Magdalene": Chorus

It is significant that the chorus is entirely sung; that is, the subject relinquishes the spoken form, which was her self-reflective mode of expression, in favor of the vocal style that was associated with the Other (or the subject's desire for the Other). This adoption of the elaborated melodic style signifies in concrete musical terms that the subject's lyrical movement toward the object is complete; she has given herself over to her desire and is in a state of emotional abandon.

The chorus is heard several times in the song, and each time it is basically the same (see figure 5.4). It thus carries a strong musical identity in the song, as contrasted with the verse, which has a less predictable design. The combined musical-lyrical identity of the chorus is critical as the repeated "message" of the song. It is also important to consider how the musical-lyrical content of the chorus relates to that of the verse. Certain musical elements carry over, most importantly the ground-bass pattern and the melodic pattern associated with it. However, Ndegéocello manipulates the structure to create a musical section with its own distinct features.

The chorus lyrics juxtapose a demand with an expression of commitment, offering a succinct expression of the subject's desire within a social context. In the first line, the subject, using the imperative, directs the Other to tell her what she wants to hear; she wants to be the "only one," implicitly invoking a larger social group. From the verse, we know that this larger group is in fact male and heterosexual, the clients of the prostitute. The second cursory line is a reminiscence of the final section of the verse ("give me"). The third line declares the subject's own desires in the form of a social commitment (marriage), thus comprising an explicit reference to a social tradition that, as Mélisse has pointed out, is typically associated with heterosexual relationships, but that is here granted a lesbian identity. This subject's concept of marriage lies outside social norms and might also be read as a form of resistance to the social system (prostitution) referenced in this song. The promise of marriage also contributes to the effect mentioned earlier in relation to the verse: the desired woman, Mary, is not an object in a pejorative sense; rather,

FIGURE 5.4 "Mary Magdalene" (Chorus)

Ndegéocello expresses a sincere commitment to marriage that takes the relationship beyond the merely sexual. The fourth line repeats the first, placing the commitment squarely in the middle of the urgent demand, and creating a rounded (statement–departure–statement) form that is enhanced by the music.

The musical formal structure of the chorus is quite unusual, despite the regularity of the continuing ground bass. The vocal line disrupts this regularity through its metric and melodic organization. In the larger formal design of the song, this section is brief, occupying just four measures of music with four ground-bass statements. However, the voice is not active for four full measures but rather occupies less than three full measures—it enters in the middle of the first ground-bass pattern, and concludes at the beginning of the fourth ground-bass statement. Within this phrase of irregular length—which disrupts the established regularity of the hypermetric structure—the subphrase parsing of the vocal line is also irregular. There are three main subphrase units: "tell me I'm the only one" is an elaborated statement of the melodic motive; "I want to marry you" is a contrasting melodic pattern; "tell me" returns for a final gesture, once again in an elaborated statement of the motive. Metrically, this rounded ABA patterning in the voice is arranged with the ground-bass support in an unpredictable way. The first "tell me" is heard on beats three and four of the measure, against A in the bass; "I want to marry you" is given downbeat emphasis; while the last "tell me" is heard against beats four and one, against the harmonic change from A to D. The final statement has a stronger effect of cadence, because of the beat-one resolution as well as the contrapuntal consonance of the vocal line (on D^4 and A^3) with the bass support (D).

The melodic content of the contrasting section commands the listener's attention with the first vocal gesture to lie outside of the established melodic range. Against the regular ground-bass pattern, the voice begins on G^4 and descends to C (G–F$\sharp$–E–D–C). The contextual dissonance of this melodic pattern cannot be overstated in a song that has been so narrowly focused on one primary melodic motive. I would interpret the lyrical significance of this pattern to exist in the subject's concept of marriage as lying outside of the social norm.

Although brief, the chorus creates a strong musical effect with its irregular metric and melodic design. Its musical strength derives, however, not from a sense of resolution, but from a feeling of irresolution, irregularity, and asymmetry. The anomolous design and melodic structure disrupt the norms established through the ground-bass formal organization.

"Mary Magdalene": Bridge

The chorus moves immediately into the bridge, with both the first harmonic contrast of the song and the abandonment of the ground bass occurring simultaneously on the hypermetric downbeat of measure 17. The bridge section is harmonically and melodically free, introducing new chromatic harmonies that lie outside the D-Mixolydian context that has been established. It runs for the irregular length of five measures, and this effect of hypermetric expansion is increased by the metric expansion in the fifth measure, which shifts from the established 12/8 meter (with four beats) to 18/8 (six beats), adding in effect two additional beats within the compound meter. The last of the six beats is treated as a silent pause for the instruments, but the voice enters with a repetition of the earlier text, "So give me what I want." When we heard this before, it was as the last part of the verse, set musically as an overlapping link to the chorus. Here it introduces the chorus once more, so that the bridge is both preceded and followed by chorus statements. The statement–departure–statement pattern (chorus–bridge–chorus) might be considered a large-scale reflection of the ABA pattern within the chorus itself.

In the chorus, a musical departure clearly coincided with Ndegéocello's lyrical efforts to suggest marriage. If one were to extend that meaning to the ABA pattern of chorus–bridge–chorus, the bridge would similarly be a musical expression of that new social construct. It certainly has the effect of exploration and freedom, and in that sense it provides a moment of musical resistance. However, the form of resistance that is suggested here is not one that engages immediately with the actual force of oppression; rather, all restrictions are forsaken to allow for a complete feeling of release (the ground bass disappears, the hypermetric organization is expanded, the harmonic and mode emphasis shifts dramatically, and the instrumental texture changes to feature a saxophone). There is an assured style to the presentation of this bridge departure, suggesting that with this passage Ndegéocello is offering an affirmative expression of Other identity and desire.

"Mary Magdalene": Verse 2 and Final Chorus Sequence

The second verse develops further the sincere involvement of the subject with her desired Other. As she returns to her original reflective mood, Ndegéocello resumes her spoken form of lyric presentation, singing at only select moments. She begins again with her observations on the object, but these comments are raised to a literary/biblical level. She now explicitly refers to Mary Magdalene, who is attributed faith and innocence ("smile / of a child") as compared with the "unworthy men" to whom she attends. She then makes her appeal that she can offer a more positive identity for Mary ("come and I'll set you free"). This material is all presented as spoken text above four ground-bass statements. She shifts to sung material only in the fifth measure of the section, at a moment in the text when her desire for Mary is expressed as an appeal: "If you must dance, dance for me." The musical gesture to which she sings these words is derived from the earlier verse material, but is really just a fragment of that material. She moves back and forth from C to A, pitches that were part of the verse's melodic pattern, but in verse 1, these two pitches never stood alone without the higher D as a point of reference. The melodic line is apparently free, and does not seem as controlled by the ground bass and its normative melodic pattern. She then returns to spoken text for a reference to God and pure faith, followed by the advice to "close your eyes and dream." That the concern is to close out dominant social systems is confirmed in the next line, "for the world will blind you." This profound recognition of the need to resist social constraints is offered once again to sung text, and here the musical melody begins on A, leaps to D, and comes back to settle on C. In the earlier "dance for me" melody, Ndegéocello avoids D; here, I feel the impact of the D on the word "blind" as a contextually dissonant note, despite its consonant D support. This poignant musical moment is followed by a return to spoken text on the low D^3 for the line "and judge not, so that I may not be judged."

The second verse leads immediately into the chorus, which is once again initiated by the demand "so give me what I want." Juxtaposed with the "judge not" lyrics, I hear this demand ("give me") as an appeal to society for acceptance, rather than as a simple repetition of the earlier sentiment of desire for the Other. The societal references and the "judge not" section create a grave mood for the ensuing chorus–bridge–chorus

165

sequence. The intensity of desire that was developed in the first verse has thus been replaced and balanced by a more reflective social commentary, confirming the sincerity with which Ndegéocello handles her literary theme.

Interpretive Conclusions

In my analysis of the song, I have frequently engaged the concept of musical power or strength. Because strength is relative and subject to evaluation, it is important to reflect on its role in my interpretive conclusions. The lyrics explore sexual power: the power of the subject and the nature of her sexual demands on the Other, but also the power of the Other—at first her weakened power in the role of prostitute, and then her attributed power in the eyes of the subject who holds the Other in sincere and committed desire. The song develops a sexual gaze in which the object is not only permitted but encouraged to assume a position of strength. Ndegéocello uses particular musical strategies to allow this narrative to emerge: the subject's gaze and the object's attributions of power within that gaze are distinguished by spoken versus sung form, each of which bears its own power as a form of musical expression. Within the spoken passages, the musical emphasis exists in the rhythmic presentation of the lyrics—the way in which the lyrics are placed within the metric scheme. In this regard, the singer explores devices such as rhythmic accents on particular words, metric elision, and hypermetric expansion. The application of these special devices can be evaluated as powerful moments in the musical discourse; that is, it is not unusual to say that a metric accent attributes strength to a musical event. Within the sung passages, the musical strategies include the virtuosic elaboration of a basic idea, the realization or denial of expectations, the introduction of dissonance, the impact of resolution, and the exploration of melodic space. Once again, these devices can be evaluated as powerful discursive strategies, permitting the interpretive evaluation of instances of musical strength. Ndegéocello's manipulation of these devices of musical power is noteworthy, because she succeeds in creating a distinct subject and object by associating each with her own musical domain; that is, the subject can celebrate her own discursive power in the domain of rhythm and meter, while the object is granted power in the domain of melody and counterpoint.

The musical ascription of power to both subject and object comprises a significant revision of a conventional construct, the sexual gaze. Ndegéocello's reinterpretation of a construct that is, in essence, an abstract perspective is a vital feature of this song and a significant conduit for her feminist discursive sabotage of race, gender, and desire.

6

P.J. Harvey, *Is This Desire?* (1998)

In fact everyone will agree that desire is not only longing, *a clear and translucent* longing *which directs itself through our body toward a certain object. Desire is defined as* trouble.
—*Jean-Paul Sartre,* Being and Nothingness

Absolute and unapprehensible, an element necessarily lacking, unsatisfied, impossible, misconstrued, an element that is called desire.
—*Jacques Lacan,* Écrits: A Selection

TERRAINS OF TROUBLE: P.J. HARVEY AND THE TOPOGRAPHY OF DESIRE (MÉLISSE LAFRANCE)

P.J. Harvey has long interrogated dominant and accepted modalities of desire through her creative work. While Harvey is routinely tight-lipped about the ultimate "meaning" of her music, a number of aesthetic themes recur in both the visual and musical works she has released for public consumption. From the early albums such as *Four-Track Demos*, *Dry*, and *Rid of Me*, to the later *To Bring You My Love*, Harvey has forged a relatively unprecedented presentation of self and work.[1] This signature presentation consists in representations of her body as bone-thin, gripped by skintight dresses, weighed down by high-heeled shoes and smeared with lipstick and other makeup. Before *Is This Desire?* Harvey's music was often hard to listen to—and her presentations-of-self often hard to look at—for both Harvey's musical and physical presentations dramatized the pain and torment associated with "proper" womanhood.

The countercultural sensibilities that characterized Harvey's earlier work are by no means absent in her 1998 album. While *Is This Desire?* turns away from more narrowly focused reflections on femininity, it expands the scope of Harvey's work to encompass issues related not only to women and their subjective and corporeal formation, but also to how heteronormative modalities of desire have both produced and relied on an acutely cultural ideal of "woman" and "man." I view the works that make up *Is This Desire?* as not only musical works denoting states of want and loss, but also as narratives with widespread cultural implications that seek to unravel contemporary gender constructs and the forms of desire produced by such constructs. Harvey's music profiles narratives inescapably invested with a careful questioning of what present-day societies have come to recognize as "woman," "man," and "desire."

Harvey's interrogation of desire goes beyond questions of who desires and how she or he does so. In *Is This Desire?* Harvey challenges her listeners by refusing to resolve her songs, either musically or thematically. In so doing, it is my contention that Harvey is asking deep-seated questions about whether desire itself can ever reach a point of satisfaction. On the album in question, desire is presented as not just complex in character, but impossible; it can never be seized in its full presence, as it is compulsively migratory, precarious, and almost invariably disappointing. Desire is, for Harvey, constituted by an array of troubled psychic states (such as pain, envy, violence, jealousy, and longing). These states exist alongside more pleasurable, albeit radically temporary, psychic states of happiness and jubilation. In this sense, Harvey's considerations of desire as impossible and of the desiring subject as contradictory or split almost uncannily resemble the theoretical positions of many contemporary philosophers. The tropological similarities between Harvey's presentation of desire and the works of, for example, Jacques Lacan and Jean-Paul Sartre are most interesting and will be discussed at length. Before making such comparisons, however, I shall briefly delineate the basic rudiments of Lacanian and Sartrian notions of desire.

Philosophical Perspectives on Desire: Jacques Lacan and Jean-Paul Sartre

Both Lacan and Sartre figure desire as an impossible project of self-recovery. For Lacan, desire emerges as a result of a fundamental hole within the self that desire attempts to fill at every turn. This hole, this lack, this absence, is established at the moment when the infant is forced out of its harmony with the mother and into the realm of language and signification. Language, for Lacan, is always symptomatic of lack as it proves that the self no longer inhabits the sphere of imaginary mother-child plenitude where language was unknown and indeed had no place.

The loss of the mother produces a split within the subject, for the moment the subject begins to speak (and to inhabit the symbolic realm of society and culture) the subject is forced to repress her desire for the mother and the blissful plenitude the mother represents. The split produced by the loss of the mother epitomizes the introduction of the unconscious, which henceforth serves as an "underground" reservoir for the young subject's repressed desire. Lacan, like his predecessor Sigmund Freud, understands the speaking subject (that is, the subject who has lost) as fundamentally split: no longer whole, but divided by the complicated and often adversarial territories of consciousness and unconsciousness. Toril Moi summarizes,

> The speaking subject that says "I am" is in fact saying "I am [she] who has lost something." . . . The sentence "I am" could therefore best be translated as "I am that which I am not," according to Lacan. This re-writing emphasizes the fact that the speaking subject only comes into existence because of the repression of the desire for the lost mother. To speak as a subject is therefore the same as to represent the existence of repressed desire: the speaking subject *is* lack. (1985, 99–100)

A Lacanian theory of desire suggests that the individual spends her entire life attempting to fill the hole produced by the loss of the mother. These attempts at self-recovery are made manifest in a range of quotidian behaviors, though they are performed most intensely in the context of romantic and sexual rituals. For Lacan, desire for an "other" is not buttressed by the other's intrinsic traits and merits as much as it is by the other's willingness and ability to reflect back to the subject an idealized self.

In formulating desire as constituted fundamentally by a search for an idealized reflection of self, Lacan draws heavily from the work of German idealist G. W. F. Hegel. According to Hegel, desire for an other is in fact desire for a recognition of self. In the terms of Hegelian desire, this is not so much a recognition of the self as the self sees itself, but rather an affirmation of the self as the self wants to be seen. For Hegel, one desires the desire of an other in order to affirm and consolidate one's own ego-ideals and, as such, to reach a point of self-certainty. On this point, Juliet Flower Maccannell explains,

> Since the ultimate value for Hegel is self-consciousness, or at least self-certainty, one's own desire would be autotelic/autoerotic (object-less) in character: desire is finally for oneself. Thus one wants to be a value for the other such that this value equals his quintessential desire, narcissistic in nature, which is the desire for himself. (1992, 64)

If desire is fundamentally a project of self-recovery and consolidation, then one can see why some Hegelians such as Alexandre Kojève (1977) have asserted that all humans will risk their biological lives to satisfy their nonbiological desires. Yet it is precisely because desire is not a biological need (and thus satisfiable) but an unstable psychic agency (and thus unsatisfiable) that it is, according to Hegel, ultimately impossible.

However, even if the other does enable the fulfillment of the subject's ego-centered fantasies, desire remains, according to Lacan, fraught with impossibility. This impossibility is rooted in the fact that the (repressed and unspeakable) euphoria of the subject's infantile attachment to the mother makes any amorous attachment in the realm of the symbolic feel deeply unsatisfying. In this sense, then, the spectre of the mother—or the Other, as Lacan terms it—is present in each and every amorous relation pursued by the subject. The Other and all of the unconscious ecstasy she represents are omnipresent in the affective life of the subject, constantly serving to remind the subject of everything that remains unfulfilled by the other. Hence, the Other always intervenes between the subject and the other, thwarting any potential for the sustained satisfaction of desire. For this reason, Lacan posits that in any dynamic of desire, "what is involved" for the subject "is not the partner, the sexed other, but a phantom" (cited in Benvenuto and Kennedy 1986, 187).

In essence, desire consists in a series of frustrated attempts on the part of the subject to find an other who will restore the subject's lost sense of neonascent wholeness and harmony. Put differently, the subject desires a "unity and completion which it imagines the other can bestow on it" (Grosz 1998, 137). Yet by virtue of the fact that the subject resides inescapably within the sphere of the symbolic (and thus the sphere of language, repression, and the unconscious), the subject is condemned to live as split and incoherent. The only way for the subject to heal its irrevocable split is to leave the symbolic, and this departure is possible only through death. It is for this reason that Freud, and Lacan after him, understand death as the logical end of desire.[2] As Moi explains,

> there can be no final satisfaction of our desire since there is no final signifier or object that can be that which has been lost forever (the imaginary harmony with the mother and the world). If we accept that the end of desire is the logical consequence of satisfaction (if we are satisfied, we are in a position where we desire no more), we can see why Freud, in *Beyond the Pleasure Principle* [(1922) 1991], posits death as the ultimate object of desire—as Nirvana or the recapturing of the lost unity, the final healing of the subject. ([1985] 1995, 101)

To summarize, then, Lacanian theory figures desire as fundamentally impossible, essentially narcissistic, prehistorically repressed, always already deferred, invariably destructive, and by nature unconscious. In addition, the Lacanian framework figures the desiring subject as inevitably split, incoherent, and incomplete. And finally, the desiring subject is, according to Lacan, actually produced by and through loss, lack, and absence. Indeed, the taxing vicissitudes of desire and the states of being they beget are viewed by Lacan as the motivational touchstone of all human behavior, no matter how loving or, conversely, how violent such behavior may appear.

Sartre's conception of desire (1966) both converges with and diverges from that of Lacan in a number of salient ways. In particular, both theorists view love and desire as fundamentally impossible and irresolvable states of consciousness, destined to frustrate the subject absolutely. Unlike Lacan, Sartre does not situate the inevitable impossibility of desire in a failed infant-child relationship, nor does he subscribe to the Freudian theory of the unconscious. He does, however, view the subject as constituted by an essential absence of foundation. While for

Lacan this foundationlessness is termed "lack" and predicated on the loss of the mother, for Sartre it is related to the subject's inability to control the way Others look at and judge her. On this subject, Sartre explains, "the Other looks at me and as such he holds the secret of my being, he knows what I am. Thus the profound meaning of my being is outside of me, imprisoned in an absence" (473).

According to Sartre, the subject's project of self-recovery—that is, of recovering a world in which the subject is not made to be by the look of the other—involves two basic intersubjective strategies. The subject's first strategy consists in an endeavor to assimilate the Other and make the Other an object.[3] By making the Other an object, I preclude the Other from making an object of me. Yet since it is the Other's ability to look at me—her freedom—that makes me be and is the condition of my freedom, reducing the Other to objectness is an inappropriate means of consolidating my being. Invariably, I realize that my first strategy is doomed, and thus I resort to a second one. My second strategy consists in an effort to incorporate the Other's freedom into me without removing its character as freedom, for "if I could identify myself with that freedom which is the foundation of my being-in-itself, I should be to myself my own foundation" (Sartre 1966, 473). I soon discover, however, that this strategy is also doomed, for I cannot absorb the Other's freedom without making an object of the Other. That is, I cannot look at the Other's look without that look becoming meaningless. Once again, my attempt to recover my freedom and establish unity with an Other is dashed. As regards the vicious circularity of the subject's relations with Others, Sartre posits,

> While I attempt to free myself from the hold of the Other, the Other is trying to free himself from mine; while I seek to enslave the Other, the Other seeks to enslave me. We are by no means dealing with unilateral relations with an object-in-itself, but with reciprocal and moving relations. [Concrete] behavior [with Others] must therefore be envisaged within the perspective of conflict. Conflict is the original meaning of being-for-others. (475)

This discussion of Sartrian concrete relations with Others is pertinent to the present discussion, as it underscores the radical impossibility of harmony with an Other.

For Sartre, love and desire constitute two of the primary attitudes toward Others. For Sartre, neither love nor desire must be seen as primarily related to the body. If love and desire were primarily related to the body, they would be easily satisfied, for the body's physiological routes to pleasure are fairly straightforward and self-directing. It is because love and desire are, first and foremost, about ensnaring the freedom or transcendence of the Other in an attempt to consolidate oneself that they become so fraught with complication.

Love, for instance, proves impossible as the lover covets the undying commitment and adoration of the beloved in order to secure its own transcendence. Without this confirmation of love, the lover feels reduced to objectness, as she feels wholly determined by the affective whims (or the look) of the Other. However, if and when the lover receives such confirmation, she grows restless and unsatisfied, because the beloved has become an object. That is, the beloved's freedom—the freedom that made the lover be—evaporates, and hence kills the objective of this amorous relation. Sartre explains,

> The total enslavement of the beloved kills the love of the lover. The end is surpassed; if the beloved is transformed into an automaton, the lover finds himself alone. Thus the lover does not desire to possess the beloved as one possesses a thing; he demands a special type of appropriation. He wants to possess a freedom as freedom. (1966, 478)

Sexual desire is similarly destined to fail. Were it to be simply an affair of bodies, it would be routinely satisfied. Desire, however, is not "all-body." It is, like love, aimed at a "special type of appropriation," one oriented toward the seizure of the beloved's freedom as freedom. But because desire is essentially related to intimate encounters with flesh and sexual relations, desire destroys itself. That is, desire begins by attempting to incarnate the Other's body so as to force her transcendence up to its bodily surface. Once the beloved's transcendence is "playing on the surface" of her body, it may be ensnared by the lover's touch. Yet in incarnating the beloved's body, the lover's desire becomes disoriented and begins focusing only on its own pleasure and satisfaction. In satisfying itself physiologically, desire squanders its chance at ensnaring the Other's freedom.

Both the Lacanian and Sartrian frameworks are based on questionable models and/or appraisals of subjective development. Moreover, they are both highly problematic due to their male-centered, heteronormative tendencies. Despite such admittedly deep-seated problems, these models do give the cultural critic working theoretical apparatuses for the interpretation of P.J. Harvey's album on desire. The fact that both the aforementioned theorists and Harvey appear to conceptualize desire as inherently laden with conflict, violence, frustration, impossibility, and dissatisfaction indicates to me that the thought of Lacan and Sartre is worth working and reworking with respect to the popular musician and the album in question. To do justice to Harvey's work, one must be enabled to think and figure the arduous affective states that Harvey most obviously associates with desire. In my view, the theories I have outlined truly enable an interpreter to make sense of desire and its many by-products as they interact in essential, tense, and negotiated simultaneity.

Having discussed the fundamentals of two major philosophical perspectives on desire, I shall now turn to a consideration of Harvey's music. Before proceeding directly to a reading of *Is This Desire?* however, I shall first situate Harvey's work and persona in the context of mainstream culture and media.

Mass Media Engagements with Is This Desire?

Is This Desire? is peopled primarily by a cast of women. The names and personages of Catherine, Angelene, Joy, Leah, Elise, and Dawn are deployed not only as song titles but as points of entry into explorations of the psychic dimensions of desire among the women in her cast.[4] In addition, there are at least five male characters on this album; three of them remain unnamed and relatively undeveloped (as in "Angelene," "Elise," "No Girl So Sweet"), while the two others appear to be involved in a homosexual tryst ("The Garden"). There can be no denying that the male presence on the album is exiguous when compared to the female presence, and this album certainly could be said to be primarily gyno-centered in its orientation.

While mainstream media may repeatedly scramble to make sense of why Harvey is singing about so many women and so few men, the same media agents are steadfast in their will to read Harvey's work as an incarnation of bizarre and unintelligible feminine angst rooted fundamentally in (failed) heterosexual desire. In that the mainstream media allows itself to work with only very minimal interpretative resources (that is, those based on a hegemonic and patriarchal conception of desire and romantic love), the female characters that make up the album are almost invariably viewed by mainstream critics as gendered cultural misfits: witches, hysterics, spinsters, or simply confused and desperate women.[5]

Regarding the female cast on the album, *Bomb* magazine writes, "Harvey's record *Is This Desire?* is HUNG UP. Obsessed. The women in her songs don't care about who knows that they're staring into the head-lights of Doomed Love" (Reid 1999). In a similar tone, a columnist for the the *Village Voice* wonders, "Are these people warped or what?" (Arnold 1998). About Harvey's character Catherine, *Request* magazine accuses, "The hushed Catherine finds her consumed by homicidal envy, sighing with the self-pitying fervor of a true nut-case."[6] And the *Minneapolis City Pages* writes the following of Harvey's cast of women: "These characters wallow in sin (read: sex) without any transgressive glee. Their desires may be the same as those of Celine Dion fans.... But Polly's princes never come, or if they do, they wind up like the loser of *A Perfect Day Elise* [*sic*]" (Harris 1998).

When the mainstream press is not busy pathologizing the women Harvey writes about, it is equally preoccupied with unreading them and, indeed, diffusing their potentially anti-heteronormative presence on an album so intimately related to desire. In a statement that appears to be fraught with contradiction, the *Financial Times* writes the following about *Is This Desire?*: "Generally, though, the effect is more discomfiting than discouraging. The apparent musical inconsistency is also given some grounding by a lyrical viewpoint that never stands still. Although a cast of women people these songs ('Angelene,' 'A Perfect Day Elise,' 'Catherine')" (Hunter-Tilney 1998). The last sentence appears to have been tacked onto a review that otherwise effaces the gynocentered ori-entation of the album. Yet the next line of the same piece in the *Financial Times* is even more puzzling. In a sentence that stands alone, it reads, "Harvey's focus slides constantly between desirer and desired, first and third person female and male."

In my view, this sort of criticism is an example of how critics who find themselves unable to make Harvey's work "mean" in heterosexual terms resort to clumsily representing it as thick with mystifying tropes of heterosexual love and melancholy. As regards the strategies of unread-ing that went into the production of mainstream Harvey criticism, the periodical *The Westword* (1998) completely elides the potentially homoerotic (sub)text in the song "Catherine." Unable to avoid reference to this stunning piece, the columnist opts to write this at the end of an unrelated and indeed chaotic paragraph: "*Catherine* quietly makes the most of an ominous scenario (Catherine De Barra / you've murdered my thinking / I gave you my heart / you left the thing stinking)."[7] Examples of this kind of unreading abound in the mainstream press about P.J. Harvey.

When it comes to Harvey's persona, mainstream journalism is similarly contestable. Regarding Polly Harvey's persona, the *San Francisco Chronicle* writes, "If Iceland's Bjork is the mercanal diva of art-pop, Polly Jean Harvey is her polar opposite—an Ice Goddess utterly detached from emotion" (Sullivan 1998). *Rolling Stone* is also harshly stereotypical in its depictions of Harvey: "A classic-rock spinster druid in Dr. Marten drag, a demon stewardess on her very own astral plane, Polly Jean Harvey knows she has a great formula.... Harvey makes her deranged fantasies of feminine evil sound like a righteous Saturday night, albeit a bleak and stormy one" (Sheffield 1998, 128). And the following example is perhaps the most shocking. Marrying fragments of sexually coercive rhetoric with images of brutally violent imagery, one columnist writes,

> Polly Jean Harvey is a tease. She knows what we want from her—what we expect—and she knows exactly how long she can toy with us before she has to deliver. When she does, the listener is jolted by both the thrill of irrational desire and the terror of becoming the object of desire. It's an effect she lands with all the subtly [*sic*] of a slasher leaping out from behind the door in a horror flick. (Harris 1998)

From this brief glance at how the mainstream (dis)engages with Harvey, it seems safe to say that her presence disturbs and disrupts. When her lyrics are not being unread by journalists, her persona is being linked to evil and the supernatural. She obviously has something that makes an awful lot of people uncomfortable. In my view, Harvey disrupts because she defies conventional forms of sex-stereotyping. She writes about violence and anger, she shows dominant norms of femininity up for what they do to women when taken to their logical extreme, she writes and produces all of her own records, and remains steadfast in her unwillingness to "explain" her songs' often abstruse character. Taken together, these traits make Harvey a difficult object of interpretation— especially for mainstream media—as she defies the many attributes commonly associated with female musicianship in late-twentieth-century popular music.

Reading Queer Desire in the Work of P.J. Harvey

While I have already explained that I am not interested in author-centered readings as much as I am in reader-centered readings, I feel that I should reiterate this position with specific reference to reading lesbian and gay desire in the works of P. J. Harvey. To be sure, I have never seen evidence of Harvey publicly identifying with lesbianism or bisexuality. Yet when analyzing her work on *Is This Desire?*—work laden with homosexual connotative value—it seems irresponsible to make nothing of such subtexts simply because the author has not publicly entertained the idea of lesbianism or bisexuality. I thus share the following position with Jennifer Rycenga when she discusses her engagement with P.J. Harvey :

> As a lesbian listener, musician, composer and scholar, I am intrigued by my strongly lesbian response to the music of three leading women composer/performers: Kate Bush, P.J. Harvey, and Tori Amos. This essay addresses how their music can be heard lesbian-i-cally, without appropriating them as pseudolesbians or critiquing their ambivalent allegiance to heterosexuality (which all three of them criticize with a mercilessness that would be labeled instantly as man-hating if sung out by a lesbian), and without suggesting that a lesbian-ic hearing is limited only to lesbians. (1997, 204)

I intend to work within the kind of framework Rycenga has delineated. Indeed, this framework allows me to read lesbian and gay desire in many of the works on *Is This Desire?* without making any insinuations regarding the author's sexual identity or her compositional intentions. Reading lesbian desire in this text is a crucial task, as it has not been performed by mainstream critics and thus remains a gap in our appreciation of both Harvey's music and the multifaceted complexity of her texts.[8] Hence, I shall turn now to a consideration of Harvey's portrayal of both straight and queer desire on the album in question.

SELECTED READINGS OF THE WORKS ON *IS THIS DESIRE?*

Is This Desire? is characterized by at least two fairly stable thematic ensembles. One of these ensembles consists of a *literal* presentation of desire as insatiable, impossible, and transient. This presentation is articulated through the use of first-person narratives related to, for instance, failed or unsatisfying relationships and/or lovers who flee their beloveds in search of something more—something they appear to have consistently lacked in their amorous encounters. The second thematic ensemble consists of what I view as a *metaphorical* presentation of desire as unapprehensible, unattainable, and in constant flux. This presentation is achieved through the deployment of specific images connoting vast but always already fleeting beauty and opportunity. Such images, which appear with unwavering frequency throughout the album, relate to water, river, wind, open road, coastline, and light. I will show that these images underscore desire as incessantly, and frustratingly, lateral in movement and passing in character. As will become apparent, the songs that I consider in this chapter bear traces of both thematics.

"Lays Open like a Road": The Transience of Desire in "Angelene"

The song "Angelene" begins with the assertion: "My first name's Angelene / Prettiest mess you've ever seen." In these first two phrases, Harvey foregrounds her protagonist's identity as bound to her "pretty" femaleness. She also discusses her protagonist in the terms of a "mess" and immediately prompts the listener to wonder why the protagonist views herself in such terms. We learn in the next two lines ("Love for money is my sin / Any man calls I'll let him in") that the protagonist deals in purely bodily desire and is cavalierly indiscriminate about those with whom she sleeps. The listener may conclude at this point that Angelene considers herself a pretty mess because she lives a life of random encounters—a messy, disorganized, and unmanageable libidinal life—linked fundamentally to the performance of a particular femininity.

In the following phrases ("Rose is my color and white / Pretty mouth, green my eyes"), Harvey once again anchors the description of her protagonist within a signifying economy of feminine aesthetics. Further, the fact that the protagonist associates herself with the quintessentially innocent and virginal colors rose and white suggests a longing on the part of the protagonist to uphold the mores of "appropriate" femininity. In my view, through these few references to Angelene's body, Harvey subtly brings into relief the ways in which women are valued and admired for their performances of conventional femininity (such as their ability to make themselves up and relate themselves to an infantilized and virginal innocence through signifiers of color).

The protagonist goes on to declare, "I've seen men come and go / But there'll be one who will collect my soul and come to me / Two thousand miles away / He walks upon the coast / Two thousand miles away / Lays open like a road." At this point, the narrative moves away from an exclusive consideration of the protagonist's femininity. Certainly the protagonist's need to have her soul "collected" by a presumably more morally upright male other is no doubt meant to represent an internalization of patriarchal norms of sexuality that position the prostitute as fallen and decadent. However, what remains of new interest in these phrases is Harvey's rendering of "true" desire. Indeed, the desire the protagonist wants, the desire that is positioned as satisfied and complete, is described as residing "two thousand miles away." This veritable and complete desire, then, is in fact a "present absence"—something the protagonist knows to be unattainable by virtue of its insurmountable distance but nevertheless holds up as her affective ideal. This allegedly true desire is also couched in terms of impossible, unstable vastness and transience. That desire is associated so markedly with a coastline and an open road—two images that connote geographic enormity and endless lateral movement, respectively—are to me clear indicators that desire is being conceptualized here as an irresistible pursuit constituted by constant, incessant movement. Such a view of desire can be mapped onto the Lacanian thesis that desire is a series of distances, all of which the subject will inevitably travel but in none of which the subject will ever find completion or satisfaction. Moreover, the notion of the present absence—of the desire that exists but is unattainable because it lies "two thousand miles away"—is also congruent with the Lacanian notion of the omnipresent Other for whom the subject waits and searches perpetually. The open road boasts the possibility of desire, but only if the protagonist is able to brave immense and most likely untravelable distances.

It is worth interrogating the significance of using an open road as a symbolic conduit to desire. First of all, a road is itself a symbol of movement. However, an *open* road is even more reminiscent of Lacanian theories of desire, as it connotes movement without determinate destinations of any kind. Further, a road is something across which one tends to move laterally—across and on the surface of terrain. It is not a vertical ascent or descent but a horizontal and superficial form of passage. Again, this kind of imagery is ripe for Lacanian interpretation, as desire is defined by Lacan as structured first and foremost by compulsive migration. And, it is worth mentioning, the song "Angelene" is saturated not only with the lateral movement presupposed by the road, but with lateral movement from birth to death ("people getting born and dying"), coast to coast ("Two thousand miles away / He walks upon the coast"), and man to man ("I've seen men come and go").

It is also worth interrogating Harvey's choice of the coast as a symbolic passageway to fulfilled desire. When one considers the properties of a coastline, one soon realizes that it is subject to constant movement and change as it is transformed by every wave and tide. While coastlines may appear relatively stable, a deeper reflection concedes that they are anything but fixed. Their borders change with each aquatic fluctuation, and their bodies vascillate constantly in width and distance. Finally, coastlines prohibit any meaningful long-term or complete marking by those who make contact with them, for even the most determined set of footprints will be washed away eventually. This sort of interrogation of Harvey's literary devices reveals the instability and impermanence that suffuses her depictions of desire.

It is interesting to note that Harvey's protagonist speaks of the realization of her true desire as "joy untold." That the joy associated with her fulfilled desire is positioned as untold recalls Lacan's assertion that desire is beyond conscious articulation. It is, for Lacan, "barred or repressed from articulation" (Grosz 1998, 65), since it is produced through repression and consequently cannot be known. Lacanian desire is quite literally unspeakable, and as such resembles the desire for which Angelene hopes and waits interminably.

I have argued that in "Angelene," Harvey subtly brings into relief the ways in which women are valued and admired for their performances of dominant femininity. I have also argued that, if viewed from a broadly Lacanian perspective, the song "Angelene" serves as an impressive commentary on the inevitable impossibility, instability, and transience of desire. As will be shown in the following interpretations, these themes are frequently used on this album.

"In Time I'd Have Won You": The Vicissitudes of Desire in "Catherine"

The song "Catherine" can be read as a powerful ode to a woman with whom the narrator is in love. For the purposes of this interpretation— and because I think the intratextual evidence supports it—I shall figure the narrator as female and read the desire in this song as particularly lesbian in its orientation.

Harvey's piece "Catherine" opens with the phrases "Catherine de Barra, you've murdered my thinking / I gave you my heart, you left the thing stinking / I'd shake from your spell, if it weren't for my drinking / the wind bites more bitter with each light of morning."[9] In this passage, the narrator evokes desperate images of longing, pain, and absence, leading the listener to the conclusion that such states of affect on the part of the narrator are due to the loss and/or the unattainability of Catherine. Indeed, the fact that Harvey chose to name the beloved Catherine de Barra is puzzling enough to warrant further discussion.

Barra is a small Scottish island situated toward the southern end of the Outer Hebrides. It is separated from larger Scottish islands by the Sound of Barra. Barra's landscape is therefore not difficult to imagine: it is wholly surrounded by bodies of water and constantly buffetted by bitter winds. The island of Barra, with its harsh climate and its history of struggle and agony, is the perfect setting for a Harvey piece, just its geographical situation and its dark, stormy weather effuse pain, isolation, and tragedy.[10] In my view, the significance of Catherine's surname is related to the harsh legacy of Barra's climate. That is, for those familiar with Barra, this surname is meant to act as yet another sign of the dark mood of impossibility associated with the narrator's desire for the beloved.

In the lyrics transcribed above, the reader is unsure as to whether there was actually a love affair between the narrator and the beloved Catherine. All the reader knows at this point is that the narrator is profoundly invested in Catherine and appears to be suffering without her. The following verse, however, thickens the narrator's story with even more emotional volatility. It reads, "I envy the road, the ground you tread under / I envy the wind, your hair riding over / I envy the pillow your head rests and slumbers / I envy to murderous envy your lover." While mainstream critics have been quick to see this last verse foremost as a homicidal fantasy, I am hard-pressed to agree unequivocally with such an assessment. I do not see any *unproblematic* evidence of homicidal phantasmagoria here. What I do see is a narrator who is sick with frustrated desire over the inaccessibility of her beloved Catherine—and it is this frustrated desire that leads her to dream of destruction. This destruction, however, is not straightforward, nor is it necessarily carried out.

The narrator is overcome with desire for Catherine, and in order to convey this at once overwhelming and desperate desire, the narrator textualizes her envy as murderous. I do not believe that the narrator has any simple or steadfast plans to destroy Catherine or her lover—as some may initially presume. It is my view that the phrase "I envy to murderous envy your lover" is one of the most arresting and complicated lyrical fragments on the album because it expresses two seemingly oppositional states of consciousness. On the one hand, this phrase crystallizes the jealousy, anger, and destruction that can overcome an individual who has been robbed of her object of desire. This phrase brings into relief what Freud, in *Mourning and Melancholia*, has frequently described as a perfectly human response to destroy that which threatens to imperil the ego's stability. In the narrator's case, that which threatens to destroy the ego's stability is Catherine's love for a third party. On the other hand, however, the "murderous envy" that consumes the narrator may also be self-directed. That is, the narrator may feel—in the face of what seems to be an irrecoverable and indeed irreparable loss—the urge to murder herself. It is worth mentioning that, when viewed from a psychoanalytic perspective, it is not terribly surprising to see death and desire so closely linked. As I discussed earlier, both Freud and Lacan see the death drive as one of the two pivotal instincts characterizing humankind.[11] Both theorists also see death as the logical end of desire, for self-annihilation consists of the only strategy that can possibly heal the insatiable and tormented subject.

In the ensuing passage, the narrator declares, "'til the light shines on me / I damn to hell every second you breathe / 'til the light shines on me." Not surprisingly, some critics have also seen this lyrical fragment as a homicidal wish on the part of the narrator. I would posit, however, that this passage is far from a straightforward homicidal wish. In my view, the aforementioned phrases are once again an expression of the narrator's uninhabitable anguish. What the narrator appears to be damning here is the disproportionate amount of pain borne by her person—a pain so intense that it resembles an excursion into hell. The narrator feels deeply wronged by whatever may or may not have transpired between her and Catherine de Barra. Consequently, the narrator—who appears to be growing increasingly disconsolate—resents any happiness experienced by her beloved. In my view, this passage is not a transparent wish for Catherine's death. It is, instead, the narrator's desperate wish for the psychic and corporeal regeneration that only light and happiness can induce.

The final lyrical installment reads as follows: "Oh my Catherine / for your eyes smiling / and your mouth singing / with time I'd have won you/with time I'd have won you / for your mouth singing." This moment is interesting as it sees a move from an acutely sombre musical style to a more resolved and pleasing one. It also marks a considerable lyrical turnaround for the narrator. While most of the song showcases the narrator's disdain for her beloved's happiness, this passage profiles the narrator's enormous tenderness for Catherine. Indeed, this instance sees the narrator recalling the beauty of Catherine's face and body and couching such recollections in warm and tranquil terms. The rather rapid and dramatic musical resolution of the piece does, however, beg a number of questions. While Lori will discuss the peculiarly musical dynamics of this moment in the song's development, I am interested in what takes place lyrically. There can be little doubt that the last section of the piece appears to signal some sort of extraordinary moment of altered consciousness.

It could be argued that this instance sees the narrator coming to grips with her love for Catherine as well as becoming able—for the first time—to gain some peaceful distance from the hurt produced by her relationship (be it real or imagined) with Catherine. That is, it sees the narrator assessing her love for Catherine retrospectively and concluding that—given more time—she would have eventually won the affections of the beloved. It could also be argued, however, that the narrator is articulating a sort of fantasy of fulfilled desire. Lori's analysis will confirm that the musical emphasis at this point signifies exactly that. This fantasy does not, however, mean that the thematics of desire have been resolved. If anything, the fantasylike musical transition and the rapidity with which it occurs make the intended resolution appear apocryphal.

The minor to major transition of this musical moment tells the reader something else about the vicissitudes of desire. That Harvey's narrator experiences her desire as a volatile oscillation between hatred and love intimates that these two states of affect exist simultaneously. The rapidity with which the lyrical and musical transitions take place at this juncture is evidence of the intimate coexistence of seemingly oppositional states of affect. The swift transition from anger to jubilation at the end of "Catherine," then, does not necessarily constitute a resolution of the protagonist's immense longing. All it truly evinces, in fact, is a testament to the vicissitudinal nature of desire.

"She Went out Looking for Someone": Searching for Fulfilled Desire in "My Beautiful Leah"

While it is a rather short piece, the song "My Beautiful Leah" articulates the sensibilities of lost and insatiable desire in a most arresting fashion. Its plot is established through the first-person narrative of the protagonist, who claims to be searching desperately for a vanished beloved. While recounting his story to a third party, the protagonist, who could be either male or female, says of the beloved Leah, "She was always so needed / Said I have no one / Even as I held her / She went out looking for someone."[12] In these few lines, Harvey's protagonist brings into relief Leah's compulsively lacking and migratory desire—a desire that searches for something more complete even as it endeavors to satisfy itself. In the final phrases of the song, the protagonist reveals the utterances made by Leah before she left. The protagonist avows, "It never leaves my mind / the last words she said / 'If I don't find it this time / Then I'm better off dead.'" Again, Harvey's bereft lover discusses the torment Leah professes to endure as she searches incessantly for fulfilled desire. These phrases also see Leah linking the impossible quality of desire to a drive toward death. In this song, then, Harvey crafts a story of two individuals suffering from lost love: the protagonist, who grieves for the absence of Leah; and Leah, who grieves for the loss of an unattainable and ultimate desire. The sensibilities of the song "My Beautiful Leah" can therefore be said to resemble the Lacanian and Sartrian positions related to desire as a constant and viciously circular struggle toward subjective consolidation and completion.

Interpretive Summary

What one sees, then, when one analyzes the work of Harvey, is at least one consistant leitmotif: unsatisfied desire. This leitmotif materializes through narratives of lost and tormented loves, as well through images of impossible and transient desire. "Angelene," "Catherine," and "My Beautiful Leah" are just three of the many songs on *Is This Desire?* that recount tales of the almost unliveable instability and insatiability of desire.

∞∞∞∞∞

THE CRAFTING OF DESIRE: MUSICAL VOICE AND MUSICAL EMBODIMENT (LORI BURNS)

P.J. Harvey crafts her songs as miniature dramatic narratives, using poetic and musical devices that captivate the listener and command both an intellectual attentiveness as well as a visceral response. In the domains of production style, instrumental and vocal techniques, as well as musical design and structure, Harvey fashions for each song an original sonic experience to complement her strange and vivid poetry.

Production. Harvey's CDs are rife with nasty hums, buzzing, distortion in the guitars, and extreme high and low volumes. It is as if the equipment is not properly plugged in, or as if the technician has not bothered to set the volume controls at a balanced level. However, this production style is surely deliberate and constitutes an essential feature of P.J. Harvey's sound. It is not a slick, highly produced sound; indeed, that is probably precisely what she is avoiding. The listener is confronted with the musicians and the problems of producing music in a very "immediate" way, such that we cannot simply treat this as musical entertainment.

Instrumental Techniques. Another element of the musical style that contributes to this ideal of musical "confrontation" is the deliberate exploitation of unique instrumental and vocal effects. Each song has its own distinctive profile, an original sound: that is, Harvey creates a musically "descriptive" setting, a lucid effect through a vocal strategy, textural arrangement, rhythmic pattern, or instrumental gesture, and then that distinctive material is repeated and developed. The listener's attention is seized by the undeniable force of the song's musical impact. The effect might be the walking electric bass (highly distorted), doubled in the synthesizer as a low accompaniment to Harvey's quiet vocal presentation in "Electric Light," or the highly rhythmic percussion texture as an accompaniment to the strained wails of the singer in "Joy."

Vocal Techniques. Harvey explores a wide range of vocal strategies. In "The Wind," she whispers, her voice recorded with a high compression so that we hear every breath, sibilant, and consonant and vowel perfectly.

One has the sense that she is controlling the placement of every syllable and word ending. In "My Beautiful Leah," Harvey uses a growly, low register in a monotonous melodic pattern to suggest the sound of a young male voice, in order to adopt that persona. At times her voice has a high, thin soprano quality, at other times a rich, low alto. In "A Perfect Day Elise," her voice is recorded with the effect that she is enclosed, but at the same time her voice is layered with an octave doubling. Some of her melodies are long-breathed and lyrical; others are insistent and repetitive. She is a versatile performer, who privileges the meaning of her music over a consistent vocal aesthetic. Inconsistency is a valuable tool here, because it allows her to develop a wide range of sonic possibilities, equal to the wide range of social possibilities that she explores. With each song on the album, the listener is caught in a unique web, entrapped by a compelling tale.

Musical Design and Structure. Musical structure plays a crucial part in the communication of Harvey's stories. Each song establishes a particular musical framework by repeating a short fragment with a distinctive harmonic, melodic, and rhythmic profile. There is a minimalist quality to her work, a shrewd use of small-cell repetition and careful manipulation. As the story develops, textural shifts and subtle musical transformations contribute to the narrative. To striking effect, Harvey sometimes steps out of the established framework to develop a new idea; these contrasts have lyrical significance. In the vocal part, there is little conventional melodic content: her songs are not "tunes" with accompaniment. As a result of this musical style, the lyrics emerge clearly, but I would not go so far as to say that the words have primacy, because the music is so uniquely presented in each song. What we experience are two powerful forces working together to make an artistic statement. I would like to stress the original content of each song: as Richard Middleton would describe them, these songs are "undercoded"; that is, they do not draw upon conventions that a listener would have heard in many other songs.

The songs that I have chosen to analyze here are "Catherine," "The Garden," and "Is This Desire?" My analytic purpose is to illustrate P.J. Harvey's perspicacious manipulation of her musical materials to explore the human condition of desire, which is the central subject of the album. With these three songs, Harvey explores three different sex/gender relationships—"Catherine" is a song that can be interpreted from a lesbian perspective, "The Garden" features a male homoerotic scene, and "Is This Desire?" is a heterosexual story. Although the sexual orientations are not the same, all three of these songs convey a similar message of unsatisfied desire.

My work here in this chapter, for this particular artist, illuminates the value of analytic attention to the details of the instrumental and vocal texture in combination with the harmonic and contrapuntal strategies. As I attend to these details, I shall invoke my theoretical category of *musical "voice" and dramatic function*. In order to capture, in music-analytical writing, the story that is recounted in each song, I find it most productive to interpret the emergent vocal/instrumental drama as a musical embodiment of the characters and their visceral experiences.

"CATHERINE"

This song explores the desire that the subject feels for a woman, Catherine, who has another lover. In the verse and chorus, the subject's desire is portrayed in negative contexts: she is envious and bitter. However, the coda shifts perspective to explore the more positive aspects of her desire as she imagines it fulfilled. The musical elements of melody and motivic structure are manipulated to depict these contrasting connotations of obsessive and unrequited love versus the fantasy of fulfilled desire. Through this structural contrast, Harvey accomplishes her critical goal of showing that desire is a complex condition.

"Catherine": Introduction

A twelve-measure introduction establishes the drum and guitar material that will be heard for most of this song. The drums begin with a steady repeated one-measure pattern in 2/4 time, for four measures. The guitar then enters, accompanied by the continuing drum pattern (transcribed in figure 6.1). The guitar plays a two-measure pattern based on B-minor harmony, heard four times. The pattern basically repeats a B-minor chord, but in the inner voice of the guitar chord, a melodic motive emerges, oscillating back and forth between D and C$\sharp$, then moving up to E before settling again on D. As a melodic outline, this pattern is repetitive and "narrow" in melodic focus. The introductory phrase comprises the repetition of this material, creating an even, static, monotonous effect. Because the guitar pattern forms the basis of the introduction, the verses, and the linking material, we hear this material for a large portion of the song; it is heard continuously until the first statement of the chorus (which introduces a new harmonic pattern) and then returns for the link and the repetition of the second verse. The emphatic presence of the guitar pattern suggests that it will carry an associative meaning in the song, but a first hearing of the introduction leaves that meaning unclarified.

"Catherine": Verse

After the twelve repetitive measures of introduction, the voice makes a startling and unsettling entry. Harvey enters off the beat; that is, one eighth-note beat late, creating one measure that is best understood in 5/8 time as opposed to 2/4. Her entry, transcribed in figure 6.2, is made even more obscure by the fact that she sings two sets of triplet eighths in each measure, against the duple subdivisions in the guitar. In the second vocal measure, the triplets continue, but she now sings on the downbeat, creating a clear triplet subdivision of a 2/4 measure.

Harvey's melodic gesture is a one-measure pattern that is heard six times, followed by two measures that offer relief through a change of melodic pattern, moving to a cadence (transcribed in figure 6.3). The vocal pattern is based on the melodic gesture F–E–D–E–B; the F to B outline is a dissonant diminished fifth against the B-minor triad in the guitar.[13] When the cadence is created at the end of the phrase, it is with a change to C, then B♭ harmony. This is an unusual harmonic progression: the C-major harmony could be explained as a "phrygian" half step above the tonic B minor, but the B♭ is a half step below the tonic, which is not a conventional harmonic relationship. The voice appears to direct this shift from B to C to B♭ by moving from B to C on the downbeat of the seventh measure of the vocal line, and then from C to B♭ on the downbeat of the cadential measure. Thus the voice appears to be in control of the direction the music will take, although that direction is unconventional and unexpected. In verse 2 (which is heard twice), the harmonic pattern for this cadence is the phrygian progression from C major to B minor (without B♭).

The lyrics of the verse establish the narrator's feelings of obsessive desire for Catherine, an unrequited desire that results in feelings of bitterness (verse 1, line four: "the wind bites more bitter"), and jealousy (verse 2, line four: "I envy to murderous envy your lover").[14] Musically, there are several ways in which the vocal line could be interpreted as

FIGURE 6.1 "Catherine" (from Introduction)

FIGURE 6.2 "Catherine" (Verse Opening)

"distraught" in relation to the instrumental backup: the voice enters in the wrong place (beat two, creating a 5/8 measure); the voice is in triplets against the duple subdivisions, an unusual strategy for popular music; the voice emphasizes the dissonant and unstable diminished-fifth F to B against the instrumental B-minor harmony with perfect-fifth F♯; and the voice introduces the chromatic and unrelated pitches C and B♭ at the cadence. At this point in the song, it is unclear exactly how to interpret the relationship between the vocal line and the guitar pattern, or what the background guitar pattern means to the subject: Is it an element of her own thoughts or something external? The ensuing chorus, however, does provide a better understanding of the relationship between the guitar and voice.

"Catherine": Chorus

Figure 6.4 transcribes the first four measures of the chorus, which begins immediately following the second verse. The guitar now has the progression E–D–B minor (a four-measure pattern with the final tonic chord lasting two measures). The vocal rhythms are based on duple subdivisions, and are thus in agreement with the accompaniment. The four-measure vocal phrase parses into two subphrases, the first emphasizing the fifth of the tonic, F♯, and the second emphasizing the lower part of the B-minor triad, B and D. However, the fifth that Harvey sings is still not a perfect fifth, F♯, but is somewhere between F♯ and F. The lyrics and music of the four-measure phrase are repeated, creating an eight-measure chorus.

Even though the original guitar motive is not present in the chorus, the lyrics here might offer an explanation of that prominent material; that is, the negative thoughts of the chorus provide an important context for the statements of desire articulated in the verses. The message of the chorus is that until her desire is requited, the narrator will "damn to hell every second" that Catherine breathes. Her desire is on her mind constantly, with this compulsion as a driving force of her existence. During the verses, which express her desire for Catherine, the singer simultaneously needs to represent the frustration that exists, in her mind, "every second." The tension felt between the voice and the guitar is thus the internal psychological tension experienced by the subject of the song: this is not an uncomplicated desire, but rather is overshadowed by her

wind bites more bit-ter with each light of mor-ning

FIGURE 6.3 "Catherine" (Verse 1 Cadence)

'til the light___ shines on me___ I damn to hell—ev-ry se-cond you___ breathe_

FIGURE 6.4 "Catherine" (Chorus Opening)

obsessive feelings. Harvey artfully represents this psychological tension through the musical drama played out between the voice and the guitar.

"Catherine": Coda

The second statement of the chorus is extended, such that the text idea "'til the light shines on me / I damn to hell every second you breathe" is heard three full times, followed by a partial fourth statement. The incomplete final statement stops on the personal pronoun, "me," and lingers there for one and a half measures, creating the longest held vocal note in the song. The part of the chorus text that is cut off is the negative content of the phrase ("I damn to hell..."), thus the chorus concludes with an optimistic reflection, "'til the light shines on me," and ushers in the gentle introspective mood of the coda.

The coda is a remarkable section of the song, as it introduces entirely new material in the music and lyrics. It is also proportionately long, lasting roughly one-third of the song's overall time. Figure 6.5 transcribes the first four measures of the coda. The guitar, after having such a prominent role in the song, finally ceases its pattern and quietly improvises around the harmony of G major for the remainder of the song. The main instrumental focus now is the synthesizer, which descends melodically in smooth quarter-note values G–F♯–E–D to a long-held B. Against this prominent line, the voice creates a counterpoint, descending as well in the pattern D–C♯–B–A. The synthesizer's line outlines the harmony of G, but the voice's melodic outline does not stay consonant with that harmony. Harvey moves from D, as fifth of G, down to the A. The melodic arrest on A sounds incomplete, as if it ought to resolve, either down to G or up to B.

The coda transports the listener from one musical and lyrical aesthetic to another; thus it is important to reflect on its meaning and message. The most striking change is that the coda drops the guitar motive, the material that I interpreted as a representation of the negative connotations of the protagonist's frustrated desire, a musical reminder of the thought ("damn to hell") that exists constantly on her mind. In the coda, we are removed from that context through new instrumental patterns, vocal patterns, and harmony, as well as smoother rhythms. Now she reflects, in a seemingly dreamy state, on the positive potential of her desire for Catherine. She imagines her "eyes smiling," her "mouth singing," for "with time [she]'d have won" Catherine. With this section of

FIGURE 6.5 "Catherine" (Coda Opening)

the song, the negative connotations of obsessive desire disappear, and we have only the positive representation of desire. As Mélisse established with her analysis, this section represents a fantasy of fulfilled desire.

"THE GARDEN"

The lyrics of this song rewrite the story of Adam and Eve in the garden in order to explore male homoerotic desire.[15] The lyrics are structured to place emphasis on the characters of the *subject* who is reflecting on desire, and the *Other* who enters into the garden, sharing an experience (presumably sexual) with the subject but then mysteriously departing, leaving the subject—as he began—alone in the garden. Once again, the theme of the song is a desire that is ultimately unresolved. Even when the desire is consummated in the song, it is problematized as "trouble taking place." This "trouble" is inferred not only to be a social response to homoeroticism, but also to be that very form of unfulfilled desire that P.J. Harvey is interrogating in this album. The music plays a significant role in the representation of these characters and their shared experience. Through a careful assignment of instrumental roles and their interaction, the music narrates the sexual plot that is only implied in the lyrics. Thus, musical texture and instrumental division of work will be primary in my analytic emphasis.

"The Garden": Verses 1 and 2

Verse 1 gives us the subject walking alone in a garden, reflecting on his being in the world; his "sad love song" is a primary expression for that reflection—in other words, his desire. The garden is a closed or contained space, and the night and the stars surround him, thus also closing him in. The songbird and the wings are symbolic of freedom, possibly here curtailed. The music for the verse is sparse. The voice is accompanied by a fretless bass guitar and drums. The drums provide one layer, setting a particular stage for the musings of the subject. The guitar and voice are more intricately bound as a unit (together forming another layer) through their use of the same motivic material. The guitar appears to be, in fact, the musical embodiment of the subject. Harvey's voice (a female voice) narrates the story, but I hear the role of the male subject to be personified by the guitar.

Harvey uses minimal melodic and harmonic content to create her subject. The voice and guitar work with the same melodic cell or motive in various elaborations and rhythmic presentations. The first motive begins on the tonic G and moves to its third B♭ and second-degree A (see figure 6.6). The voice introduces the pattern in an anacrusic upbeat and in an embellished form to present the first line of text: "And he was walking in the garden." The guitar, however, presents the pattern, beginning on the downbeat, with a clear rhythmic profile, without melodic embellishment, and repeats the pattern for several measures. The guitar's version has such a strong motivic profile that I hear it to be projecting the role of subject. The motivic material changes for the second half of the verse, when "the stars come out," but the process is similar: the voice elaborates and rhythmically varies a melodic pattern, now a rising gesture with a major third, G–B♮–C, while the bass repeats the same two-measure unit, G–B♮–E♭, with a clear rhythmic profile. The rising gesture of this second motive (to C in the voice and to E♭ in the bass) creates a feeling of anticipation or musical antecedent, to be followed immediately by a second verse, which will introduce a new narrative element.

The second verse introduces "another," or rather an Other, who shares the protagonist's identity ("another with his lips"). Sexual desire is suggested, and invitations are offered ("Won't you come and be my lover?"), but it is only, at this stage, a *promise* of fulfillment ("I will give you gold and mountains"). When the second verse introduces the Other ("there inside the garden, came another"), the piano enters with a syncopated and dissonant chord (A–D–G) that is full of musical promise (see figure 6.7). That is, its offbeat rhythmic placement and dissonance suggest the potential for movement. We hear the piano chord's syncopated entry at the beginning of each vocal phrase, after which it is sustained throughout the phrase. At the same time, an organ (synthesized) enters with a melodic line that is based on the very first melodic motive (G–B♭–A). Thus, the lyrical Other is musically represented by the keyboard sound, the piano being a clear embodiment of the Other, and the organ having a more general role in the communication of desire that is the theme of this verse. At the end of the second verse, the piano makes one small change to its chordal pattern. Just after the lyrics "if you stay a while with me," the piano moves the highest note of its three-note chord up one step (G to A), an anticipatory gesture that suggests that the piano is about to fulfill expectations. Thus, verses 1 and 2 establish the setting,

FIGURE 6.6 "The Garden" (Verse Opening)

FIGURE 6.7 "The Garden" (Verse 2 Opening)

the theme of desire, and the two characters (the subject in verse 1 and the Other in verse 2). The music and lyrics both establish a sense of anticipation, setting the stage for the chorus to fulfill or deny expectations.

"The Garden": Chorus

The chorus expresses the fulfillment of desire, although it is ascribed a negative connotation as "trouble taking place." The lyrics only imply that the desire is fulfilled, but the music creates an explicit union through the clever use of the guitar and the piano, as the personification of the subject and the Other, respectively. Here, they "move" together in total agreement. Although it is a difficult musical gesture to perform, these two instruments move in perfect union. The gesture, shown in figure 6.8, is a rhythmically syncopated pattern, with distinctive rhythmic repetition, articulated in warm parallel tenths between the upper voice of the piano and the bass. The melodic material is based on the first melodic motive, but rearranged to move A–G–B♭ in the piano and F–E♭–G in the bass. It is a strikingly unusual musical gesture, and thus commands our attention. After two statements of the pattern, establishing the union, the voice sings "ah" on pitches belonging to the dominant harmony (F♯–A–D), the first such harmonic change in the entire song (see figure 6.9). Against the voice's pattern, the piano takes the same melodic line, but draws it out in longer note values, while at the same time continuing to move through the repeated and syncopated rhythmic pattern that articulates the melodic line A–G–B♭. The guitar moves again in rhythmic unity with the piano chords, but the melodic and harmonic emphasis changes here from parallel thirds to a more independent contrapuntal relationship. The bass moves D–F–G, suggesting dominant–tonic movement (without leading tone), against the piano's A–G–B♭. There is a sense of harmonic resolution here, but the prominent F♯–A–D (dominant harmony) pattern in the voice and in the higher register of the piano does not resolve harmonically to a tonic.

"The Garden": Verse 3 and Final Chorus

Following the chorus, the third and final statement of the verse begins with the lovers still in the garden. The piano and bass continue to play material derived from their union, but they are no longer in rhythmic or contrapuntal agreement (see figure 6.10). The first half of this verse sug-

FIGURE 6.8 "The Garden" (Chorus Opening)

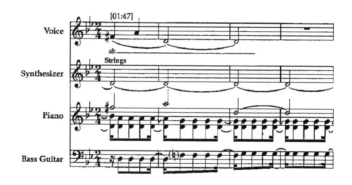

FIGURE 6.9 "The Garden" (from Chorus)

gests that they are still together, although beginning to separate, and at the end of the fourth line of the lyrics, the subject finds himself alone. At that point, the piano dramatically cuts out and the bass is left alone. When he realizes he is alone, he becomes aware again (as he was in the first verse) of the garden's enclosure and containment of him (the wind gathers around him). In the instrumental texture, the entry of the wind is represented by the entry of the strings (synthesized), which take over for the organ melody that represented the subject's sexual desire.

After this final verse, there is a sudden drop back to the drum texture that introduced the song. Several measures of drums form a link that clears the sonic stage for the final statement of the chorus. The final chorus brings us back to the fulfillment of the desire, but this sounds (after the hollow linking passage) like a distant memory. The final chorus concludes with the "ah" section, ending the song on dominant harmony. This dominant is both resolved and unresolved: it is resolved in the piano and bass counterpoint, but unresolved in the voice and upper piano melody. Thus the song ends with a question, a lack of clear resolution, in keeping with the concept of "troubled" desire.

"IS THIS DESIRE?"

This is the final song of the album, one that presents its own individual narrative while at the same time offering a broader reflection on the central interrogation of the album. The lyrics of the song rewrite the story of Mary and Joseph's travel to Bethlehem.[16] The CD liner confirms the biblical context by providing both a picture of Mary and Joseph as well as a quotation from the Bible.[17] In this revision of the story, Mary is replaced by Dawn, and the couple's interest in finding a place to rest for the night is not for Dawn to give birth, but for Dawn and Joseph to consummate their desire. The verses and pre-chorus establish the scene and the characters, and develop the narrative of this intense moment in their relationship, while the chorus offers a reflection on the nature of their desire: "Is this desire enough, to lift us higher, to lift above?" This question can be received as a concluding question to all of the songs on the album, thus to all of the individual situations portrayed on the album. My analysis will discuss the musical meaning of the song both from the perspective of the individual song as a closed text, and as the concluding element of a larger artistic statement.

FIGURE 6.10 "The Garden" (Verse 3 Opening)

FIGURE 6.11 "Is This Desire?" Vocal Line (Verse Opening)

"Is This Desire?": Introduction and Verses 1 and 2

On first listening, the final track on this album seems to have a delayed start: there are nineteen seconds of apparent silence before the song proper begins. Closer listening, however, reveals a high-frequency sustained pitch ($F\sharp^6$) in the synthesizer during these nineteen seconds, which then continues through the first verse. By using this extremely quiet and high-pitched sound for the introduction, Harvey asks her audience to listen very attentively and sensitively, to focus on subtle sounds. An associative meaning for this high $F\sharp$ is not explicitly understood in the first verse, but its return in the final verse creates an explicit connection: the high $F\sharp$ returns in the last verse at the text "the sun set"; the first verse also refers to the sunset while the synthesizer sustains the high pitch. Thus, the introductory section of the song establishes a physical setting, an attempt to evoke a visceral or sensory response to the song. During the first two verses, Harvey uses many words that evoke the senses: the concepts of movement (walking), temperature (coldness, fire), sight (green trees, golden hair), and the body (Dawn's neck, bare feet).

As the verses are presented, the structural patterns and form of the music also evoke a physical response. The first verse begins with the voice accompanied only by drums (and the background high $F\sharp$ in the synthesizer). The recording is dry, with little reverberation, which brings Harvey's voice very close. The eight-measure vocal phrase comprises four statements of a two-measure pattern that, in its melodic design, creates a falling then rising gesture (see figure 6.11). As this pattern is repeated, we hear a repeated cycle of descent–ascent–descent–ascent. In the first statement of the pattern, the voice begins on low $F\sharp^3$ on beat one, then waits until the second beat of measure 2 to continue. The continuation is a rising pattern, from A^3, to B^4, falling back momentarily to A, then moving up to C. This C creates a diminished fifth with the original pitch and tonic $F\sharp$, and is a note that requires resolution (a "tendency" tone). For the remaining statements, the first measure of the pattern is not just the repeated $F\sharp$ of the first measure, but rather is altered to become a falling gesture (B–A–$F\sharp$), resolving the tendency tone C and confirming the descending function of that measure in the two-measure pattern. The accompanying drum pattern also conveys a "down–up" gesture, although at the level of a single measure. In each measure, the drummer creates a strong beat one on the snare, then a stressed upbeat to beat three on its rim (a syncopation), with constant

FIGURE 6.12 "Is This Desire?" (Link)

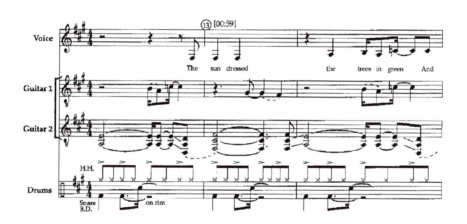

FIGURE 6.13 "Is This Desire?" (Verse 2 Opening)

eighth-note subdivisions on the high hat. This sense of down–up cyclic patterning continues through the eight-measure phrase, stopping with the ascending gesture: at "let's build a fire," the flat fifth in the vocal line does not resolve, leaving the implications unspoken.

The anticipation created by the unresolved ending of the verse continues into and is developed by a short (four-measure) linking passage that introduces a distinctive guitar pattern (shown in figure 6.12). The two-measure guitar progression (repeated) is basically a shift from the open fifths on F♯ to A to D. The F♯ harmony is heard for one full measure, then the second measure sustains A with the addition of a quick shift to D on the very last eighth note. The D moves immediately to F♯ harmony, for the pattern to begin again. A melodic guitar gesture creates an interesting counterpoint to this harmonic progression: against the F♯ harmony, the guitar melody descends from G♯ to F♯ in a 9–8 dissonance resolution, then against the A harmony, the melody descends in another 9–8 pattern, B–A, but rises to C, creating a momentary A-minor triad (the listener might have been expecting A major in the F♯-minor context). This guitar pattern once again creates a kind of "down–up" gesture. The descending 9–8 patterns are powerful in their evocation of movement, and the rising gesture to C creates a feeling of anticipation. Coming immediately after Dawn says "let's build a fire," I would interpret this guitar pattern as a representation of Joseph and Dawn's accumulating desire.

The material from this guitar link continues as an accompaniment for the second verse, and carries with it the associative meaning of their desire. As is shown in figure 6.13, the vocal line is now heard against the moving 9–8 resolutions and the anticipatory rising gesture to C. Indeed, the guitar and vocal line unite in the pattern B–A–C. This gesture is connected to lyrics such as "I feel like a king" and "her feet were bare" and thus is associated with their bodies, and so with their feelings of desire.

"Is This Desire?": Pre-chorus

Just four measures long and heard only once, as an introduction to the first statement of the chorus, the pre-chorus builds an even greater sense of anticipation for the fulfillment of Joesph and Dawn's desire. The lyrics expand a moment in time, the moment when they look into each other's eyes and are about to embrace. Several musical elements contribute to the increased sense of expectation and the suggested effect of a short moment in time standing still. These individual elements command very close attention and draw the listener into the urgency of the moment:

1. Each of the four measures contain basically the same material (with small rhythmic differences in the vocal presentation of the lyrics), until the final measure when the synthesizer makes a slight change. (The first measure of the pre-chorus is transcribed in figure 6.14.)
2. The guitar progression is the same F♯–A–D pattern that we have heard continuously since the link between verses 1 and 2, but the harmonic rhythm is increased such that the entire progression occurs within the space of one measure (as opposed to two).
3. The guitar melody is also altered to fit within the span of one measure, but it receives yet another modification that increases its expressive tension: the F♯ of the G♯–F♯ (9–8) pattern is not heard; that is, the ninth is unresolved.
4. The synthesizer returns, playing an F♯-minor triad with F♯ in the highest position until the last measure of the pre-chorus, when it rises to a dissonant G♯ that is left unresolved.
5. The voice stays mainly on one pitch for the entire pre-chorus, always leaving the downbeat empty, as if Harvey is breathing at a faster rate. The pitch she sings is the third of the F♯-minor tonic triad (A), an "active" pitch in the conventions of contrapuntal usage.

"Is This Desire?": Chorus

The pre-chorus leads immediately into the chorus with no intervening material. The chorus has been prepared by the lyrics of the verses and pre-chorus as the section that will articulate the sexual union; however, the lyrics of the chorus do not directly address this goal. The lyrics pose a question concerning the nature of Dawn and Joseph's desire and its potential to satisfy or to transport them: "Is this desire? Enough enough to lift us higher, to lift above?" Thus, rather than being presented with a confirmation of satisfied desire, we are discomforted by a critical interrogation; after all of the lyrical and musical appeals to the visceral, the final statement is intellectual. The music confirms that the culminating moment of the chorus is not a representation of fulfilled sexual desires. Indeed, the music defies expectations on a number of counts (see figure

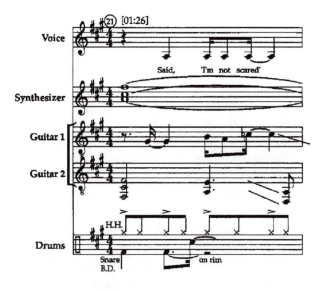

FIGURE 6.14 "Is This Desire?" (Pre-chorus Opening)

6.15). The material is minimal and repetitive rather than expansive and luxuriant. The harmony in the guitar is dissonant and unresolved: in each measure the guitar slides from D_9 to $F\sharp_9$ (the ninth chords here are simply two stacked open fifths). Harvey's voice disengages from the previous melodic material and lifts itself out of the expected range of movement to reiterate a high $F\sharp^4$; the verse and pre-chorus material worked within the range of $F\sharp^3$ to C^4. In addition, her vocal quality shifts from being deep and "throaty" to thin and distant. Her repetition of $F\sharp$ continues until the last gesture of the chorus, when she rises to the high A and falls to $G\sharp$, the dissonant ninth above the harmony of $F\sharp$.

This melodic $G\sharp$–$F\sharp$ gesture has carried an associative meaning throughout the song: it was heard in the guitar as a representation of Joseph and Dawn's desire during the link between the two verses, and then as an accompaniment to the second verse. During the pre-chorus, we hear an abbreviated form of the guitar pattern in which the $G\sharp$ does not resolve to $F\sharp$, and this unresolved ninth builds anticipation. Now it accompanies the fundamental question of the chorus, but it is a disquieting form of question, because the music does not establish a context in which the answer is expected. That is, the repetitive planing of the ninth chords from D_9 to $F\sharp_9$ establish the ninth as a point of reference. In these four measures, the ninth is not an active pitch, with the potential to "move" contrapuntally as it did in the guitar link and verse. It is a static dissonance; the only movement expected is the repetition of the pattern back and forth from D_9 to $F\sharp_9$. When the voice joins in to take the ninth in the final gesture of the chorus, it is an unsettling stop on the dissonant vertical harmony, but I do not expect Harvey's voice to resolve that dissonance.

"Is This Desire?": Verse 3 and Final Chorus

The chorus ends with the hollow question and the stacked fifth or ninth harmony on $F\sharp$. That harmony is carried over into the next measure, as the guitar link material returns, with some significant modifications from its first appearance: the melodic line does not resolve the 9–8 dissonance, but rather sustains the ninth ($G\sharp$), and the subsequent 9–8 pattern does not move on to its anticipatory C. There is a feeling of calm here, a sense of slowing down, as opposed to the sense of intensification that was created by the first statement of this material after verse 1.

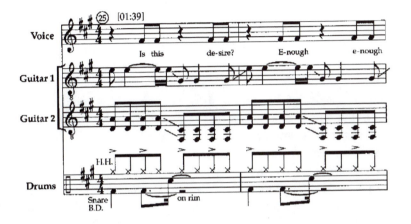

FIGURE 6.15 "Is This Desire?" (Chorus Opening)

The third verse continues the mood of reflection and critical interrogation that developed during the chorus by referring to the passing of time ("Hour long by hour may we two stand / When we're dead") and the setting of the sun. The instrumental texture now includes an element that was not present in the earlier verse statements: the synthesizer sustains the vertical harmony of A–C–G♯. This harmony is derived from the F♯-minor harmony that was heard in the synthesizer during the pre-chorus; in the last measure of that section, the high F♯ moved up to a G♯, creating this very structure. Thus, the G♯ can be understood as a dissonant substitute for F♯, but it is significant that the G♯ does not come directly from an F♯. Just as the chorus used the G♯ ninth as a static dissonance, here the G♯ does not suggest movement. In this song, as I have discussed, the ninth G♯ is used in different contexts. When it moves to or from F♯, that movement is symbolic of desire; when it is heard as a static pitch, it suggests isolation.

The final chorus arrives without its preparatory pre-chorus and offers the final reflection on the central question, "Is this desire enough?" It features the same instrumentation as the first statement, with the addition of high rolled chords in the synthesizer. Against the planing ninths in the guitar, the synthesizer moves from an A-major triad to an F♯-minor triad, spaced closely so that the common tones hold over while the highest voice moves up from E to F♯. This progression could create an effect of resolution, as it is directed toward the tonic; however, the guitar progression at the same time leads to a tonic with a dissonant ninth. In addition, the final gesture in the voice leaves the melodic G♯ unresolved.

Asking, "Is this desire?" the chorus appears to move outside of the immediate narrative of the story of Dawn and Joseph, in order to pose that profound question on behalf of all of the characters and situations explored on the album. With this final song, the listener is left with a question and the musical effect of irresolution. As I suggested in my analysis of the song's narrative, the chorus does not fulfill the expectations created by verses 1 and 2 and the pre-chorus. That is, as desire accumulates during these sections, the listener anticipates the consummation of desire through the lyrical and musical expression. When the chorus avoids that expected resolution, and offers instead the critical question, this constitutes, in effect, a fracture within the song. This rupture serves a narrative purpose not only at the level of this particular song, but at the level of the entire album. We are lifted out of the immediate context of Dawn and Joseph's story to be reminded of the loftier pursuit of Harvey's artistic endeavor. The chorus of the final song is her opportunity to punctuate an album that explores manifold representations of desire.

Appendix **1**

Song Lyrics

TORI AMOS, "CRUCIFY" (1991)

Instrumentation: Voice, backup vocals, piano, bass, drum kit (snare, high hat, low tom-tom, bass drum) and percussion (shaker, woodblock), ukelele, mandolin
Meter: 4/4

Lyrics copyright 1991 by Sword and Stone, A Division of Music Sales Corporation. Used by permission. This presentation of the text respects Amos's treatment of punctuation and her use of capitalization.

Verse 1   00:00 (8 measures, 1–8)
Every finger in the room is pointing at me
I wanna spit in their faces then I get afraid of what that could bring
I got a bowling ball in my stomach I got a desert in my mouth
Figures that my COURAGE would choose to sell out now

Pre-chorus   00:23 (8 measures, 9–16)
I've been looking for a savior in these dirty streets
Looking for a savior beneath these dirty sheets
I've been raising up my hands drive another nail in
Just what GOD needs one more victim

Chorus   00:46 (14 measures, 17–30)
Why do we crucify ourselves every day
I crucify myself
Nothing I do is good enough for you

I crucify myself everyday
I crucify myself
My heart is sick of being
I said my HEART is sick of being in chains

Verse 2   1:26 (8 measures, 31–38)
Got a kick for a dog beggin' for LOVE
I gotta have my suffering so I can have my cross
I know a cat named Easter he says will you ever learn
You're just an empty cage girl if you kill the bird

Pre-chorus   1:49 (8 measures, 39–46)
I've been looking for a savior in these dirty streets
Looking for a savior beneath these dirty sheets
I've been raising up my hands drive another nail in
Got enough GUILT to start my own religion

Chorus   2:12 (14 measures, 47–60)

Bridge   2:51 (8 measures, 61–68)
Please be Save me I CRY

Pre-chorus   3:14 (8 measures, 69–76)
I've been looking for a savior in these dirty streets
Looking for a savior beneath these dirty sheets
I've been raising up my hands drive another nail in
Where're those angels when you need them

Chorus   3:37 (14 measures, 77–90)

Coda   4:14 (14 measures, 90–103)

COURTNEY LOVE (HOLE), "VIOLET" (1994)

Instrumentation: Voice, back-up vocals, 2 guitars, bass, drums
Meter: 4/4
Lyrics © 1994 by Mother May I Music (BMI). Used by permission.

N.B. In the recording, it is possible to make out the line of text given for the bridge, but it is not included in the published song score. In verse 2, Love pronounces the word "violet" as "violence."

Verse 1   00:00 (32 measures, 1–32)
And the sky was made of amethyst.
And all the stars look just like little fish.
You should learn when to go.
You should learn how to say no.
Might last a day.
Mine is forever.
Might last a day.
Mine is forever.

Pre-chorus   00:45 (8 measures, 33–40)
When they get what they want they never want it again.
When they get what they want, well, they never want it again.

Chorus   00:57 (8 measures, 41–48)
Go on, take ev'rything, take ev'rything, I want you to.
Go on take ev'rything, take ev'rything, I want you to.

Verse 2   1:09 (32 measures, 49–80)
And the sky was all violet.
I want it again, but violet more violet [violence].
And I'm the one with no soul,
One above and one below.
Might last a day.
Mine is forever.
Might last a day.
Mine is forever.

Pre-chorus   1:55 (8 measures, 81–88)

Chorus   2:06 (8 measures, 89–96)
Go on take ev'rything, take ev'rything, I want you to.
Go on take ev'rything, take ev'rything, I dare you to.

Pre-chorus   2:18 (8 measures, 97–104)
Ooh, I told you from the start just how this would end.
When I get what I want, well, I never want it again.

Chorus   2:30 (8 measures, 105–112)

Bridge   2:41 (8 measures, 113–120)
[As I lie on my bed now]

Chorus   2:53 (8 measures, 121–128)

Coda   3:05 (9 measures, 129–137)

ME'SHELL NDEGÉOCELLO, "MARY MAGDALENE" (1996)

Instrumentation: Voice, back-up vocals, guitar, bass, synthesizer, piano,
drums, saxophone
Meter: 12/8

Introduction   00:00 (4 measures, 1–4)

Verse 1   00:24 (8.5 measures, 5–13.5)
I often watch the way you whore yourself
You're so beautiful, you flirt and tease
enviously, I wish you'd flirt with me.
Perhaps I'm enticed by what you are
I imagine us jumpin' the broom foolish I know
'Cause that's not the life you live
You live alone in a crowded bed
never remembering faces, conversations
just a body for the lonely.
Spend one night with me
satisfy me for free

and I'll love you endlessly.
You always tell them you'll give them what they want
So give me what I want.

Chorus   1:13 (3.5 measures, 13.5–16)
Tell me I'm the only one
give me
I want to marry you
Tell me I'm the only one.

Bridge   1:34 (5 measures, 16–21)
So give me what I want
[lyrics in last measure, which is expanded to 18/8 meter]

Chorus   2:06 (4 measures, 22–25)

Verse 2   2:30 (8.5 measures, 26–34.5)
In a harlot's dress you wear the smile
of a child with the faith of Mary Magdalene.
Yet you wash the feet of unworthy men.
Come and I'll set you free
into an endless valley of fruits both sweet and sour
and whatever displeases your palate
my kisses will wash away. Stay.
If you must dance, dance for me.
So blessed are the pure of heart
for the they shall see God.
So close your eyes and dream
for the world will blind you.
And judge not so that I may not be judged
So give me what I want.

Chorus   3:16 (3.5 measures, 34.5–37)

Bridge   3:40 (5 measures, 38–42)
[last measure expanded to 18/8 meter]

Chorus   4:12 (3.5 measures, 43–46.5)

Coda   4:32 (8.5 measures, 46.5–54, plus instrumental fade-out)

P.J. HARVEY, "CATHERINE" (1998)

Instrumentation: Voice, guitar, drums, synthesizer
Meter: 2/4

Lyrics © 1998 by Hot Head Music, Ltd., and EMI Music Publishing, Ltd.
Used by permission.

Introduction   00:00 (12 measures, 1–12)

Verse 1   00:24 (8 measures, 13–20)
Catherine de Barra, you've murdered my thinking
I gave you my heart, you left the thing stinking
I'd [shake] from your spell if it weren't for my drinking
the cold wind bites more bitter with each light of morning

Link   00:40 (4 measures, 21–24)

Verse 2   00:48 (8 measures, 25–32)
I envy the road, the ground you tread under
I envy the wind, your hair riding over
I envy the pillow your head rests and slumbers
I envy to murderous envy your lover

Chorus   1:03 (8 measures, 33–40)
'til the light shines on me
I damn to hell every second you breathe
'til the light shines on me
I damn to hell every second you breathe

Link   1:19 (8 measures, 41–48)

Verse 2   1:35 (8 measures, 49–56)

I envy the road, the ground you tread under
I envy the wind, your hair riding over
I envy the pillow your head rests and slumbers
I envy to murderous envy your lover

Chorus   1:51 (16 measures, 57–72)
'til the light shines on me
I damn to hell every second you breathe
'til the light shines on me
I damn to hell every second you breathe
'til the light shines on me
I damn to hell every second you breathe
'til the light shines on me...

Coda   2:22 (44 measures, 73–116)
Oh my Catherine
for your eyes smiling
and your mouth singing
with time I'd have won you
with wile I'd have won you
for your eyes smiling
and your mouth singing
with time I'd have won you
Oh, my Catherine
with time I'd have won you
with wile I'd have won you [fade]

P.J. HARVEY, "THE GARDEN" (1998)

Instrumentation: Voice, bass, piano, drums, synthesizer
Meter: 2/4

Lyrics © 1998 by Hot Head Music, Ltd., and EMI Music Publishing, Ltd.
Used by permission.

Introduction   00:00 (4 measures, 1–4)

Verse 1   00:06 (24 measures, 5–28)
and he was walking in the garden
and he was walking in the night
and he was singing a sad love song
and he was praying for his life
and the stars came out around him
he was thinking of his sins
and he's looking at his song bird
and he's looking at his wings

Link   00:45 (4 measures, 29–32)

Verse 2   00:52 (24 measures, 33–56)
there inside the garden
came another with his lips
said, "Won't you come and be my lover?"
"Let me give you a little kiss?"
and he came, knelt down before him
and fell upon his knees
said, "I will give you gold and mountains
if you stay a while with me ... "

Link   1:30 (2 measures, 57–58)

Chorus   1:34 (24 measures, 59–82)
and there was trouble taking place
trouble taking place ... ah ...

Verse 3   2:13 (24 measures, 83–106)
there inside the garden
they kissed, and the sun rose
and he walked a little further
and he found he was alone
and the wind, it gathered round him
he was thinking of his sins
and he was looking [for] his song bird
and he was looking [for] his wings

Link   2:51 (6 measures, 107–112)

Chorus   3:01 (24 measures, 113–136)
and there was trouble taking place
trouble taking place . . . ah . . . [fade]

P.J. HARVEY, "IS THIS DESIRE?" (1998)

Instrumentation: Voice, guitars, drums, synthesizer
Meter: 4/4

Lyrics © 1998 by Hot Head Music, Ltd., and EMI Music Publishing, Ltd.
Used by permission.

Introduction   00:00

Verse 1   00:19 (8 measures, 1–8)
Joseph walked on and on
The sunset went down and down
Coldness cooled their desire
And Dawn said, "Let's build a fire"

Link   0:46 (4 measures, 9–12)

Verse 2   0:59 (8 measures, 13–20)
The sun dressed the trees in green
And Joe said, "[Dawn] I feel like a king"
And Dawn's neck and her feet were bare
Sweetness in her golden hair

Pre-chorus   1:26 (4 measures, 21–24)
Said, "I'm not scared"
Turned to her and smiled
Secrets in his eyes
Sweetness of desire

Chorus   1:39 (4 measures, 25–28)
Is this desire?
Enough enough
To lift us higher
To lift above?

Link   1:53 (4 measures, 29–32)

Verse 3   2:05 (8 measures, 33–40)
How long, by hour may we two stand
When we're dead, between these lands
The sunset behind his eyes
And Joe said, "Is this desire?"

Link   2:32 (2 measures, 41–42)

Chorus   2:39 (8 measures, 43–50)
Is this desire?
Enough enough
To lift us higher
To lift above?
Is this desire?
Enough enough
Enough inside
Is this desire?

Appendix **2**

Reductive Analysis: Notation Terminology

Reduction, or Voice-Leading Graph. Graphic representation (in musical notation) of the principal voice-leading connections and hormonic prolongations. An analysis of the contrapuntal relations between vocal line and bass support, including elaborative pitches and unique voice-leading events.*

Bar Lines. Note values do not represent actual rhythmic events, but the bar lines make it possible to determine approximate metric emphasis.

Stemmed Notes and Note Heads. Stemmed notes indicate pitches that belong to the prevailing harmony for that metric unit (measure or part of the measure. Unstemmed note heads are elaborative pitches.

Solid Slurs. Solid slurs are analytic slurs, which connect elaborative pitches to structural pitches, group notes into a linear progression, or outline an arpeggiation.

Dotted Ties. The structural attack—that is, the moment when the bass and voice are in harmonic agreement—is notated as a stemmed note. Suspensions or anticipations are notated as note heads. A dotted tie connects the structural "attack" to the suspension or anticipation.

Open Note Heads. Open note heads indicate the prolongational structure for any given section of the work. That is, for each section of the song, open note heads will illustrate harmonic or voice-leading emphasis.

Notes

Preface
1. The verse-chorus design in rock music (post-1950) is not equivalent to and therefore should not be confused with Tin Pan Alley or other early popular forms. See, for instance, Everett 1999 (15–17).
2. Although this assertion is based more on opinion than on fact, we do believe that many would agree that Lennox's androgynous, hypersensual presentation of self on the album covers and concepts of the Eurythmics' *Touch* (1983) and *Revenge* (1986) were probably her most important articulations of countercultural body politics. Moreover, we believe that most would concur that Chapman's eponymous album release (1988)—which included the hits "Fast Car" and "Talking about a Revolution"—constituted her most significant moments of political subversion.
3. See Britzman 1998 for an exposition of the unintelligible and/or unknowable intricacies of psychic life.

Chapter 1
1. Nehring (1997) does not sanction this perspective, but at this particular juncture in his work, he is merely explicating it. Nehring proceeds to reveal that "[the post-modern incorporation thesis isn't] really postmodern at all, however. Since the eighteenth century and the birth of aesthetics (or the philosophy of art), academics and other intellectuals have held that meaningless emotional appeals are characteristic of the low or popular arts produced by the marketplace" (xi). For examples of critical and postmodern theorists who subscribe to the incorporation thesis, see, for example, Adorno and Horkheimer [1969] 1993, Grossberg 1992, Jameson 1983 and 1991.
2. We have not conducted any empirical investigations related to the discomfort produced in listeners when they are subjected to the musics in question. Nor have we drawn on any like-natured studies to support the claim that our disruptive divas disquiet those who engage with their creative work. I am quite confident, however, that the following chapters will bring into relief the extent to which the musicians selected for this volume boldly capsize the grand mythological edifices from which so many of us draw our appreciations of reality and "common sense." If that does not produce discomfort within the listener, then what does?
3. See Nehring 1997 for a discussion of these musical cultures.
4. Nehring echoes this view in his discussions of the potentialities of subversive agency through popular music, though he couches it more explicitly in a critique of

the alleged "postmodern death of the subject." He asserts, "We ought to move on to a post-postmodern effort to restore a belief in agency, although a more examined belief, alive to contradictions, than that of the Enlightenment" (1997, 19–20).

5. Some of these comments regarding postmodernism require further debate and will consequently be taken up later.

6. From what I can gather, the use of literary theories of interpretation is not widespread academic practice when it comes to analyzing popular music and lyrics. In fact, very few critics of song lyrics address the problems associated with viewing language as in any way inherently meaningful or transparent.

7. This is an admittedly superficial historicization of how reader-response theories emerged. Certainly one could trace incipient reader-response sensibilities back to the work of Stephane Mallarmé—as Barthes does in his essay. The point of this explanation, however, is not to provide an exhaustive historical account of reader-oriented criticism. It is intended merely to situate the reader in the texts that have structured my approach to the musics in question.

8. While I could not pretend to completely answer all of these questions in *Disruptive Divas*, I shall be approaching each of them to varying degrees in each chapter of the volume.

Chapter 2

1. David Lewin chooses the verb *enact*, as opposed to *read* or *allegorize*, "because the term emphasizes gestural—often bodily—aspects of the interrelation (Lewin, in press).

2. Covach (1997b) discusses this problem extensively.

3. Covach made this comment at the conference entitled "Border Crossings: New Directions in Musicology," held in Ottawa in 1995.

4. For lengthy discussions of the connections between popular and classical music, please see Allan Moore 1993, chapters 1 and 2, and Walser 1992.

5. Allan Moore does not go so far as to explore Schenkerian reductive theory in his 1993 book, and indeed has some negative comments about its applicability to popular music (10–12). He also discusses Schenkerian theory in his 1995 article and puts into play a modified form of voice-leading analysis. In addition, his 1997 Beatles study uses voice-leading reduction as an integral part of his analytic method.

6. The criticism has been both explicit and implicit; that is, when musicologists speak of the negative effects of formalism in tonal analysis, Schenker may not be named but is undoubtedly implied. For instance, Schenker is surely the unnamed offender when Middleton says, "the main problem felt to attach to mainstream methods has been the tendency to *formalism*" (1993, 177).

7. I have responded in greater detail to Middleton's and Moore's critiques of Schenkerian theory in Burns 2000.

8. Please see in particular Allan Moore 1995, Everett 1999, and Lori Burns 1999 and 2000.

9. Middleton cites Stefani 1987 as an important influence. The interested reader will also find a nice summary of codes and competences in Brackett 1995, 9–14.

10. Middleton cites Stefani 1987. On this same issue, Allan Moore (1993, 23–24) discusses Adorno's categories of listening (Adorno 1976, 3–14).

11. Middleton bases these categories on the model of Stefani (1987).

12. In this regard, Middleton's discussion of codes is worth mentioning: he suggests that the codes in a given work "may vary in *strength*. That is, the patterns they organize may be very familiar and predictable—heavily coded—or they may be rather ambiguous and unpredictable—subject to weak or newly invented codes" (1990, 173). In other words, a given piece of music will negotiate the codes and conventions of the style to which it belongs to varying degrees, sometimes conforming absolutely to paradigms, sometimes eschewing paradigms, and presumably sometimes taking a middle position on conventionality or unconventionality.

13. For a nice summary of the verse/chorus form, see Everett 2000, 272–73, and for definitions of the individual sections, verse, chorus, bridge, etc., see Everett 1999, 313–15.

14. In this regard, see Winkler 1978, Allan Moore 1992, 1993, 1995, and Everett 1999 and 2000.

15. For further discussion of these issues, the reader will find the following references of great value: Bobbitt 1976, Winkler 1978, Allan Moore 1992 and 1993, Everett 2000, and Lori Burns 2000.

16. Middleton (1990, 203–11) gives considerable theoretical attention to melodic design in popular music.

17. McClary discusses binary opposites in musical constructs as they are mapped onto gender opposites (McClary 1991, 9–18).

18. Shepherd and Wicke (1997, 160–62) and Middleton (1990, 183) discuss the concepts of equivalence and difference as fundamental to musical meaning.

19. Allan Moore expresses his similar displeasure with the word *aberrant* (1995, 186).

20. I would be cautious here about all instances where closure is avoided, because of the inherent "problem" in popular music that closure can be achieved in one section of the song (the bridge, for instance) but disrupted with the return to the chorus. In my individual analyses, I will discuss ways to interpret the problems of cyclic repetition and of the "fade-out" in popular song expression.

21. Cusick's remark pertains to Fanny Hensel's *Piano Trio*.

22. Walser also suggests such potential when he asserts that vocal syncopation can signify "resistance with respect to the context constructed by instruments" (1993b, 50).

Chapter 3

1. It must, of course, be borne in mind that any act of reading invariably engages and is mediated by the reader's biography. In cases where the text is especially abstruse, however, it might be said that the reader's biography plays a more important role as she is less restricted by the explicit narrative of the text.

2. In this instance and throughout this study I have been careful to avoid appealing to a universal and coherent category of "woman" due to recent theoretical challenges to the culturally and historically stable "female" subject. According to Butler (1990) and Fraser and Nicholson (1990), the early feminist claim of a universal

woman's experience was based on a privileged range of Western women's experiences (for example, white, bourgeois, heterosexual, able-bodied) and their corresponding experiences of oppression. Because feminist discourse is performative (that is, it effectively produces what it names), its universal and coherent categories of femaleness invariably homogenize those within it and marginalize their differences. For these reasons, Butler asserts: "by conforming to a requirement of representational politics that feminism articulate a stable subject, feminism thus opens itself to charges of gross misrepresentation" (5). For Butler, then, representational politics can only be useful to feminism when the category of "woman" is nowhere presumed. Butler's "subject skepticism," however, does not reside unchallenged. Other feminist scholars (for instance, Bordo 1989, Wendy Brown 1987, DiStefano 1990, Harstock 1987) remain profoundly wary of calls for a feminism whose foundation omits and/or excludes the possibility of a unified female subject. These feminists have proposed two central problems with postmodernism's "impossible subject" thesis. The first relates to what some feminists perceive to be a reaction against recent gains made by feminists and other marginalized groups. Nancy Harstock (1987) summarizes the first problem when she asks, "Why is it, just at the moment in Western history when previously silenced populations have begun to speak for themselves and on behalf of their subjectivities, that the concept of the subject and the possibility of discovering/creating a liberating 'truth' become suspect?" (cited in DiStefano 1990, 75; see chapter 1 of this volume for more on this question). The second problem with the "impossible subject" thesis pertains to its arguable but plausible androcentric bias. In this regard, DiStefano (1990) and Wendy Brown (1987) wonder whether "the subject under fire from postmodernism may be a more specifically masculine self than postmodern theorists have been willing to admit" (DiStefano 1990, 75). Despite these criticisims, however, I believe that it is important to remain alive to the problems associated with positing a universal and coherent category of "woman."

3. Reynolds and Press's (1995) discussion of Tori Amos is problematic on many counts. As I mentioned, these authors often grant legitimacy to thematic organizing categories—for example "confessional"—without interrogating their sociocultural implications or even superfically reflecting on whether these categories can be soundly applied to the artist in question.

4. Inspired by Hogeland (1994), Lafrance (in press) delineates the distinction between gender consciousness and feminist consciousness: "In the Western world, there is no doubt that women are now more visible in the public sphere than they once were. This visibility, however, does not necessarily provoke a widespread acceptance of feminism. When discussing women with regard to feminism, it is important that we emphasize the distinction between feminist consciousness and gender consciousness, and concede that these two terms are in no way interchangeable. While women have recently begun to explore their womanhood, thus making it more visible, they have also discovered an increased vulnerability to male power and control." In this study, I use *gender consciousness* to denote the increased visibility Amos brings to the once "private problems" of women's lives. Although this visibility may accomplish some solidarity between women, it does

not *essentially* lead to heightened feminist consciousness. In fact, some depoliticized, hyperindividualized interpretations of Amos's gender consciousness (see Reynolds and Press 1995, DeMain 1994, Fleissner 1996) have actually, in my estimation, hindered the feminist project.

5. The complete lyrics for "Crucify" are provided in appendix 1.

6. It is difficult to interpret this piece without mapping Amos's identity onto that of her protagonist, because the song's narrative is presented in the first person. For argumentative purposes, the terms *Amos* and *the protagonist* will be used interchangeably.

7. This is not to posit that patriarchal forces do not interfere concretely to regulate women's behavior, nor is it intended to underestimate the social importance of such sanctions. Many second-wave feminist scholars argue (Brownmiller 1975, Mary Daly 1978, Griffin 1981, MacKinnon 1989) that violence against women constitutes a concrete manifestation of patriarchal disciplining. For example, Humm (1995) discusses the disciplinary nature of sexual violence against women: "Feminist theory defines rape as an *act* and a *social institution* which perpetuate patriarchal domination and which are based on violence rather than specifically as a crime of violence. . . . In feminist analysis rape is the logical conclusion of sexism" (234).

8. As Butler (1990), Burstyn (1999), and Messner and Sabo (1992) have already noted, the concept of patriarchy is problematic on many counts. On the one hand, it has tended to falsely universalize women's experiences. That is, proponents of patriarchy theory have sometimes presumed that all women, irrespective of nationality, race, class, sexuality, creed, ability, and/or age, share the same experiences of gender subordination. In this sense, patriarchy theory sometimes minimizes the importance of other forms of oppression while hierarchizing oppressions in general. On the other hand, as Burstyn outlines, patriarchy is only one form of male domination. She prefers the term *male supremacist*, as it underscores the various systems of domination and subordination controlled by and beneficial to men. With these terminological criticisms in mind, we have decided to use both the concepts "patriarchy" and "male supremacy," as they appear to be equally appropriate for the purposes of this argument.

9. These words are in quotation marks because they are the same words as those employed by Foucault (1979) in his discussion of modern power's strategies and tactics.

10. The violent sanctions that compel women to choose to perpetually sustain and renew their genders attests not only to the contingency of gender, but to its role in maintaining social relations of domination (Bartky 1993, Butler 1989).

11. The word "courage" appears in uppercase letters in the album inlay. One could argue that the emphasis put on the word courage denotes that Amos also saw this concept as (in some way) problematic.

12. I have chosen Beauvoir ([1949] 1953) and more importantly Butler's (1989 and 1990) revision of theories of the cultural making and becoming of women, as they neither remove nor efface women's agency in social processes of subordination. Contrary to some traditional feminist accounts of socially constructed femininity

that see women's role in socialization processes as passive and determined, new scholars of gender, while not always in perfect agreement, are nonetheless theoretically mindful of women's primordial active participation in the creation and renewal of dominant gender modalities. I will show that this feminist framework is most appropriate for understanding that which underlies the most important concepts in "Crucify." That is, neglecting to focus on both Amos's subjectivity-at-work and her subjectivity-in-discourse inevitably prohibits a complete understanding of the range of implication in "Crucify."

13. This conceptualization of women, religion, and violence is problematic on many counts. In brief, concepts such as "victim" and "consent" do not account for resistance, agency, and a more feminist-Foucauldian conceptualization of power used by scholars such as Fisher and Davis (1993) and Beausoleil (1994). One must remember nonetheless that Mary Daly's (1968, 1973, and 1978) work emerged before scholars of culture and feminism began discussing possibilities for resistance in situations of constraint. Despite these important conceptual problems, I have deemed Daly's work on women and religion indispensable to my argument.

14. Certainly it would be difficult to attack organized religion without attacking its male supremacist nature. This contention is further supported by the range of femininities represented in the video version of "Crucify."

15. For excellent discussions of how feminine agency is often found at the (uncomfortable) theoretical crossroads of action, freedom, and resistance, see Davis's (1993) elaboration of the dilemma of cosmetic surgery, and Beausoleil's (1994) problematization of femininity, makeup, and resistance.

16. It could be argued that it is no coincidence that in Christian tradition, Easter is the commemoration of when Christ rose from the cave where he was buried after his crucifixion. The emptiness of the cave after Christ's resurrection could be mapped onto the "empty cage" of which the cat speaks in verse 2.

17. There are occasional filmed inserts of her torso and arms, dressed in this outfit, but soaking wet, with water running over her body. The meaning of these will be explained by later events in the video.

18. This is the primary image of the first pre-chorus, although there are occasional filmic inserts of images that will be explained by later events in the video: the images are of water, with immersed objects, such as chains and a high-heeled shoe.

19. One of the viewed items is unusual in this context: a water nozzle. Its presence will be explained by later events in the video.

20. This scene offers an explanation for some of the earlier images of the video: the inserted images of water and the prostitute bathing from earlier scenes are derived from this scene.

21. The narrative timeline is altered at several points, through the use of filmed inserts that foreshadow later events. For example, we see immersed objects long before we see the bathtub.

22. Reverberation can be defined as the effect of the sound reflection as the soundwaves hit the enclosing surfaces and then decay. The quality of the reverberation is affected by the delay (how soon the first reflection occurs), the decay (the length

of time that the sound takes to die away), and the proximity of the sound-producing instrument to the surface. Quite simply, these measurements of reverberation would tell the listener in what sort of room the sound was being produced: a small room in which the decay time might be 0.5 to 1.5 seconds, a concert hall (1.9 to 2.5 seconds), or a cathedral (3 to 4 seconds). For my purposes, the effect of reverberation is a noteworthy strategy for vocal production and the communication of the song's story.

23. Figure 3.1 provides a simplified bass line and a reduction of the vocal line to those pitches that receive the greatest emphasis and the strongest harmonic support. The interested reader can refer to appendix 2 for an explanation of my reductive method.

24. Allan Moore (1993) discusses period structures in rock, identifying the open-closed pattern, or period design, as the normative rock position. In discussing the different possible combinations of open and closed phrases, he comments that he is "unaware of any songs using closed/open pairings" (53).

25. I would add, however, that a section change is not the only analytic possibility for contrast; some of the analytic commentary on the content of the verse also held the potential for such contrast; for instance, the closed, then open design of the phrase structure.

26. In making these comparative remarks about the verse and pre-chorus, I must caution the reader that I am doing so in order to identify different discursive strategies; I do not mean to assume a corrective view of these strategies.

Chapter 4

1. This section of the chapter does not purport to be an exhaustive account of Courtney Love's media representations. There are numerous other significant and arguably highly apocryphal representations of Love's personal and musical trajectory, such as the documentary *Kurt and Courtney*. In that the present chapter is not intended to be a content analysis of press related to Love but a close reading of her lyricism—which happens to be strengthened by a brief discussion of Love's media portrayal—I do not claim to have wholly assessed the various ways in which Love has been framed by the global entertainment apparatus.

2. In this chapter, I will be using terms such as *mainstream media, the press,* and *dominant representations* to both denote the actual apparatuses of such media and connote their intrinsic and inextricable relationship to broader structural and discursive regimes.

3. I am going to discuss Hole's music with primary reference to Love for two reasons. First, Love was by far the band member most involved in the lyric-writing process (Jason Cohen 1995). Since my analysis pertains mainly to lyrical content, it seems perfectly justifiable to discuss them with primary reference to Love. Second, this article endeavors to write Love's fierce intelligence and insurgence back into empowering discussions of Hole's work and success. To do so, I am deliberately highlighting Love's central involvement in Hole's lyrical production.

4. For more on this subject, see Susan Bordo's introduction to her *Unbearable Weight* (1993).

5. See Fisher and Davis 1993 for a critical discussion of Bordo's position on this matter.
6. The complete lyrics for "Violet" are provided in appendix 1. This song will be analyzed in detail by Lori in the second section of this chapter.
7. See Smith 1989 for a discussion of male fantasies of female mutilation.
8. See Dinnerstein 1978 and Wolf [1990] 1997 for interesting discussions of how patriarchal societies keep women from forming meaningful bonds with one another.

Chapter 5

1. *Peace beyond Passion* was released in 1996 on the record label Maverick, owned by Madonna and operated by Warner Bros. Incorporated. Madonna's personal and professional "interests" in the promotion of an artist as disruptive as Ndegéocello would constitute, it seems to me, an interesting area of future study for scholars of popular culture.
2. See Roberts 1996 for a relatively extensive, albeit somewhat atheoretical, synthesis of Ndegéocello's first album, *Plantation Lullabies*.
3. The lyrics for "Mary Magdalene" are provided in appendix 1.
4. See the Gospel according to Luke 7.36–50.
5. The complete lyrics for "Mary Magdalene" are provided in appendix 1.
6. See the Gospel according to Deuteronomy.
7. As I raise the issue of the gaze, it is useful to recall my discussion of Tori Amos's song "Crucify" (chapter 3). In her treatment of the gaze, she is the one being watched, thus her song explores the tension felt by the object of the gaze, but also her resistance to that gaze.

Chapter 6

1. One of the only other popular female artists who has presented herself in ways akin to Harvey is Courtney Love. Both artists tend to work a great deal with the primary signifiers of femininity (such as lipstick, body size and image, dresses, and high-heels). Their appropriation of such signifiers, however, is not in any way a pure appropriation. Indeed, both artists dramatize the trappings of femininity in disconcerting ways so as to reveal the injury caused by such trappings when they are taken to their extreme, albeit logical, conclusions.
2. Freud's most important assertion related to desire as bound up with the death drive is delineated in "Beyond the Pleasure Principle" ([1922] 1991). See also Richard Boothby's *Death and Desire: Psychoanalysis in Lacan's Return to Freud* (1991).
3. The strategies exploited by the subject in an attempt to consolidate her being (that is, her freedom) do not unfold in a linear progression in the way that I have delineated them. Instead, these strategies function cyclically and indeed chaotically. It is merely for the sake of argumentation that I have delineated them as taking place in a first and second instance. On this issue, Sartre writes, "These two attempts which I am are opposed to one another. Each attempt is the death of the other; that is, the failure of the one motivates the adoption of the other. Thus there is no dialectic for my relations toward the Other but rather a circle—although each attempt is

enriched by the failure of the other" (1966, 474). See the first section of "Concrete Relations with Others" in *Being and Nothingness* for more on this question.

4. These names, the reader may have noticed, bode potentially hagiographic significance. While I am unable to discuss this dimension of Harvey's work in any depth, it remains another interesting component to the songwriting on this album.

5. Interestingly, the male personages on the album, who are represented as either homosexual ("The Garden") or weak and pathetic ("Elise," "Angelene," "No Girl so Sweet"), are absent from nearly all mainstream criticism of *Is This Desire?*

6. Review of *Is This Desire?* 1998. *Request Magazine* (November).

7. Review of *Is This Desire?* 1998. *The Westword* (December 3).

8. It should be noted that Harvey is highly supportive of reader-oriented interpretation and reader-response criticism. In a recent article in the British daily *The Guardian*, Harvey is reported to have reiterated her long-held view that "once she has released her songs, it is up to the listeners to interpret them" (Baker 2000, 44). In fact, Harvey directly refuses to speak of the meaning of her lyrical works. It should thus seem obvious that not only is a reader-oriented critique of *Is This Desire?* appropriate, but it is also necessary and unavoidable.

9. The complete lyrics for "Catherine" are provided in appendix 1.

10. The Island of Barra has been inhabited variously by the English druids and the Irish and Scottish Celts and Gaels. There have been a number of rather noteworthy Catherines who were born and lived in Barra. One, née Catherine de Clanclavald, was married to a man from Barra who died in the mid-1500s. There was also a Catherine MacPhee, from Barra, who testified in the nineteenth century that she was driven from her home in the Clearances. This testimony, however, does not seem to tell the reader much about why Harvey would have chosen to name her narrator's beloved Catherine de Barra. Finally, on a fan-posted website devoted to Harvey, the custodian of the site thanks Catherine de Barra for some of the information included on the site. This could suggest that there is a living Catherine de Barra who is presently linked to Harvey. But again, one cannot be certain of this supposition. While the genealogy of Catherine de Barra does not necessarily determine the course of my interpretation (considering that my interpretation is reader-centered rather than author-centered and most readers will neither know who Catherine de Barra is nor take the time to investigate her identity), I thought it would be important to, at the very least, mention this rather mysterious allusion.

11. The other fundamental instinct, according to Freud, is the life instinct (embodied in eros, in the way that the death instinct is embodied in desire).

12. For this song, Harvey appears to go out of her way to sing in an unnaturally low register. This could be construed as her way of communicating a male voice. However, her vocal strategies could have little to do with gender—in which case the song could be read as lesbian in its orientation.

13. In the repetition of verse 2, this dissonance is felt even more acutely, as a sustained F♯ in the synthesizer is added to the texture. The F♯ is at first dissonant against the vocal line, which strikes the F♮ at the downbeat for the first four bars of this final verse; however, the voice does sing F♯ in bars 5 and 6 of this last verse.

14. The complete lyrics for "Catherine" are provided in appendix 1.
15. The complete lyrics for "The Garden" are provided in appendix 1.
16. The complete lyrics for "Is This Desire?" are provided in appendix 1.
17. "Mary and Joseph went on and on. The sun went down. It was getting cold. They saw fire."

Appendix 2

*For the purpose of this study, I will use the terms *reduction* and *voice-leading graph* interchangeably, even though I have elsewhere (Burns 2000) made a careful distinction between the two.

Bibliography

Abbate, Carolyn. 1991. *Unsung Voices: Opera and Musical Narrative in the Nineteenth Century*. Princeton, NJ: Princeton University Press.

Adorno, Theodor, and Max Horkheimer. [1969] 1993. "The Culture Industry: Enlightenment as Mass Deception." In *The Cultural Studies Reader*, ed. Simon During. London: Routledge, 29–44. Extracted from *Dialectic of Enlightenment*, trans. John Cumming. New York: The Seabury Press, 1972. Originally published in German by Fischer Verlag GmbH.

_____. 1976. *Introduction to the Sociology of Music*. New York: Seabury Press.

Agawu, Kofi. 1997. "Analyzing Music under the New Musicological Regime," in *Journal of Musicology* 15/3 (Summer): 297–307.

Allen, Virginia. 1983. *The Femme Fatale: Erotic Icon*. Troy, NY: Whitson Publishing.

Althusser, Louis. 1969. *For Marx*. Harmondsworth: Penguin.

Amos, Tori. 1995. "Biography," in *Atlantic Recording Corporation*. Atlantic Records <http://www.atlantic-records.com>.

Arnold, Gina. 1998. "Love Taps." *The Village Voice*, September 30–October 6.

Baker, Lindsay. 2000. "Let There Be Light." *Guardian*, October 21, 40–46.

Balsamo, Ann. 1996. *Technologies of the Gendered Body: Reading Cyborg Women*. Durham, NC: Duke University Press.

Barkin, Elaine, and Lydia Hamessley, ed. 1997. *Audible Traces: Identity, Gender, and Music*. Zurich: Carciofoli Verlagshaus.

Barthes, Roland. [1970] 1974. *S/Z*, trans. Richard Miller. Reprint New York: Noonday Press.

Bartky, Sandra Lee. [1984] 1990. "Feminine Mashochism and the Politics of Personal Transformation." In *Femininity and Domination: Studies in the Phenomenology of Oppression* New York: Routledge. Originally published in *Women's Studies International Forum* 7/5: 323–34. (Page references are to the original edition.)

_____. 1990. *Femininity and Domination: Studies in the Phenomenology of Oppression*. New York: Routledge.

_____. 1993. "Foucault, Femininity, and the Modernization of Patriarchal Power." In *Women and Values: Readings in Recent Feminist Philosophy*, ed. Marilyn Pearsall. Belmont, CA: Wadsworth, 151–65.

Bataille, Georges. 1962. *Death and Sensuality*. New York: Walker.

Beardsley, Monroe C. and William K. Wimsatt. 1954. *The Verbal Icon: Studies in the Meaning of Poetry*. Lexington: University Press of Kentucky.

Beausoleil, Natalie. 1994. "Make-up in Everyday Life: An Inquiry into the Practices of Urban American Women of Diverse Backgrounds." In *Many Mirrors: Body Image and Social Relations,* ed. Nicole Sault. New Brunswick, NJ: Rutgers University Press, 33–57.

_____. 1996. "Parler de soi et des autres femmes minoritaires: Problèmes rattachés aux catégories d'identité dans la recherche féministe." In *Femmes francophones et pluralisme en milieu minoritaire,* ed. Dyane Adam. Ottawa: University of Ottawa Press, 7–16.

Beauvoir, Simone de. [1949] 1953. *The Second Sex,* trans. and ed. H. M. Parskley. New York: Knopf. Originally published in Paris by Gallimard.

Benjamin, Jessica. 1983. "Master and Slave: The Fantasy of Erotic Domination." In *Powers of Desire: The Politics of Sexuality.* New York: Monthly Review Press.

_____. 1988. *The Bonds of Love: Psychoanalysis, Feminism, and the Problem of Domination.* New York: Pantheon Books.

Bennett, Tony, Simon Frith, Lawrence Grossberg, John Shepherd, and Graeme Turner, eds. 1993. *Rock and Popular Music: Politics, Policies, Institutions.* London and New York: Routledge.

Benvenuto, B., and Kennedy, R. 1986. *The Works of Jaques Lacan: An Introduction.* London: Free Association Books.

Berger, John. 1988. *Ways of Seeing.* London: Penguin Books.

Betrock, Alan. 1982. *Girl Groups: The Story of a Sound.* New York: Delilah Books.

Betterton, Rosemary. 1987. *Looking On: Images of Femininity in the Visual Arts and Media.* London and New York: Pandora.

Björnberg, Alf. 1994. "Structural Relationships of Music and Images in Music Videos," in *Popular Music* 13/1: 51–74.

Blundell, Valda, John Shepherd, and Ian Taylor, eds. 1993. *Relocating Cultural Studies: Developments in Theory and Research.* London and New York: Routledge.

Bohlman, Philip V. 1993. "Musicology as a Political Act," in *Journal of Musicology* 11/4 (Fall): 411–36.

Boone, Graeme. 1997. "Tonal and Expressive Ambiguity in 'Dark Star.'" In *Understanding Rock: Essays in Musical Analysis,* ed. John Covach and Graeme Boone. New York: Oxford University Press, 171–210.

Boothby, Richard. 1991. *Death and Desire: Psychoanalysis in Lacan's Return to Freud.* London: Routledge.

Bordo, Susan. 1989. "Feminism, Postmodernism, and Gender-Scepticism." In *Feminism/Postmodernism,* ed. Linda J. Nicholson. New York: Routledge, 133–57.

_____. 1993. *Unbearable Weight: Feminism, Western Culture, and the Body.* Los Angeles: University of California Press.

_____. 1995. "Material Girl: The Effacements of Postmodern Culture." In *Free Spirits: Feminist Philosophers on Culture,* ed. Kate Mehuron and Gary Percesepe. Toronto: Prentice-Hall, 66–81.

Brackett, David. 1995. *Interpreting Popular Music.* Cambridge: Cambridge University Press.

Bradby, Barbara. 1990. "Do-Talk and Don't-Talk: The Division of the Subject in Girl-Group Music." In *On Record: Rock, Pop, and the Written Word,* ed. Simon Frith and Andrew Goodwin. New York: Pantheon Books, 341–70.

Bravmann, Scott. 1996. "Postmodernism and Queer Identities." In *Queer Theory/Sociology*, ed. Steven Seidman. London: Blackwell, 333–62.

Brett, Philip, Gary Thomas, and Elizabeth Wood, eds. 1994. *Queering the Pitch*. New York: Routledge.

Britzman, Deborah. 1998. *Lost Subjects, Contested Objects: Toward a Psychoanalytic Inquiry of Learning*. Albany: State University of New York Press.

Brooks, Ann. 1997. *Postfeminisms: Feminism, Cultural Theory, and Cultural Forms*. London: Routledge.

Brown, Matthew. 1997a. "'Adrift on Neurath's Boat': The Case for a Naturalized Music Theory," in *Journal of Musicology* 15/3 (summer): 330–42.

_____. 1997b. "'Little Wing': A Study in Musical Cognition." In *Understanding Rock: Essays in Musical Analysis*, ed. John Covach and Graeme Boone. New York: Oxford University Press, 155–70.

Brown, Wendy. 1987. "Where Is the Sex in Political Theory?" in *Women and Politics* 7/1: 3–23.

Brownmiller, Susan. 1975. *Against Our Will: Men, Women, and Rape*. New York: Simon and Schuster.

_____. 1984. *Femininity*. New York: Linden Press/Simon and Schuster.

Bührer, Emil, Dorothee Sölle, Herbert Haag, and Joe Kirchberger. 1993. *Great Women of the Bible in Art and Literature*. Grand Rapids, MI: William B. Eerdmans Publishing.

Burnham, Scott. 1997. "Theorists and 'the Music Itself.'" in *Journal of Musicology* 15/3 (summer): 316–29.

Burns, Gary. 1987. "A Typology of Hooks," in *Popular Music* 6/1: 1–20.

Burns, Lori. 1997. "'Joanie' Get Angry: k.d. lang's Feminist Revision." In *Understanding Rock: Essays in Musical Analysis*, ed. John Covach and Graeme Boone. New York: Oxford University Press, 93–112.

_____. 1999. "Genre, Gender, and Convention Revisited: k.d. lang's Cover of Cole Porter's 'So in Love,'" in *repercussions* 7 (in press).

_____. 2000. "Analytic Methodologies for Rock Music: Harmonic and Voice-Leading Strategies in Tori Amos's 'Crucify.'" In *Expression in Pop-Rock Music: A Collection of Critical and Analytical Essays*, ed. Walter Everett. New York: Garland, 213–46.

_____. In press. "Meaning in a Popular Song: The Representation of Masochistic Desire in Sarah McLachlan's 'Ice.'" In *Analysis Primer: Essays in Music Theory*, ed. Deborah Stein and Cynthia Gonzales. New York: Oxford University Press.

Burstyn, Varda. 1999. *The Rights of Men: Masculinity, Politics, and the Culture of Sport*. Toronto: University of Toronto Press.

Butler, Judith. 1989. "Gendering the Body: Beauvoir's Philosophical Contribution." In *Women, Knowledge, and Reality: Explorations in Feminist Philosophy*, ed. Ann Garry and Marilyn Pearsall. Boston: Unwin Hyman.

_____.1990. *Gender Trouble: Feminism and the Subversion of Identity*. New York: Routledge.

_____.1993a. *Bodies That Matter: The Discursive Limits of Sex*. New York: Routledge.

_____.1993b. "Gender as Performance: An Interview with Judith Butler. *Radical Philosophy* 67, 32–9.

Caplan, Paula J. 1993. *The Myth of Women's Masochism*. Toronto: University of Toronto Press. Originally published by E. P. Dutton, 1985.

Carty, Linda, and Dionne Brand. 1993. "Visible Minority Women: A Creation of the Canadian State." In *Returning the Gaze*, ed. Himani Bannerji. Toronto: Sister Vision Press, 169–81.

Case, Sue-Ellen. 1990. *Performing Feminisms: Feminist Critical Theory and Theatre*. Baltimore: Johns Hopkins University Press.

Chancer, Lynn S. 1992. *Sadomasochism in Everyday Life: The Dynamics of Power and Powerlessness*. New Brunswick, NJ: Rutgers University Press.

Citron, Marcia. 1993. *Gender and the Musical Canon*. New York: Cambridge University Press.

Clarke, Eric F. 1999. "Subject-Position and the Specification of Invariants in Music by Frank Zappa and P.J. Harvey," in *Music Analysis* 18/3: 347–74.

Cohen, Jason. 1995. "Lollapalooza: Hole Is a Band, Courtney Love Is a Soap Opera," *Rolling Stone* 715 (August 24): 46–51.

Cohen, Sara. 1991. *Rock Culture in Liverpool: Popular Music in the Making*. New York: Clarendon Press.

Cole, Cheryl L. 1996. "American Jordan: P.L.A.Y., Consensus, and Punishment," in *Sociology of Sport Journal* 13/4, 366–98.

_____. 1998. "Representing Black Masculinity and Urban Possibilities: Racism, Realism, and *Hoop Dreams*." In *Sport and Postmodern Times*, ed. Geneviève Rail. Albany: State University of New York Press, 49–86.

Cole, Cheryl L., and Amy Hribar. 1995. "Celebrity Feminism: Nike Style, Post-Fordism, Transcendence, and Consumer Power," in *Sociology of Sport Journal* 12/4: 347–69.

Cook, Susan, and Judy S. Tsou, eds. 1994. *Cecilia Reclaimed: Feminist Perspectives on Gender and Music*. Urbana and Chicago: University of Chicago Press.

Covach, John. 1997a. "Progressive Rock, 'Closer to the Edge,' and the Boundaries of Style." In *Understanding Rock: Essays in Musical Analysis*, ed. John Covach and Graeme Boone. New York: Oxford University Press, 3–32.

_____. 1997b. "We Won't Get Fooled Again: Rock Music and Musical Analysis." In *Keeping Score: Music, Disciplinarity, Culture*, ed. David Schwarz, Anahid Kassabian, and Lawrence Siegel. Charlottesville and London: University Press of Virginia, 75–89.

_____. 2000. "Jazz-Rock? Rock-Jazz? Stylistic Crossover in Late-1970s American Progressive Rock." In *Expression in Pop-Rock Music*, ed. Walter Everett. New York: Garland, 113–34.

Cubitt, Sean. 1991. *Timeshift: On Video Culture*. London: Routledge.

Cusick, Suzanne. 1993. "Of Women, Music, and Power: A Model from Seicento Florence." In *Musicology and Difference: Gender and Sexuality in Music Scholarship*, ed. Ruth Solie. Berkeley: University of California Press, 281–304.

_____. 1994a. "'There Was Not One Lady Who Failed to Shed a Tear': Arianna's Lament and the Construction of Early Modern Womanhood," in *Early Music* 22: 21–41.

_____. 1994b. "Feminist Theory, Music Theory, and the Mind/Body Problem," in *Perspectives of New Music* 32/1 (winter): 8–27.

_____. 1994c. "On a Lesbian Relationship with Music: A Serious Effort Not to Think Straight." In *Queering the Pitch: The New Gay and Lesbian Musicology*, ed. Philip Brett, Elizabeth Wood, and Gary C. Thomas. New York: Routledge, 67–83.

Daly, Mary. 1968. *The Church and the Second Sex*. New York: Harper and Row.

_____. 1973. *Beyond God the Father: Toward a Philosophy of Women's Liberation*. Boston, MA: Beacon.

_____. 1978. *Gyn/Ecology: The Metaethics of Radical Feminism*. Boston, MA: Beacon.

Daly, S. 1998. "Tori Amos: Her Secret Garden," *Rolling Stone* 789 (June 25): 38–41.

Davis, Kathy. 1993. "Cultural Dopes and She-Devils: Cosmetic Surgery as Ideological Dilemma." In *Negotiating at the Margins: The Gendered Discourses of Power and Resistance*, ed. Sue Fisher and Kathy Davis. New Brunswick, NJ: Rutgers University Press, 23–47.

de Lauretis, Teresa. 1988. "Displacing Hegemonic Discourses: Reflections on Feminist Theory in the 1980s," in *Inscriptions* 3/4: 127–45.

DeMain, Bill. 1994. "The Inner World of Tori Amos," in *Performing Songwriter* (March/April) <http://mglz19a@prodigy.com>.

Derrida, Jacques. 1976. *Of Grammatology*. Baltimore: Johns Hopkins University Press.

Diekmann, Katherine. 1995. "Frost Me," *Village Voice* (March 15), 65.

Dines, Gail, and Jean M. Humez. 1995. "A Cultural Studies Approach to Gender, Race, and Class in the Media:" In *Gender, Race, and Class in Media A Text-Reader*, ed. Gail Dines and Jean M. Humez. Thousand Oaks, CA: Sage Publications, 1–4.

Dinnerstein, Dorothy. 1978. *Mermaid and the Minotaur: Sexual Arrangements and Human Malaise*. New York: Harper and Row.

DiStefano, Christine. 1990. "Dilemmas of Difference: Feminism, Modernity, and Postmodernism." In *Feminism/Postmodernism*, ed. Linda J. Nicholson. New York: Routledge, 63–83.

Dolan, Jill. 1988. *The Feminist Spectator as Critic*. Ann Arbor: University of Michigan Press.

Dubiel, Joseph. 1997. "On Getting Deconstructed," in *Journal of Musicology* 15/3 (summer): 308–15.

During, Simon, ed. 1992. *The Cultural Studies Reader*. London: Routledge.

Eagleton, Terry. [1983] 1996. *Literary Theory: An Introduction*. Oxford: Blackwell.

Ebert, Teresa L. 1996. *Ludic Feminism*. Ann Arbor: University of Michigan Press.

Edwards, Anne. 1987. "Male Violence in Feminist Theory: An Analysis of the Changing Conceptions of Sex/Gender Violence and Male Dominance." In *Women, Violence, and Social Control*, ed. Jalna Hanmer. London: MacMillan Press, 12–29.

Esterberg, Kristin G. 1996. "A Certain Swagger when I Walk: Performing Lesbian Identity." In *Queer Theory/Sociology*, ed. Steven Seidman. London: Blackwell, 259–80.

Evans, Liz. 1994. *Women, Sex, and Rock Music*. London: Pandora.

Everett, Walter. 1992. "Voice Leading and Harmony as Expressive Devices in the Early Music of the Beatles: 'She Loves You,'" in *College Music Symposium* 32/1: 19–35.

_____. 1995. "Text-Painting in the Foreground and Middleground of Paul McCartney's Beatle Song 'She's Leaving Home': A Musical Study of Psychological Conflict," in *In Theory Only* 9: 5–13.

_____. 1997. "Swallowed by a Song: Paul Simon's Crisis of Chromaticism." In *Understanding Rock: Essays in Musical Analysis*, ed. John Covach and Graeme Boone. New York: Oxford University Press, 113–54.

_____. 1999. *The Beatles as Musicians: Revolver through the Anthology*. New York: Oxford University Press.

_____. 2000. "Confessions from Blueberry Hell, or Pitch Can Be a Sticky Substance." In *Expression in Pop-Rock Music*, ed. Walter Everett. New York: Garland, 269–346.

Fast, Susan. 2000. "Music, Contexts, and Meaning in U2," in *Expression in Pop-Rock Music*, ed. Walter Everett. New York: Garland, 33–58.

Finn, Geraldine. 1985. "Patriarchy and the Pornographic Eye/I," in *Canadian Journal of Political and Social Theory* 9/1–2: 81–95.

_____. 1993. "Why Are There No Great Women Postmodernists?" In *Relocating Cultural Studies: Developments in Theory and Research*, ed. Valda Blundell, John Shepherd, and Ian Taylor. London and New York: Routledge, 123–55.

Firestone, Shulamith. 1970. *The Dialectic of Sex: The Case for Feminist Revolution*. New York: William Morrow.

Fisher, Sue, and Kathy Davis. 1993. *Negotiating at the Margins: The Gendered Discourses of Power and Resistance*. New Brunswick, NJ: Rutgers University Press.

Fiske, John. 1992. "Cultural Studies and the Culture of Everyday Life." In *Cultural Studies*, ed. Lawrence Grossberg, Cary Nelson, and Paula A. Treichler. New York: Routledge, 154–65.

Flax, Jane. 1987. "Re-membering the Selves: Is the Repressed Gendered?" in *Michigan Quarterly Review* 26/1: 92–110.

_____. 1990. "Postmodernism and Gender Relations in Feminist Theory." In *Feminism/Postmodernism*, ed. Linda J. Nicholson. New York: Routledge, 39–63.

Fleissner, Jen. 1996. "Deep Space Tori," *Village Voice* (February 13), 53.

Forte, Allen. 1993. "Secrets of Melody: Line and Design in the Songs of Cole Porter," in *Musical Quarterly* 77/4: 625–47.

_____. 1995. *The American Popular Ballad of the Golden Era*. Princeton, NJ: Princeton University Press.

Foucault, Michel. 1979. *Discipline and Punish: The Birth of the Prison*. New York: Vintage.

_____. [1976] 1990. *The History of Sexuality*, vol. 1. Reprint New York: Vintage. Translated into English in 1978. Originally published in French in 1976.

Frankenberg, Ruth. 1993. *White Women, Race Matters: The Social Construction of Whiteness*. Minneapolis: University of Minnesota Press.

Fraser, Nancy, and Linda J. Nicholson. 1990. "Social Criticism without Philosophy: An Encounter between Feminism and Postmodernism." In *Feminism/ Postmodernism*, ed. Linda J. Nicholson. New York: Routledge, 19–39.

Freud, Sigmund. [1922] 1991. "Beyond the Pleasure Principle." In *On Metapsychology*, ed. James Strachey and Angela Richards. London: Penguin, 269–339.

_____. [1957] 1991. "Mourning and Melancholia." In *On Metapsychology*, ed. James Strachey and Angela Richards. London: Penguin, 245–269. Originally published in *The Standard Edition of the Complete Works of Sigmund Freud*. London: Hogarth Press and The Institute of Psychoanalysis.

Freund, Elizabeth. 1987. The Return of the Reader: Reader-Response Criticism. London: Methuen.

Frith, Simon. 1981. *Sound Effects: Youth, Leisure, and the Politics of Rock 'n' Roll*. New York: Pantheon.

Frith Simon, and Andrew Goodwin, eds. 1990. *On Record: Rock, Pop, and the Written Word*. New York: Pantheon.

Frith, Simon, Andrew Goodwin, and Lawrence Grossberg, eds. 1993. *Sound and Vision: The Music Video Reader*. London and New York: Routledge.

Gaar, Gillian G. 1992. *She's a Rebel: The History of Women in Rock and Roll*. Seattle, WA: Seal Press.

Goldman, Ruth. 1996. "Who Is That 'Queer' Queer: Exploring Norms around Sexuality, Race, and Class in Queer Theory." In *Queer Studies: A Lesbian, Gay, Bisexual, and Transgender Anthology*, ed. Brett Beemyn and Mickey Eliason. New York: New York University Press, 169–83.

Goodwin, Andrew. 1992. *Dancing in the Distraction Factory: Music Television and Popular Culture*. Minneapolis: University of Minnesota Press.

Greig, Charlotte. 1989. *Will You Still Love Me Tomorrow: Girl Groups from the 50s On*. London: Virago.

Griffin, Susan. 1981. *Pornography and Silence: Culture's Revenge against Nature*. New York: Harper and Row.

Grossberg, Lawrence. 1992. *We Gotta Get Out of This Place: Popular Conservatism and Postmodern Culture*. New York: Routledge.

———. 1993. "The Formations of Cultural Studies: An American in Birmingham." In *Relocating Cultural Studies: Developments in Theory and Research*, ed. Valda Blundell, John Shepherd, and Ian Taylor. London and New York: Routledge, 21–67.

Grossberg, Lawrence, Cary Nelson, and Paula Treichler, eds. 1992. *Cultural Studies*. New York: Routledge.

Grosz, Elizabeth. 1990. "Contemporary Theories of Power and Subjectivity." In *Feminist Knowledge: Critique and Construct*, ed. Sneja Gunew. London and New York: Routledge, 59–120.

———. 1994. *Volatile Bodies: Toward a Corporeal Feminism*. Bloomington: Indiana University Press.

———. 1998. *Jaques Lacan: A Feminist Introduction*. London: Routledge.

Guck, Marion. 1994. "A Woman's (Theoretical) Work," in *Perspectives of New Music* 32/1 (winter): 28–43.

———. 1997a. "Music Loving: Or the Relationship with the Piece," in *Journal of Musicology* 15/3 (summer): 345–52.

———. 1997b. "Two Types of Metaphoric Transference." In *Music and Meaning*, ed. Jenefer Robinson. Ithaca, NY: Cornell University Press, 201–12.

Guillaumin, Colette. 1981. "The Practice of Power and Belief in Nature, Part I," in *Feminist Issues* 1/2: 3–28.

———. 1983. "The Practice of Power and Belief in Nature, Part II," in *Feminist Issues* 1/3: 87–109.

Hakim, Albert B. 1992. *Historical Introduction to Philosophy*. Toronto: Maxwell MacMillan Canada.

Hale, Sylvia. 1995. *Controversies in Sociology*. Toronto: Copp Clarke.

Hall, Stuart. 1992. "Cultural Studies and Its Theoretical Legacies." In *Cultural Studies*, ed. Lawrence Grossberg, Cary Nelson, and Paula Treichler. London: Routledge, 277–86.

Hanmer, Jalna, and Mary Maynard. 1987. *Women, Violence, and Social Control*. Basingstoke, UK: MacMillan.

Harris, Keith. 1998. "Please Release Me," *Minneapolis City Pages* 19/993 (October 21).

Harrison, Daniel. 1997. "After Sundown: The Beach Boys' Experimental Music." In *Understanding Rock: Essays in Musical Analysis*, ed. John Covach and Graeme Boone. New York: Oxford University Press, 33–58.

Harrison, Daphne Duval. 1987. *Black Pearls: Blues Queens of the 1920s*. New Brunswick, NJ: Rutgers University Press.

Harstock, Nancy. 1987. "Rethinking Modernism: Minority vs. Majority Theories," in *Cultural Critique* 7: 187–206.

———. 1990. "Foucault on Power: A Theory for Women?" In *Feminism/Postmodernism*, ed. Linda J. Nicholson. London: Routledge, 157–76.

Hart, Linda. 1998. *Between the Body and the Flesh*. New York: Columbia University Press.

Hawkins, Stan. 1992. "Prince: Harmonic Analysis of 'Anna Stesia,'" in *Popular Music* 11/3: 325–36.

———. 1996. "Perspectives in Popular Musicology: Music, Lennox, and Meaning in 1990s Pop," in *Popular Music* 15/1: 17–36.

Headlam, David. 1997. "Blues Transformations in the Music of Cream." In *Understanding Rock: Essays in Musical Analysis*, ed. John Covach and Graeme Boone. New York: Oxford University Press, 59–92.

Hebdige, Dick. 1987. "The Impossible Object: Towards a Sociology of the Sublime," in *New Formations* 1.

Hegel, G. W. F. 1952. *The Phenomenology of Spirit*. Hamburg: Felix Meiner.

Hirsch, E. D. Jr. 1969. *Validity in Interpretation*. New Haven: Yale University Press.

———. 1976. *The Aims of Interpretation*. Chicago: University of Chicago Press.

Hirshey, Gerri. 1997. "The Backstage History of Women Who Rocked the World," *Rolling Stone* 773 (November 13): 85–89.

Hisama, Ellie. 1993. "Postcolonialism on the Make: The Music of John Mellencamp, David Bowie, and John Zorn," in *Popular Music* 12/2: 91–105.

———. 1995. *Gender, Politics, and Modernist Music: Five Analyses of Compositions by Ruth Crawford (1901–53) and Marion Bauer (1887–1955)*. Ph.D. dissertation, City University of New York.

———. 1999. "Voice, Race, and Sexuality in the Music of Joan Armatrading." In *Audible Traces: Gender, Identity, and Music*, ed. Elaine Barkin and Lydia Hamessley. Zürich and Los Angeles: Carciofoli Verlagshaus, 115–132.

———. 2000. "From *L'Étranger* to 'Killing an Arab': Representing the Other in a Cure Song." In *Expression in Pop-Rock Music*," ed. Walter Everett. New York: Garland, 59–74.

Hogeland, Lisa Maria. 1994. "Fear of Feminism: Why Young Women Get the Willies," in *Ms.*, November–December, 18–21.

hooks, bell. 1981. *Ain't I a Woman: Black Women and Feminism*. Boston, MA: South End Press.

———. 1992a. *Black Looks: Race and Representation*. Boston: South End Press.

———. 1992b. "Representing Whiteness in the Black Imagination." In *Cultural Studies*, ed. Lawrence Grossberg, Cary Nelson, and Paula A. Treichler. New York: Routledge, 338–47.

_____. 1994. *Outlaw Culture: Resisting Representations*. New York: Routledge.

Hubbs, Nadine. 2000. "The Imagination of Pop-Rock Criticism." In *Expression in Pop-Rock Music,* ed. Walter Everett. New York: Garland, 3–30.

Humm, Maggie. 1995. *The Dictionary of Feminist Theory.* 2nd ed. New York: Prentice Hall.

Hunter-Tilney, Ludovic. 1998. "Don't Look Here for the Answer: Pop Is This Desire?" *Financial Times,* September 25.

Hutcheon, Linda. 1989. *The Politics of Postmodernism.* New York: Routledge.

Jackobson, Roman. 1990. *On Language.* Cambridge, MA: Harvard University Press.

Jaggar, Alison M., and Susan R. Bordo. 1992. *Gender/Body/Knowledge: Feminist Reconstructions of Being and Knowing.* New Brunswick, NJ: Rutgers University Press.

Jameson, Frederic. 1983. "Postmodernism and Consumer Society." In *The Anti-Aesthetic: Essays on Postmodern Culture,* ed. Hal Foster. Seattle, WA: Bay Press, 111–26.

_____. 1991. *Postmodernism, or, the Cultural Logic of Late Capitalism.* Durham, NC: Duke University Press.

Jhally, Sut. 1992. *Dreamworlds: Desire/Sex/Power in Rock Video.* Toronto: Kinetic.

Johnson, Christopher. 1997. *Derrida: The Scene of Writing.* London: Phoenix.

Kaminsky, Peter. 1992. "The Popular Album as Song Cycle: Paul Simon's 'Still Crazy after All These Years,'" in *College Music Symposium* 32: 38–54.

Kant, Immanuel. [1790] 1951. *Critique of Judgment,* trans. J. H. Bernard. New York: Hafner.

Kaplan, E. Ann. 1983. *Women and Film: Both Sides of the Camera.* New York: Methuen.

_____. 1987. *Rocking Around the Clock: Music Television, Postmodernism, and Consumer Culture.* New York and London: Methuen.

_____. 1988. "Whose Imaginary? The Televisual Apparatus, the Female Body, and Textual Strategies in Select Rock Videos on MTV." In *Female Spectators: Looking at Film and Television,* ed. Deidre E. Pribram. London: Verso, 132–56.

Kearney, M. C. 1997. "The Missing Links: Riot Grrrl—Feminism—Lesbian Culture." In *Sexing the Groove: Popular Music and Gender,* ed. Sheila Whiteley. New York: Routledge, 207–30.

Kellner, Douglas. 1995. "Cultural Studies, Multiculturalism, and Media Culture." In *Gender, Race, and Class in Media: A Text-Reader,* ed. Gail Dines and Jean M. Humez. Thousand Oaks, CA: Sage Publications, 5–17.

Kelly, Liz. 1987. "The Continuum of Sexual Violence." In *Women, Violence, and Social Control,* ed. Jalna Hanmer. London: MacMillan, 46–60.

Kerman, Joseph. 1980. "How We Got into Analysis, and How to Get Out," in *Critical Inquiry* 7/2: 311–31.

Kielian-Gilbert, Marianne. 1994. "Of Poetics and Poesis, Pleasure, and Politics: Music Theory and Modes of the Feminine," in *Perspectives of New Music* 32/1 (winter): 44–67.

Killam, Rosemary. 1993. "Calamity Jane: Strength, Uncertainty, and Affirmation," in *Women and Music Quarterly* 1/3 (November): 17–25.

Kingsbury, Martha. 1972. "The Femme Fatale and Her Sisters." In *Woman as Sex Object: Studies in Erotic Art,* ed. Thomas B. Hess and Linda Nochlin. New York: Newsweek, 182–205.

Kojève, Alexandre. 1977. *Introduction to the Reading of Hegel: Lectures on "The Philosophy of the Spirit."* Ithaca, NY: Cornell University Press.

Koozin, Timothy. 2000. "Fumbling towards Ecstasy: Voice Leading, Tonal Structure, and the Theme of Self-Realization in the Music of Sarah McLachlan." In *Expression in Pop-Rock Music,* ed. Walter Everett. New York: Garland, 247–66.

Kramer, Lawrence. 1997. *After the Lovedeath: Sexual Violence and the Making of Culture.* Berkeley: University of California Press.

Lacan, Jacques. 1977. *Écrits: A Selection,* trans. Alan Sheridan. London: Tavistock.

Lafrance, Mélisse R. 1998. "Colonizing the Feminine: Nike's Intersections of Postfeminism and Hyperconsumption." In *Sport and Postmodern Times,* ed. Geneviève Rail. Albany: State University of New York Press, 117–39.

_____. In press. "Narrow Notions of Freedom: Some Reflections on Why Young Women Fear Feminism," in *Who's That Girl? Turbo Chicks Meet Feminist Theory,* ed. Allyson Mitchell. Toronto: Second Story Press.

Lafrance, Mélisse R., and Geneviève Rail. 1998. "Denis Rodman—Cultural Imposter—Paper Doll," in *Borderlines* 46, 8–11.

Leppert, Richard, and Susan McClary, eds. 1987. *Music and Society: The Politics of Composition, Performance, and Reception.* Cambridge: Cambridge University Press.

Lester, Paul. 1992. "Beauty or Beast?" *Melody Maker,* September 19, 45.

Lévi-Strauss, Claude. [1971] 1981. *The Naked Man.* London: Jonathan Cape. Originally published in French.

Levy, Janet. 1987. "Covert and Casual Values in Recent Writings about Music," in *Journal of Musicology* 5/1 (winter): 3–27.

Lewin, David. 1982. "*Auf dem Flusse*: Image and Background in a Schubert Song," in *19th Century Music* 6/1 (summer): 47–59.

_____. 1986. "Music Theory, Phenomenology, and Modes of Perception," in *Music Perception* 3/4: 327–92.

_____. 1991. "Some Problems and Resources of Music Theory," in *Journal of Music Theory Pedagogy* 5/2: 111–32.

_____. 1992a. "Musical Analysis as Stage Direction." In *Music and Text: Critical Inquiries,* ed. Steven Paul Scher. Cambridge: Cambridge University Press, 163–76.

_____. 1992b. "Women's Voices and the Fundamental Bass," in *Journal of Musicology* 10/4 (fall): 464–83.

_____. In press. *Analyses of Texted Music in the German Tradition with Some Broader Theoretical Considerations.*

Lewis, Lisa A. 1990. *Gender Politics and MTV: Voicing the Difference.* Philadelphia: Temple University Press.

Lorde, Audre. 1990. "Age, Race, Class, and Sex: Women Redefining Difference." In *Out There: Marginalization and Contemporary Cultures,* ed. Russell Ferguson, Martha Gever, Trinh T. Min-ha, and Cornel West. Cambridge, MA: MIT Press, 281–89.

Lull, James, ed. 1992. *Popular Music and Communication.* 2nd ed. Newbury Park, CA: Sage Publications.

MacKinnon, Catherine. 1989. *Toward a Feminist Theory of the State.* Cambridge, MA: Harvard University Press.

Maccannell, Juliet Flower. 1992. "Desire." In *Feminism and Psychoanalysis: A Critical Dictionary*, ed. Elizabeth Wright. Oxford: Blackwells, 63–68.

Macy, Laura. 1996. "Speaking of Sex: Metaphor and Performance in the Italian Madrigal." *The Journal of Musicology* 14/1 (winter): 1–34.

Matthews, Eric. 1996. *Twentieth-Century French Philosophy*. Oxford: Oxford University Press.

Maus, Fred. 1993. "Masculine Discourse in Music Theory," in *Perspectives of New Music* 31/2 (summer): 264–93.

McClary, Susan. 1991. *Feminine Endings: Music, Gender, and Sexuality*. University of Minnesota Press.

_____. 1992. *Georges Bizet: Carmen*. Cambridge and New York: Cambridge University Press.

_____. 1994. "Music: Blood Rites," *Village Voice* (December 6).

McCreless, Patrick. 1997. "Contemporary Music Theory and the New Musicology," in *Journal of Musicology* 15/3 (summer): 291–96.

McDonnell, Evelyn, and Ann Powers, ed. 1995. *Rock She Wrote*. New York: Delta Trade Paperbacks.

Messner, Michael, and Don Sabo. 1992. *Sport, Men, and the Gender Order*. Champaign, IL: Human Kinetics Press.

Middleton, Richard. 1990. *Studying Popular Music*. Buckingham: Open University Press.

_____. 1993. "Popular Music Analysis and Musicology: Bridging the Gap," in *Popular Music* 12/2: 177–88.

Millett, Kate. 1970. *Sexual Politics*. Garden City, NY: Doubleday.

Minh-Ha, Trinh T. 1995. "Writing Postcoloniality and Feminism." In *The Postcolonial Studies Reader*, ed. Bill Ashcroft, Gareth Griffiths, and Helen Tifflin. New York: Routledge, 264–69.

Mitchell, Juliet. 1974. *Psychoanalysis and Feminism*. Harmondsworth: Penguin.

Moi, Toril. 1985. *Sexual/Textual Politics: Feminist Literary Theory*. Reprint 1995, London: Methuen.

Moore, Allan. 1992. "Patterns of Harmony," in *Popular Music* 11/1: 73–106.

_____. 1993. *Rock: The Primary Text*. Buckingham: Open University Press.

_____. 1995. "The So-Called 'Flattened Seventh' in Rock," In *Popular Music* 14/2: 185–201.

_____. 1997. *The Beatles: Sgt. Pepper's Lonely Hearts Club Band*. Cambridge: Cambridge University Press.

Moore, John. 1989. "'The Hieroglyphics of Love': The Torch Singers and Interpretation," in *Popular Music* 8/1: 31–58.

Morgan, Robin, ed. 1970. *Sisterhood Is Powerful: An Anthology of Writings from the Women's Liberation Movement*. New York: Vintage.

Morrison, Toni. 1992. *Playing in the Dark: Whiteness and the Literary Imagination*. New York: Vintage.

Mulvey, Laura. 1975. "Visual Pleasure and Narrative Cinema," in *Screen* 16 (fall): 6–18.

Nead, Lynda. 1992. *The Female Nude: Art, Obscenity, and Sexuality*. London and New York: Routledge.

Nehring, Neil. 1997. *Popular Music, Gender, and Postmodernism: Anger Is an Energy*. London: Sage Publications.

Nichols, Jeanette, Darlene Pagano, and Margaret Rossoff. 1982. "Is Sadomaschsim Feminist? A Critique of the Samois Position." In *Against Sadomasochism: A Radical Feminist Analysis*. ed. Robin Ruth Linden, Darlene R. Pagano, Diana E. H. Russell, and Susana Leigh Star. Palo Alto: Frog in the Well Press, 137–46.

Noyes, John K. 1997. *The Mastery of Submission: Inventions of Masochism*. Ithaca and London: Cornell University Press.

Oakley, Ann. 1972. *Sex, Gender, and Society*. London: Temple-Smith.

O'Brien, Lucy. 1995. *She Bop: The Definitive History of Women in Rock, Pop, and Soul*. New York: Penguin.

O'Dair, Barbara, ed. 1997. *Trouble Girls: The Rolling Stone Book of Women in Rock*. New York: Random House.

Peraino, Judith. 1998. "PJ Harvey's 'Man-Size Sextet' and the Inaccessible, Inescapable Gender," in *Women and Music:" A Journal of Gender and Culture* (spring): 47–63.

Perkins, William Eric, ed. 1996. *Droppin' Science: Critical Essays on Rap Music and Hip Hop Culture*. Philadelphia: Temple University Press.

Phillips, Marlene N. 1989. *She Tries Her Tongue: Her Silence Softly Breaks*. Charlottetown, PEI: Ragweed Press.

Potter, Russell A. 1995. *Spectacular Vernaculars: Hip-Hop and the Politics of Postmodern*. Albany: State University of New York Press.

Pratt, Ray. 1990. *Rhythm and Resistance: The Political Uses of American Popular Music*. New York: Praeger.

Probyn, Elspeth. 1993. "True Voices and Real People: The 'Problem' of the Autobiographical in Cultural Studies." In *Relocating Cultural Studies: Developments in Theory and Research*, ed. Valda Blundell, John Shepherd, and Ian Taylor. London and New York: Routledge, 105–23.

Rail, Geneviève. 1998. "Introduction." In *Sport and Postmodern Times*, ed. Geneviève Rail. Albany: State University of New York Press, 5–20.

Réage, Pauline. 1965. *The Story of O*, trans. Sabine d'Estrée. New York: Grove Press.

Reece, Douglas. 1996. "Int'l Fan Base Propelling Tori Amos' Atlantic Set," in *Billboard* 108 (February 17): 108.

Reid, Vernon. 1999. "Revenge Effect," in *Bomb* 67 (spring): 22–23.

Reynolds, Simon, and Joy Press. 1995. *The Sex Revolts: Gender, Rebellion, and Rock 'n' Roll*. Cambridge, MA: Harvard University Press.

Roberts, Robin. 1996. *Ladies First: Women in Music Videos*. Jackson: University Press of Mississippi.

Robinson, Thomas. 1899. *The Life and Death of Mary Magdalene*. London: Kegan Paul and Trench Trubner.

Rolling Stone. 1994. Review of *Live through This*, in *Rolling Stone* 680 (April 21): 84–85.

Rolling Stone. 1994–95. Review of *Live through This*, in *Rolling Stone* 698–99 (December 29–January 12): 190.

Rowley, Hazel, and Elizabeth Grosz. 1990. "Psychoanalysis and Feminism." In *Feminist Knowledge: Critique and Construct*, ed. Sneja Gunew. London and New York: Routledge, 175–204.

Ruether, Rosemary Radford. 1974. *Religion and Sexism: Images of Women in the Jewish and Christian Traditions*. New York: Simon and Schuster.

Rycenga, Jennifer. 1997. "Sisterhood: A Loving Lesbian Ear Listens to Progressive Heterosexual Women's Rock." In *Keeping Score: Music, Disciplinarity, Culture*, ed. David Schwartz, Anahid Kassabian, and Lawrence Siegel. Charlottesville and London: University Press of Virginia, 204–28.

Said, Edward. 1995. "Orientalism." In *The Postcolonial Studies Reader*, ed. Bill Ashcroft, Gareth Griffiths, and Helen Tifflin. New York: Routledge, 87–92.

Sanjek, David. 1997. "Can a Fujiyama Mama Be the Female Elvis? The Wild, Wild Women of Rockabilly." In *Sexing the Groove: Popular Music and Gender*, ed. Sheila Whiteley. New York: Routledge, 137–68.

Sartre, Jean-Paul. 1966. *Being and Nothingness*. New York: Washington Square Press.

Saussure, Ferdinand. 1974. *A Course in General Linguistics*. London: Fontana.

Scher, Steven Paul. 1992. *Music and Text: Critical Inquiries*. Cambridge: Cambridge University Press.

Schottroff, Luise. 1996. "Through German and Feminist Eyes: A Liberationist Reading of Luke 7.36–50." In *A Feminist Companion to the Hebrew Bible in the New Testament*, ed. Athalya Brenner. Sheffield, UK: Sheffield Academic Press, 332–42.

Schwichtenberg, Cathy, ed. 1993. *The Madonna Connection: Representational Politics, Subcultural Identities, and Cultural Theory*. Denver, CO: Westview Press.

Seidman, Steven, ed. 1996. *Queer Theory/Sociology*. London: Blackwell.

Sheffield, Rob. 1998. Review of *Is This Desire?* in *Rolling Stone* 797 (October 15): 128.

Shepherd, John. 1991. *Music as Social Text*. Cambridge: Polity Press.

Shepherd, John, and Peter Wicke. 1997. *Music and Cultural Theory*. Cambridge: Polity Press.

Shuker, Roy. 1994. *Understanding Popular Music*. London and New York: Routledge.

Silverman, Kaja. 1992. "*Histoire d'O*: The Construction of a Female Subject." In *Pleasure and Danger: Exploring Female Sexuality*, ed. Carole Vance. London: Pandora, 320–49.

Simon, Roger. 1991. *Gramsci's Political Thought: An Introduction*. London: Lawrence and Wishart.

Snead, James. 1994. *White Screens, Black Images*. New York: Routledge.

Smith, Joan. 1989. *Misogynies: Reflections on Myths and Malice*. London: Faber and Faber.

Smith, Dorothy. 1990. *Text, Facts, and Femininity: Exploring the Relations of Ruling*. London: Routledge.

Snitow, Ann, Christine Stansell, and Sharon Thompson, eds. 1983. *Powers of Desire: The Politics of Sexuality*. New York: Monthly Review Press.

Solie, Ruth A. 1980. "The Living Work: Organicism and Musical Analysis," in *Nineteenth-Century Music* 4/2 (fall): 147–56.

———. 1992. "Whose Life? The Gendered Self in Schumann's Frauenliebe Songs." In *Music and Text: Critical Inquiries*, ed. Stephen Paul Scher. Cambridge: Cambridge University Press, 219–40.

———, 1993. *Musicology and Difference: Gender and Sexuality in Music Scholarship*. Berkeley: University of California Press.

Spicer, Mark. 2000. "Large-Scale Strategy and Compositional Design in the Early Music of Genesis." In *Expression in Pop-Rock Music,* ed. Walter Everett. New York: Garland, 77–112.

Spivak, Gayatri C. 1988. *In Other Worlds: Essays in Cultural Politics.* New York: Methuen.

_____. 1990. *The Postcolonial Critic: Interviews, Strategies, Dialogues.* London: Routledge.

Stefani, Gino. 1987. "A Theory of Musical Competence," in *Semiotica* 66/1–3: 7–22.

Stein, Deborah, and Robert Spillman. 1996. *Poetry into Song: Performance and Analysis of Lieder.* New York: Oxford University Press.

Steussy, Joe. 1990. *Rock and Roll: Its History and Stylistic Development.* Englewood Cliffs, NJ: Prentice Hall.

Steward, Sue, and Sheryl Garratt. 1989. *Signed, Sealed, and Delivered of Pop.* Boston: South End Press.

Strauss, Neil. 1995. "A Singer Spurns the Role of Victim," *New York Times,* Feburary 18, L14.

Sullivan, James. 1998. Review of *Is This Desire?* in *San Francsico Chronicle,* September 27.

Tagg, Philip. 1982. "Analysing Popular Music: Theory, Method, and Practice," in *Popular Music* 2: 37–67.

Tavris, Carol. 1989. *Anger: The Misunderstood Emotion.* New York: Simon and Schuster.

Tomlinson, Gary. 1984. "The Web of Culture: A Context for Musicology," in *Nineteenth-Century Music* 7/3: 350–62.

Troost, Anne. 1996. "Elisabeth and Mary—Naomi and Ruth: Gender-Response Criticism in Luke 1–2." In *A Feminist Companion to the Hebrew Bible in the New Testament,* ed. Athalya Brenner. Sheffield, UK: Sheffield Academic Press, 159–97.

Udovitch, Mim. 1994. "Mothers of Invention: Women in Rock Talk about Scents, Sensibility, and Sexism," in *Rolling Stone* 692 (October 6): 49-53, 81, 96.

Vance, Carole S., ed. 1989. *Pleasure and Danger: Exploring Female Sexuality.* London: Pandora.

Walser, Robert. 1992. "Eruptions: Heavy Metal Appropriations of Classical Virtuosity." In *Popular Music* 11/3: 263–308.

_____. 1993a. "Forging Masculinity: Heavy-Metal Sounds and Images of Gender." In *Sound and Vision: The Music Video Reader,* ed. Simon Frith and Lawrence Grossberg. London: Routledge, 153–81.

_____. 1993b. *Running with the Devil: Power, Gender, and Madness in Heavy Metal Music.* Hanover: Wesleyan University Press.

Waugh, Patricia. 1984. *Metafiction: The Theory and Practice of Self-Conscious Fiction.* London: Methuen.

Weedon, Chris. 1997. *Feminist Practice and Poststructuralist Theory.* Oxford: Blackwell.

Weeks, Jeffrey. 1996. "The Construction of Homosexuality." In *Queer Theory/Sociology,* ed. Steven Seidman. Oxford: Blackwell, 41–64.

Weinburg, Thomas, ed. 1995. *S&M: Studies in Dominance and Submission.* New York: Prometheus Books.

Whitely, Sheila, ed. 1997. *Sexing the Groove: Popular Music and Gender.* London: Routledge.

Wicke, Peter. 1990. *Rock Music: Culture, Aesthetics, and Sociology,* trans. Rachel Fogg. Cambridge: Cambridge University Press.

Winkler, Peter. 1978. "Toward a Theory of Popular Harmony," in *In Theory Only* 4/2: 3–26.

_____. 1997. "Writing Ghost Notes: The Poetics and Politics of Transcription." In *Keeping Score: Music, Disciplinarity, Culture*, ed. David Schwarz, Anahid Kassabian, and Lawrence Siegel. Charlottesville and London: University Press of Virginia, 169–203.

Wittig, Monique. 1990. "The Straight Mind." In *Out There: Marginalization and Contemporary Cultures*, ed. Russell Ferguson et al. Cambridge, MA: MIT Press, 51–57.

Wolf, Naomi. [1990] 1997. *The Beauty Myth*. Reprint Mississauga: Random House, Canada. (Page references are to the reprint edition.)

Young. Iris M. 1990. *Throwing Like a Girl and Other Essays in Feminist Philosophy and Social Theory*. Bloomington: Indiana University Press.

Index